People are talking

The Teenagers' Guide to Scho

D0371355

"Rebecca Greene's *The Teenagers' Guide to School Outside the Box* captures the best of the alternative learning model. This is a very helpful book." **Paul Wellstone,** U.S. Senator

"This book shows teens how to expand their high school horizons—and get ready for their future." **Julianne Dueber,** author of *The Ultimate High School Survival Guide*

"*The Teenagers' Guide to School Outside the Box* is a roadmap to the adventurous world of alternative learning. Using this book, teens can plot their own course to seek out and get the most from real-world experiences." **Gail Grand,** author of *Free (and Almost Free) Adventures for Teenagers*

"From deciding what you want, to finding out how to get it, this guide has it all for teens wanting to 'break out of the box'!" **Jill F. VonGruben,** author of *College Countdown: The Parent's and Student's Survival Kit for the College Application Process*

"Rebecca Greene opens windows inside the imagination. For any teen with the desire to get more out of high school than just the standard fare, this book spells out the benefits and the practical steps for finding those life-altering learning experiences. It's all about choices, knowing yourself, and what's out there!" **Annie Fox,** author of *Can You Relate? Real-World Advice on Guys, Girls, Growing Up, and Getting Along*

The Teenagers' Guide to School Outside the Box

By Rebecca Greene

Edited by Elizabeth Verdick

At the time of this writing, all facts and figures cited are the most current available, and all Web site URLs are accurate and active. Please keep in mind that URLs change and sites come and go. When in doubt, use a search engine.

NOTE: Parents, teachers, and other adults who are working with children using the Internet should make sure that the exploration of Web sites is age-appropriate and acceptable. We have done our best to identify sites that meet these criteria, but we cannot guarantee their contents.

Library of Congress Cataloging-in-Publication Data

Greene, Rebecca
    The teenagers' guide to school outside the box / by Rebecca Greene
        p. cm.
Includes bibliographical references and index.
ISBN 1-57542-087-2 (pbk.)
1. Alternative education—United States. 2. Education, Secondary—Activity programs—United States. 3. Active learning—United States. I. Title.

LC46.4 .G74 2001
373.2'14—dc21
                              2485 1130 8/01

00-031699

Assistant editor: KaTrina Wentzel
Illustrations by Jeff Tolbert
Cover design by Percolator
Interior design by Marieka Heinlen
Index prepared by Randl Ockey

10 9 8 7 6 5 4 3 2 1
Printed in the United States of America

Free Spirit Publishing Inc.
217 Fifth Avenue North, Suite 200
Minneapolis, MN 55401-1299
(612) 338-2068
help4kids@freespirit.com
www.freespirit.com

Dedication

For my parents, Merle and Phillip Greene, and my grandparents,
Florence and Raymond Manusow, and Fae and David Greene, with love.

Acknowledgments

This book could not have become a reality without the wonderful staff at Free Spirit Publishing. My sincere appreciation goes out to Judy Galbraith, for all her encouragement and support. I am also enormously grateful to my editor, Elizabeth Verdick, for her inspiration, wisdom, and insight. Your suggestions were right on target, and you helped take this book to a whole new level. Thank you also to the rest of the staff at Free Spirit (current and former) for their literary counsel and limitless efforts, especially Tim Woessner, Nancy Robinson, Marieka Heinlen, Caryn Pernu, Margie Lisovskis, Trina Wentzel, and Marsha Collins. A special thank you to Michael Landes, whose passionate foreword and invaluable advice helped stoke the fires for this book.

Many people contributed their advice, experiences, and knowledge to this project. Warmest thanks go out to everyone who provided interviews for this book. I also want to thank Ingrid Anderson for her enduring friendship and editing prowess, Sean McNee for his computer wizardry and revision ideas, and Paul Abosh and Scott Schwartz for their help and inspiration. Thank you also to Jeanie Pullen of Mentor Connection, Dr. Tom Greenspon, Darnell Green of 100 Black Men, Melynda DuVal at PETA, Cornelius Bull of The Center for Interim Programs, Alden Mahler, Lara Zielin, Courtney Colville, Frank Morral, the Carleton Career Center, Margit Johnson, Jill VonGruben, Annie Fox, Gail Grand, Senator Paul Wellstone, Dave Denman at Time Out, Julie Dueber, Mark Oldman of Vault.com, John Katzman of the Princeton Review, Michael Shapiro, Suzette Tyler, and Ron and Caryl Krannich. A final thank you goes out to Carleton College, my wonderful alma mater, for providing me with so many opportunities to take advantage of alternative learning.

Contents

Foreword by Michael Landes, Career Counselor, Pace University, NY, Author of *The Back Door Guide to Short-Term Job Adventures* viii

Introduction 1
What Exactly *Is* Alternative Learning? 1
Why I Wrote This Book—and How to Use It 5

Part 1: What You Can Do While Living at Home 9

Chapter 1: Give More of Yourself—Volunteer Your Time 10
What You Can Learn from Volunteering 13
Volunteering and School 16
Volunteering Abroad 30

Chapter 2: Take Courses Outside the High School Classroom . . 35
Dual Enrollment—What Does It Mean? 37
Summer Options 45
Early Admission—Are You Ready? 48
Distance Learning 53
Other Educational Alternatives 54
Other Ways of Learning 57

Chapter 3: Get a Mentor, Be a Mentor 60
Why Have a Mentor? 62
How to Choose a Mentor 65
Making the Most of Your Mentorship 85
Touch Someone's Life: Be a Mentor 86

Chapter 4: Job Shadow a Professional 91
Ready to Shadow? 96

Chapter 5: Find an Internship 113
What's an Internship—and What Can It Do for You? 118
Applying for an Internship—What Does It Take? 129
Acing Your Interview 142
Making the Most of Your Internship 149

Chapter 6: Become a Youth Apprentice 158
How to Get an Apprenticeship 162

Part 2: What You Can Do Away from Home . . . Or Far, Far Away 177

Chapter 7: Go to Camp, Go on an Adventure, Go Overseas . . 178
Heading Off to Summer Camp 179
Getting Adventurous 190
Traveling Overseas 197

Chapter 8: Study Abroad 216
16 Good Reasons to Study Abroad 218
Choosing a Program That's Right for You 228
Get Ready, Get Set, Go 240
Making the Most of Your Experience 246

A Final Word 252

Index 255

About the Author 261

Foreword

So, you're in high school. You're probably doing the things that are expected of you: spending time on homework assignments, studying for tests, participating in extracurricular activities, developing friendships, and maintaining your responsibilities at home. But is there more to life than this traditional path that most of us seem to follow? If you often find yourself wondering if there *is* something more out there—activities that really interest you—you're about to indulge in a book that could forever change your life. Really.

Enter Rebecca Greene—your new alternative-learning coach. She has filled the pages of this guide with a world of possibilities, along with "been there, done that" advice from teen readers who have actually gone "outside the box" with much success. You can do the same, because you'll soon have the know-how to take your life to a higher level.

I must admit that my own life would have bloomed in my teenage years if only I'd had the tools and resources within this guide. It wasn't until my final year of college that the light bulb went off for me . . . You can study abroad? Do a summer internship? Network? Get a mentor? Job shadow? Volunteer? Do an independent study? Get involved in a service-learning project? *Why didn't anybody tell me about these things?*

Well, like many young people, I thought that by doing what was expected of me, I was doing the right things in my education. It wasn't until the day I asked myself this very important question that my life began to change in ways I had never dreamed possible: "Are the things I'm studying and doing right now preparing me for what I want to do with my life after graduation?" That was an important day for me; sure enough, it will be for you, too. Go ahead, ask yourself that question. If you're unsure of the answer, read on, because your life is about to get really exciting.

You might not realize it right now, but the teen years are the ideal time to take advantage of the world of alternative learning. Now is the time to start exploring what's important to you: to develop your talents and see where you "belong" in this world. It's time to trade in your security blanket for opportunities that stretch your mind, body, and soul. Rebecca coins this time as your call to introspection: a time to really take a hard look at what you're doing, where you're going, and how you want your life to unfold.

It's not a simple process, and the answers don't come overnight. That's why *The Teenagers' Guide to School Outside the Box* paves the path of success by asking you lots and lots of questions—questions that will challenge you and push you into unknown terrain. You'll begin to learn things your education could never teach you—primarily, how to stretch and test your limits. It's up to you to uncover what it is that gets you excited; then to pursue it, experience it, and see how the opportunity unfolds. This may all sound like scary stuff, but now you have the resources to ease those fears. You'll learn how to take your education into your own hands and reach for something more. You can begin to think about your life differently—to do and see things that you've never imagined. Why settle for less?

As the author of a book on short-term job adventures and a career counselor for many years, I've witnessed firsthand the changes that occur in people who challenge their abilities and look at life through curious eyes. All that it takes to begin is one small risk. By making the decision to take part in one alternative learning experience, your whole life can change over the course of a few days or a few months. You'll have pursued something that interests you; and that one experience will most likely lead to something else that excites you. What you're doing is creating a momentum for your life, which will give you the confidence to do even more.

Each risk—each new path—brings you closer to doing what you love. You're growing. You're learning. You're maturing. It feels good. There may be times when you ask yourself, "What the heck am I doing?" But by living and looking at your life with a long-haul approach, you'll find that each new risk and experience will bring you closer to your dreams. You'll be doing the things that begin to harmonize with your natural gifts, abilities, and skills. That's a refreshing thought.

So, what are you waiting for? Turn the page and let Rebecca share with you her passion for alternative learning, the endless possibilities that exist, and how you can begin to do the things that really, really interest you.

Michael Landes
Career Counselor, Pace University, NY
Author of *The Back Door Guide to Short-Term Job Adventures* (*www.backdoorjobs.com*)

Introduction

> "Life is either a daring adventure or nothing."
> **Helen Keller**

Do you want to get more out of life? Sure. Don't we all? But you're in high school, and maybe you haven't had opportunities to explore subjects and activities that *really* interest you—yet.

Think you're too young to get out there, see the world, and discover what you're capable of? Think again! Rosha Forman, a student from New York, spent six weeks in Kenya after her junior year. Henry Brock of Bemidji, Minnesota, apprenticed under a blacksmith during the summer between ninth and tenth grades. Beth Scott, from Nebraska, interned as an aide at a zoo all through high school; she spent weekends and summers working in the zoo's aquarium, caring for the fish and aquatic birds. Imagine what *you* might do when you give alternative learning a try.

What Exactly Is Alternative Learning?

When you hear the word *alternative*, what do you think of? Skateboarders? Radio stations? Body piercing? New-age spas? Here's a simple definition:

alternative: (adjective) offering a choice of two things.

The key word here is *choice.*

Alternative learning doesn't necessarily have to mean education that's edgy, way out there, or on the fringes. (Although it can, if that's what you're into.) Alternative learning simply means going beyond what's offered in classrooms and through extracurricular activities. In other words, *you* choose what you want to learn. You take your education into your own hands.

Alternative learning is for teens who want something more. Maybe you enjoy school, but you crave real-world experiences. On the other hand, maybe your high school isn't challenging enough for you or doesn't offer much in the way of resources, equipment, or hands-on learning. Maybe you're bored or feeling lost, and you really want to try something new. Or maybe you're looking for guidance from experienced adults in your particular field of interest. Perhaps you want to learn about other people and places, other cultures, and the world. Whatever your situation, this book can show you how to create your own choices—your own learning path.

Let's face it: lots of high school students feel boxed in. Are you one of them? You rush off to school, go to class, eat lunch, go to class, hang out in the halls, go to class, talk with your friends, and—you guessed it—go to class. After school, maybe you're involved in sports, drama, a club, the yearbook committee, school government, art, a service project, a job, or some other activity. (If you are, great! All of these extracurriculars help you learn and grow.) *But* have you ever just felt like doing something different, something nontraditional, something out of the ordinary . . . or even extraordinary? Maybe you could:

- work as an intern at a recording studio
- take an auto repair class at a community college
- "job shadow" an artist to see what he or she does in the studio day-to-day

F. Y. I.

Throughout this book you'll see lots of references to teens, teenagers, and high school. You might be a teenager in high school, but you might also have graduated already, or be eleven or twelve and in middle school or junior high. When I use the terms *teenager* and *high school,* I don't mean to exclude readers whose situations are different. It's just simpler to say "teens" than it is to say "eleven-year-olds, twelve-year-olds, and teenagers," and easier to say "high school" than to say "middle school, junior high, high school, or just out of high school." I've tried to make this book friendly to as many readers as possible. If you're interested in any of the choices alternative learning has to offer, this book is for you.

- study a foreign language not offered at your school
- find a mentor who can help you in your favorite hobby or your potential career
- become an activist in your community
- travel overseas as a student or volunteer

All of these adventures in learning are within your grasp.

You can go way beyond your familiar high school routine—no matter what kind of student you are right now. Whether you're struggling in school or acing every class, you have the power to reach for something more. Alternative learning experiences let you branch out in new and unexpected directions. You can enhance your learning in a particular subject, or you can seek hands-on experience in the real world. Alternative learning—or school outside the box—is a way to discover the things you *want* to know, as opposed to focusing only on what your school *requires* you to know. Alternative learning can make your high school years a lot more fun and fulfilling. In fact, you might even wake up to a whole new way of life.

F. Y. I.

Of course, if you want to graduate, you'll still have to spend plenty of time inside the classroom (unless you're a homeschooler). This book *isn't* about creative ways to skip school and still get your diploma! Instead, it's about enhancing the education you're already getting and making the most of your time in and out of school.

High school is typically designed so that students are taught the same things in more or less the same way. But who says you have to go through four straight years of classes, lectures, discussions, homework, tests, and final exams? During that time, you're expected to work at a set pace, pay attention, listen, and discuss a topic probably chosen by your teacher. In that kind of environment, you don't often have the chance to get out and experience life in a hands-on way. Your natural curiosity and love for learning may be squelched. Alternative learning lets you break out of the standard mold. Your goal can be to focus on a particular interest, explore an unusual subject, learn a new skill, get a cool hobby, or simply satisfy a curiosity. Whatever you choose, the objective is to experience life *beyond the classroom walls.*

Many alternative learners discover that trying something out of the ordinary renews their energy and helps them feel more in charge of their education. In fact, students who decide to take the nontraditional route often say it was the most rewarding and exciting time of their lives (so far!). This may be because learning something on your own—or with the help of an adult who has special knowledge to share—is a fascinating experience. This is the type of learning that sticks with you for life. In fact, for many people, it's what makes life worth living.

Here are a few more benefits of alternative learning:

- You'll feel proud when you do something important and exciting.

- You'll gain a sense of satisfaction after following through with something you started on your own.

- You'll feel more confident and mature.

- You'll increase your understanding of the world, or of yourself.

- You'll become more independent, more of an individual.

- You'll be better prepared for your future—whatever it may hold.

- You could discover an interest, a talent, or an ability that you didn't even know you had.

- You'll impress your friends, peers, parents, teachers, and other people when you try new things and share what you've learned.

- You may finally find an answer to that persistent question, "What do you want to do with your life?"

- You can kiss boredom and indifference good-bye.

And it doesn't hurt that alternative learning experiences happen to look *great* on a résumé or college application. College admissions officials and employers admire teens who are involved in alternative learning. When you look for a job, start applying to colleges, or pursue other educational opportunities, you can take pride in knowing that your application will stand out. Employers and review boards often look beyond the usual credentials to find someone who seems unique, diverse, or highly motivated. This person can be *you*.

Why I Wrote This Book—and How to Use It

In high school, I was involved in alternative learning without even realizing it. I did an internship at a suburban newspaper, volunteered at a senior citizens' care center and at a local science museum, and participated in several summer writing and journalism programs. No one called these activities "alternative learning experiences" or directed me to resources where I could discover more about what I was doing. Instead, I located these opportunities mainly on my own because I was in search of creative ways to spend my summers or my time after school. I enjoyed this "outside" work; I felt I was doing something of value and playing a positive role in other people's lives. These learning experiences helped me make friends with people of different ages and backgrounds—including senior citizens, newspaper editors, writers, and kids I met at the museum.

It wasn't until college that I was officially bitten by the "alternative learning bug." I was fortunate to have opportunities to study abroad—in England, Germany, and Japan. I learned how to deal with culture shock, follow local customs, and live in foreign countries where nearly everything was unfamiliar to me, including how people talked, what they ate, how they got from place to place, and what kind of money they used. The survival skills I gained helped me feel more knowledgeable and worldly. They gave me greater confidence in myself.

During college, I became even more interested in writing. I wanted to go beyond writing academic papers for my classes and explore what career possibilities might lie ahead. I got an internship at a TV station to gain a close-up look at the world of broadcast journalism. As I soon discovered, the internship wasn't very structured, and no one was going to "take me under their wing." I decided to look at this as an opportunity, not a disappointment. With little supervision and few responsibilities, I had plenty of freedom to meet the reporters, the anchors, and the meteorologist, and to spend time observing how a newsroom operates. I was able to go out with the camera crew on their shoots, too—some of the locations included a local jail, the home of a crime victim, and an apartment building ablaze with fire. I witnessed real-life events I wouldn't ordinarily be exposed to, and I saw firsthand how reporters have to act fast to release breaking news and meet their tight deadlines. While this was exciting, I decided that a fast-paced career in broadcast news wasn't for me.

F. Y. I.

This book isn't another directory of programs; there are many of those available already. *The Teenagers' Guide to School Outside the Box* is about a world of possibilities that awaits you—if you know what to look for and are willing to experiment.

The pace was slower at my internship with a monthly regional magazine. There, my main duty was fact-checking, which meant I was responsible for verifying information and details. I would spend days at the library poring over records and reading historical documents. I enjoyed working one-on-one with the editors and phoning people for interviews—I even got to write several pieces for the magazine!

Of course, these internships weren't 100 percent fun-filled and glamorous. At both, I was expected to master the standard gofer duties: running errands, getting people coffee, and—every intern's crowning glory—making crisp and clear photocopies. But no matter how big or small the task, I learned the importance of efficiency and teamwork. I saw how things were run in the world of business. And I got a chance to test my writing skills in a whole new way.

I loved every moment of my college work experiences and my travels, but I couldn't help feeling a twinge of regret that I didn't know sooner about the many learning opportunities the world held. My high school years weren't nearly as fun and interesting as my college years—but now I know they could have been. That's why I decided to write a book, the one I wish had existed when I was in high school. My mission was to create a comprehensive guide of alternative learning experiences that are available to teens, plus: (1) how to scout them out, (2) what to expect from them, and (3) how to make the most of them.

I strongly believe in the value of going beyond a traditional four-year high school curriculum to try out new opportunities. But how do you figure out what you want to do, and what you'll most enjoy? College students have access to lots of resources and information about internships, mentorships, study abroad programs, and more. Your high school may not have this kind of information—mine didn't. And there may be other obstacles as well:

What if I can't afford the costs of going abroad?
What if I miss my friends and family when I'm away?
What if my parents don't support my desire to travel?

What if what I really want to do is make the world a better place?

What if I don't know what to talk about with a mentor?
What if I have no idea what I want to do in life?

What if I'm nervous about doing a résumé and interviewing for a job or an internship?
What if I live far from a university or college, but I still want to take higher-level courses?

All good questions! This book is designed to be your definitive, one-stop shop for exploring your what ifs—and finding answers that are right for you.

Part 1, "What You Can Do While Living at Home," presents a variety of fun, challenging learning experiences you can try while living with your family. Part 2, "What You Can Do Away from Home . . . Or Far, Far Away," explores travel adventures and study abroad programs that are available to high school students. You can start anywhere in this book, depending on what type of learning experience you feel ready for. If you're enthusiastic about travel, go right to Part 2. If you're looking for activities closer to home, begin with Part 1. Not sure *what* you want? Dip in anywhere—you're sure to find something that will pique your interest. Throughout the book, you'll read about other high school students who have gone "outside the box." You'll also find lots of resources that can help you go further in your search for opportunities that match your needs and interests.

So, what if no one you know has ever tried an alternative learning experience? What if your school doesn't offer anything like internships or job shadowing? What if your high school guidance center is seriously lacking? Relax. Armed with the knowledge in this book, you can be the first of your friends to pursue these innovative opportunities. That's what being an alternative learner is all about.

If you choose an alternative learning experience from this book—or use this book as a starting point for brainstorming your own idea—write and tell me about what you learned. How did you decide on your alternative learning experience? How did it go? What impact did it have on you? What would you have done differently? You can also write to me with questions or comments about this book. You can reach me at this address:

Free Spirit Publishing Inc.
217 Fifth Avenue North, Suite 200
Minneapolis, MN 55401-1299
email: help4kids@freespirit.com

I look forward to hearing from you!

Rebecca Greene

Part 1:

What You Can Do While Living at Home

Chapter 1

Give More of Yourself—
Volunteer Your Time

"Everybody can be great because anybody can serve. You don't
have to have a college degree to serve. You don't have to
make your subject and verbs agree to serve. You only
need a heart full of grace, a soul generated by love."

Martin Luther King, Jr.

- A high school freshman in Pennsylvania started a
  clothing drive for people who are homeless.
- In Wisconsin, a high school junior spent a semester in
  Chile inoculating children against disease.
- A Florida teenager began a project to feed the hungry
  every Thanksgiving.

In towns, cities, and states across the nation, teens are doing their
part to make the world a better place. Volunteering is *everywhere*.
Are you lending a hand?

You can volunteer on a large scale, like the teenagers you just
read about. But if you're not sure you're ready to organize a big
project on your own, you may decide to donate your time to
a nonprofit organization like the United Way, People for the
Ethical Treatment of Animals, or Habitat for Humanity, for

example. Volunteers keep the cogwheels of organizations like these greased and running. Churches, synagogues, and other religious organizations also lead a variety of service projects, from fundraisers to mentoring programs to delivering meals to people in need.

And what do all of the volunteers get for offering their services? Money? No. Fame and glory? Probably not. Gratitude? Definitely. A deep-down sense of personal fulfillment? You better believe it! Not only do volunteers feel good about pitching in for a cause they care about, but they also learn more about themselves, and the world, through their hard work and dedication.

Maybe you want to volunteer, but you'd prefer to start small. No problem. You can give your time in a very personal way by working one-on-one with someone who's in need. Is there an elderly person in your apartment building or neighborhood who could use help running errands, cleaning, reading the newspaper, or preparing meals? A parent who might need some free babysitting? Is there a child you know who's going through a difficult time at home or at school? What might you do to help? Giving your time—giving of *yourself*—definitely has rewards. You'll learn to be more compassionate as you realize that people in your community need help. And you'll become more confident when you find out that *you* are the right person to give it.

It's not just people who need help. You could volunteer on behalf of animals, donating time at a local shelter. You could focus on the environment by getting involved in a community garden or a tree-planting program. Or you could spend some time picking up litter in your neighborhood. All of these activities add up to time well spent.

Need more ideas? Brainstorm a list using the suggestions on page 12 for inspiration. You can organize your list by categories like People, Animals, and Community/Environment. If you want to get more specific, you can further divide your list into topics like Kids, Wildlife, Recycling, and so on.

F.Y.I.

Volunteering is one kind of work that you don't have to be a certain age to do. Few volunteer organizations will turn you down because of how old you are. You might even get to set your own schedule and work as many hours as you wish.

People

- Donate time at a soup kitchen.
- Read to someone who's blind.
- Become a reading tutor.
- Help out at a homeless shelter.
- Set up a free baby-sitting service for low-income families.
- Participate in a blood drive.

Animals

- Contact your local zoo to find out about adopting or sponsoring an animal.
- Walk dogs or clean cages at a shelter.
- Provide a foster home for animals awaiting adoption.
- Offer free pet care to families on vacation.

Community/Environment

- Encourage others to recycle.
- Hold an environmental fair at your school.
- Plant some flowers in a park.
- Adopt an acre of rain forest.
- Beautify a vacant lot.

One of the best things about volunteering is that *anyone* can do it. You don't need experience or expertise—all you need is a wish to help. In fact, for many teens, volunteering is a good introduction to alternative learning experiences. Donating your time is an easy—and inspiring—place to start.

What You Can Learn from Volunteering

Volunteering is a wonderful opportunity to challenge yourself physically, emotionally, and mentally—and to connect with yourself and others at a deeper level. End result? You feel good. But beyond that, you expand your view of the world. Volunteering is alternative learning in action. Here's why:

1. You'll meet people of diverse ages and backgrounds. High schools are filled with teens. (Obviously!) So, most often, you're interacting with people who are your age or just a little older or younger. Aside from parents, siblings, teachers, and administrators, you may have little interaction with adults or young children during the day. Volunteering can change that. Depending on what type of project you decide to pursue, you may get a chance to work with people of a variety of ages, races, religions, and socioeconomic backgrounds. This can open your eyes to other ways of life, new friendships, and fresh ways of thinking.

2. You may encounter a variety of viewpoints and outlooks. If you're volunteering on behalf of a cause that's political or controversial, you'll most likely run into people who have strong opinions and beliefs. This can help open your mind and raise your awareness. Fifteen-year-old Ben, for example, volunteered at an environmental organization that was often harassed by companies wanting to shut it down. People representing these companies picketed outside the organization Ben worked for. Although he was committed to his work and the cause it supported, Ben wanted to remain open to other points of view. He often talked to the picketers and other opponents to see the issue from both sides. Like Ben, other teens have discovered that getting involved in a cause makes the issue come alive. You're not just reading about it, you're *participating* in it, along with other people—that's hands-on learning.

3. You'll see how people deal with problems and adversity. When you're in school all day, you're insulated from the broader world. It's easy to forget that there's more to life than tests and homework assignments. But when you get out there and volunteer, you see things you might not ordinarily see: patients who are ill in the hospital, children who have learning problems or physical disabilities, adults who are learning to read or speak English, people who are committed to rehabilitating injured wildlife or polluted waterways. Sixteen-year-old Robert found that volunteer work helped him put life in perspective: "I used to get upset when I'd get a bad grade, but after I volunteered at a food bank and saw how brave and full of hope people were even though they had been hungry for days, I decided not to sweat the small stuff." You too may learn a lot about hardship—and the human spirit—when you become a volunteer.

4. You'll be tested and realize you're capable of more than you thought. You'll be tested, but not in the same way you are in a high school classroom. As nearly every volunteer discovers, the duties change, expand, and grow like crazy. If you work at a senior citizens' care center, for example, the people in charge may ask you to answer phones one day, sort mail the next, and help out in the recreation room the day after that. You might quickly find yourself running the evening bingo game, leading an arts and crafts group, or encouraging seniors to participate in an exercise class—even if you've never done anything like that before. Some tasks will be easy; others may seem difficult. Stretching yourself is part of learning.

5. You'll gain new skills. In school, you're focusing on subjects like math, science, English, history, and so on. Much of this learning involves reading, memorizing, and writing. But what if you love to work with your hands—molding clay, painting, taking apart electronic equipment, grooming animals, sewing, planting—and you wish you could incorporate these activities into your day? What if you enjoy exercise and being outdoors—can you combine learning with things you love to do? Of course! Getting involved in a volunteering project gives you a chance to explore your interests, while doing something that benefits other people or the earth. As you work with and on behalf of others, you sharpen your people skills. As you use your hands or your body, you make them stronger. As you try new things and take on more challenges, you grow.

6. You'll think about your life differently. Maybe you'll be more grateful for what you have. Maybe you'll feel more energized and excited about what you're able to give. Maybe you'll think about your future in a whole new light. All of this can open your mind and heart, making you more receptive to learning opportunities that come your way.

7. You'll have a new activity to talk about. A valuable part of volunteering is sharing what you've learned. Your family, friends, and teachers will want to hear about your experiences, and when you share this information, you may encourage them to get involved, too. Plus, when you volunteer, you automatically have something in common with the other volunteers you meet. Some of these people may be adults who can help you evaluate your future plans and give you insights into a potential career. Added bonus: you'll now have something to put on your résumé!

F. Y. I.

Volunteer work is generally regarded with as much respect as paid work. Employers consider volunteering to be as valuable as job experience because they know that volunteers have a range of duties and are highly motivated. College admissions officers are also impressed by teens who volunteer. Donating your time shows you're a dedicated and compassionate person, a characteristic that can set you apart from other applicants.

GETTING YOUR FOOT IN THE DOOR

Do you have a special interest or ideas for a career? Maybe you want to explore veterinary medicine, accounting, newspaper publishing, dentistry, or social services. Plenty of companies, organizations, and offices could use a helping hand, so offer your services as a volunteer. Explain that you're looking for a chance to learn more about what interests you and to acquire new skills. If you're hired, you'll get to meet new people, observe what they do at work, pitch in where you can, prove what you're capable of, and learn something new. Sure, you work for free, but there are still rewards. You may connect with someone in your field of interest—someone who could become a mentor. (To read more about this, see Chapter 3, "Get a Mentor, Be a Mentor.") You may even receive a glowing recommendation from your boss, which means you'll have something to take to future job interviews. Time well spent, in other words!

Volunteering and School

Convinced you want to volunteer, but you still don't know where to begin? Actually, starting at school can be helpful. Does your high school have a service club or a volunteer fair? Many high schools have national clubs that focus on service, including Interact Club (sponsored by Rotary International), Leo Club (Lions Club International), and Key Club (Kiwanis International). If your school has these clubs, it's likely that regularly scheduled volunteer opportunities are part of the activities. Join in! This is a simple way to add volunteering into your schedule.

If you've got a great idea for a volunteer project but you know you'll need lots of help, a school service club might just be the answer. Other members will probably want to lend a hand. Talk to the president or organizer of the service club to see who might be able to help and what resources are available. Another option is to talk to a teacher or an administrator about what you'd like to do, and see if you can start your *own* service club. You may soon be on your way to turning your idea into a reality.

> **F. Y. I.**
>
> In 1992, Maryland became the first state to require that students complete a certain number of hours of community service in order to graduate. Since then, many states have followed Maryland's lead.

Does your school have a community service requirement, meaning you have to complete a certain number of hours of community service—or volunteer work—in order to graduate? If your school requires that all students perform community service as a graduation requirement, you'll want to start thinking about your options. First, determine what causes you're most interested in or where you'd like to make a difference. Create a list of possibilities. Next, think about where in your community help is needed most.

- Are there areas of your neighborhood that look neglected?
- Do the sidewalks need repair?
- Is there a lot of graffiti in your community? A building that might be beautified with a mural?
- Does a local park need more trees? Is there a playground that requires better equipment?
- Are many people in the community hungry or homeless?
- Is there a group of people you're interested in serving: the elderly, infants, children, people with disabilities?

Where could you make the most difference?

Next, contact organizations that focus on the kind of help you'd like to give and explain your interest in volunteering. The American Red Cross, the Sierra Club, and the YMCA/YWCA are examples of large organizations that have branches in cities and communities across the country. Many such organizations welcome high school volunteers. Find out what opportunities are open to you and ask to meet the volunteer coordinator. You might also call a local parks and recreation department, a care center for senior citizens, or a hospital to ask about volunteering.

When meeting with a representative from the organization, explain your school service requirement and your specific skills and interests. Talk about your schedule, how many hours you can give, and what you hope to gain from the experience. Ask any questions that come to mind. Be sure to bring along paper and a pen, so you can take notes.

To make the most of your volunteering experience, think about what you can offer and what the activity can offer *you.* What do you want to learn and accomplish? Why does this particular cause or effort matter to you? You may not have the answers right away, especially if you're a first-time volunteer. Keep the questions in the back of your mind. Ask them of yourself every so often to determine what you're getting out of the experience. This helps keep your learning goals in sight.

SPOTLIGHT ON

David Hendler
Greenhill School
Dallas, Texas

During the summer before my freshman year, I donated about seventy-five hours at Trinity Ministry to the Poor, a nonprofit organization that hosted several programs. I worked in the kitchen and helped with lunch and cleanup. The Ministry had a thrift shop, job training, and other programs to help people get back on their feet. Volunteering turned out to be a lot of fun. The head cook was a good guy, I learned how to make mass quantities of food, and I got to know the people who came through every day.

My school has a good community service program. At least twice a year, the entire school participates in a community service day, and we also have a community service requirement. I have volunteered with many organizations, including Head Start (an early childhood program) and the

Science Place. The Science Place is a science museum in Dallas; I had been there many times as a kid and loved it. As a volunteer, I shadowed employees to see what they did while on the job. I also helped with cleaning and other day-to-day tasks.

I spent many hours in the Hands On Physics area, where the harmonograph was. This device demonstrated harmonic motion as well as friction. It's a big table with a piece of paper on it that has four wires connecting the corners of the table to the ceiling about 20 feet up. There's a pen that doesn't move, which traces the motion of the table onto the paper. If you haven't ever seen a harmonograph, it's hard to imagine, but it makes cool designs. During my time at the museum, I got to know the people and the exhibits better, and I was given more responsibility. I got to talk to visitors about the exhibits and even perform some demonstrations.

My advice to other volunteers is to try out different things. Every volunteer experience will be different. Work hard at whatever you get involved in. The more you try, the more likely you'll find something you enjoy!

Tips for Successful Volunteer Work

- **Sit down with your volunteer supervisor and discuss the expectations.** What will your responsibilities be? Are you comfortable with them? Would you like to do more (or less)? Be clear about what you expect to learn from the experience.

- **Take on as much responsibility as you feel you can.** The more you put into it, the more you'll get out of it. But this doesn't mean that you have to jump right in and do everything at once. At first, you may just want to observe, so you can learn more about the people you're working with or the organization you're now a part of. Little by little, you can get more involved.

- **Keep the lines of communication open with your supervisor and the other volunteers.** Are you having fun? Contributing as much as you can? Do you have ideas to share? Suggestions for improvement? Do you want more responsibility? Are you feeling overwhelmed? Don't be afraid to speak up.

- **Take your duties seriously.** You won't be paid, but volunteer work is still important work. Show up on time. Do your share. Put forth your best effort. Act responsibly. Remember, people are counting on you!

- **Keep a log of your volunteer work.** (This may even be part of your community service requirement.) A log or journal is a good place to keep track of your experience and will serve as a record to look back on. This will come in handy when you're putting together a résumé or preparing for a job interview where you'll talk about your volunteering. You may also want to take photos, so you can always remember the people you worked with or helped.

- **Be friendly, open, and honest.** Volunteering is really about community building. It depends on the teamwork and camaraderie of the volunteers themselves.

- **Make contacts.** Personal contacts are important when you need a recommendation letter, a lead for an internship, or advice about a potential career. Your colleagues—other volunteers, staff members at the organization, your supervisor—can be your contacts. You may even want to ask your volunteer supervisor to write you a recommendation letter at the conclusion of your volunteer work—then you'll have something on file that you can use when applying to colleges or for a job.

SPOTLIGHT ON

Hannah Chapin
Chapel Hill High School
Chapel Hill, North Carolina

I worked on many volunteer projects during high school, logging in a total of about 300 hours. In those four years, I became more and more invested in community service for the joy of it. It became part of my life.

I worked on everything from collecting trash on the side of roads near my house, to tutoring, to helping with the public television station's yearly pledge drive. I was also involved in a local festival of Hispanic culture that happens every year in Chapel Hill: La Fiesta del Pueblo. I noticed that the festival, while having an abundance of food, games, and music, was lacking in its recycling practices, so I set out to improve them.

I entered the project with big dreams, modeled on practices at another local outdoor festival. I envisioned composting all of the food and paper waste, and recycling cans and bottles. This was a bit ambitious, as I soon learned, because of our facilities and short time frame. I decided to focus on recycling cans and bottles at the festival, realizing we would have our hands plenty full with that.

I worked with the county's recycling coordinator because she had more experience and professional contacts than I did. She really handled all of the logistics, but I acted as a catalyst for the project and was responsible for organizing high school volunteers to manually collect the recyclable materials from stations around the festival. We created a recycling display to get people's attention; we also put out recycling bins, labeled in both Spanish and English. It was hot and difficult work, but I felt that it was beneficial. By the end of the festival, we had recovered a large volume of recyclable materials, which helped reduce waste. But the other important aspect was educating the public about this environmental issue.

I believe that the recycling program at the festival will continue to expand and improve, even though I'm no longer a part of it. And as with most environmental causes, the evidence of any positive effects may come years down the road. I couldn't have run the entire program on my own. Sometimes the best thing a person can do is plant the seed of an idea and actively help it grow. If one is lucky, the project will then take on a life of its own, and the effects will spread far beyond anything that one single person could accomplish.

Dealing with Problems

- **How do you handle those first-day fears?** You might feel nervous or jittery just thinking about the day you start your volunteer work. Keep in mind that everyone has these fears from time to time. So how do you deal with them? First, remind yourself that it's normal to feel at least a little scared when introduced to a new situation. The moment you walk in the door on the first day, take a few deep breaths to calm down. A good way to get accustomed to an unfamiliar situation is to ask a lot of questions. You can ask your supervisor, the other volunteers, or the people themselves—no question is too silly when you're showing genuine interest and curiosity. Share some information about yourself and your background, so everyone can get to know you. You'll eventually start to feel more comfortable.

- **What if your parents don't support the volunteer work you've chosen?** Maybe you're working on behalf of a cause that your parents strongly disagree with. Without their support, you might feel pressured to quit. Seventeen-year-old Shana volunteered at a clinic that performed abortions, even though her parents believed abortion was wrong. At first, her parents tried to convince her to volunteer somewhere else.

Shana explained that, although she valued their opinion, she wanted to be open-minded about the abortion issue. Talking things over helped. Discuss your point of view with your parents and try to peacefully resolve any conflicts that come up.

- **What if you have trouble dealing with the hardships you're witnessing?** Teens who volunteer at crisis centers, homeless shelters, hospitals, and animal shelters often express that they weren't completely prepared for the realities their volunteer work forced them to face. At times, you too may feel overwhelmed by what you see and experience. Talk with someone you trust: your supervisor, another volunteer, a friend, a parent, or a teacher. Often, just getting your feelings out in the open can be a relief.

SPOTLIGHT ON
Erika Greisman
Wilmington Friends
Wilmington, Delaware

The summer after my junior year in high school, I volunteered at a women's shelter, where I cared for the children of women who'd been victims of domestic violence. I wish I'd gone into the shelter with more realistic expectations. Many people decide to help with the expectation that they'll be able to do some concrete good and walk away with a satisfaction similar to finishing a huge batch of dishes. I went to the shelter expecting to cure the women's and the children's problems by sharing my wisdom and love with them. I was an idealist—but the reality I faced was much different. I learned about the complexities surrounding abuse and the nature of human suffering. I realized that I couldn't solve these issues as just one individual. There are no easy answers or quick fixes.

- **What if you make a mistake on the job?** Mistakes are embarrassing when they happen, but don't let them prevent you from trying new things or feeling good about the work you do. The people you volunteer with will know that you're human like everyone else—they aren't expecting perfection. Besides, even the most seasoned professionals make mistakes. If you goof up, think of it as a learning experience, not a failure. Try to make amends by fixing your error or simply apologizing.

 ## FIND OUT MORE

Volunteering is one of the most accessible learning experiences covered in this book. So here's a "mega-list" of resources describing some of the many ways you can get involved.

Community Service for Teens by Bernard Ryan Jr. (Chicago: Ferguson, 1998). This multi-volume set discusses a wide variety of community service options in eight different fields, such as caring for animals, participating in government, expanding education, and serving with the police. Your high school or a local college career center may have the entire set, but the books are also available individually.

The Future Is Ours: A Handbook for Student Activists in the 21st Century, edited by John W. Bartlett (New York: Henry Holt, 1996). This book will show you everything you need to know to be an effective activist. Its step-by-step approach, complete with case studies and worksheets, will help you take charge and make change happen. You'll also find a resource directory and descriptions of the most effective ways to implement change, including community education, demonstrations, and fund-raising.

Generation React: Activism for Beginners by Danny Seo (New York: Ballatine Books, 1997). This book includes suggestions on starting your own activist group or reenergizing an existing one. There are helpful hints on how to publicize efforts, raise funds, organize a protest, lobby government officials, and more. The nineteen-year-old author of this inspiring guide knows what he's talking about—he founded a national organization of youth concerned about animal rights and the environment when he was twelve.

It's Our World, Too! Stories of Young People Who Are Making a Difference by Phillip Hoose (Boston: Joy Street Books, 1993). This book shares the stories of teens who are making a difference and tells you how to do the same. If you're interested in social action, make sure to add this title to your reading list.

150 Ways Teens Can Make a Difference by Marian Salzmann and others (Princeton, NJ: Peterson's Guides, 1991). In this book, teens discuss their volunteer experiences in an honest, "tell-all" manner. Topics range from bringing volunteerism into a busy schedule to sharing personal accomplishments. Though out of print, the book is worth searching for at your local public library.

Volunteer America, edited by Harriet Clyde Kipps (Chicago: Ferguson, 1997). This comprehensive directory lists almost 1,500 organizations that are looking for volunteers. Each listing includes information on the organization, the address, a contact person, objectives, services, and publications.

Volunteering: 101 Ways You Can Improve the World and Your Life by Douglas M. Lawson (San Diego: Alti Publishing, 1998). This book answers questions on volunteering, such as "How can I raise money as a volunteer?" and "Can volunteering help me build new skills?" It's full of inspiring quotes that will motivate you to do your part to make the world a better place. The book is out of print, but it should be available at your local public library.

The Volunteer's Survival Manual: The Only Practical Guide to Giving Your Time and Money by Darcy Campion Devney (Cambridge, MA: Practical Press, 1992). There are many great—and sometimes surprising—rewards to volunteering. This book examines how volunteering can improve many aspects of your life, including relationships and career options. It also gives information on how nonprofit organizations work, plus helpful tips on becoming a successful volunteer.

Corporation for National Service
1201 New York Avenue NW
Washington, D.C. 20525
(202) 606-5000
www.cns.gov

The Corporation for National Service is a public-private partnership that engages people of all ages in service through three national initiatives: Americorps, Learn & Serve, and Senior Corps. Visit the CNS Web site to find out information about these programs and more.

Do Something!
423 West 55th Street, 8th Floor
New York, NY 10019
(212) 523-1175
www.dosomething.org

Do Something! is a national program that funds and trains teens to be leaders in their communities. The organization's comprehensive and fun Web site allows you to apply for grants and awards, get new volunteering ideas, and read inspiring stories of other young volunteers.

Key Club International
3636 Woodview Trace
Indianapolis, IN 46268-3196
1-800-549-2647
www.keyclub.org

Key Club International is an organization that promotes citizenship, service to school and community, and leadership training for high school students. Check out the Key Club Web site to find out if your school is already a member. If not, you can contact the organization and learn how to start a chapter at your school.

National Service-Learning Clearinghouse
University of Minnesota
954 Buford Avenue, Room R-460
Saint Paul, MN 55108
1-800-808-SERVE (1-800-808-7378)
www.nicsl.coled.umn.edu

The NSLC is a national storehouse for service-learning resources. The Web site lets you look up events and programs by state, read the "Learn & Serve America" grant guidelines, and look up frequently asked service-learning questions by topic. The site also has links to other Web addresses.

National Youth Leadership Council
1910 West County Road B
Roseville, MN 55113
(651) 631-3672
www.nylc.org

This organization's mission is to help teens and youth participate in their communities and schools through learning, service, leadership, and public policy. NYLC supports several schoolwide programs and is a great resource if you're thinking about service-learning.

Points of Light Foundation
1400 I Street NW, Suite 800
Washington, D.C. 20005
(202) 729-8000
www.pointsoflight.org

This foundation provides technical assistance, training, consulting, information sharing, research, and advocacy on behalf of youth service, service-learning, and youth leadership. In other words, a good place to get information!

YMCA Teen Leadership Programs
101 North Wacker Drive
Chicago, IL 60606
1-800-872-9622
www.ymca.net

You'll find plenty of opportunities to do service projects here, such as the Earth Service Corps groups that combine environmental awareness with volunteering. The Web site will also lead you to your local YMCA and projects.

Youth Service America
1101 15th Street
Suite 200
Washington, D.C. 20005
(202) 296-2992
www.ysa.org

Youth Service America is a resource center dedicated to increasing the quantity and quality of opportunities for teens to serve locally, nationally, and globally. The organization also sponsors many initiatives including National Youth Service Day (see below).

The Virtual Volunteering Project
www.serviceleader.org/vv/

Want to volunteer but have difficulty with transportation? Try virtual volunteering where the tasks are completed in whole or part via the Internet. The Virtual Volunteering Project Web site gives you information including the history of the project, answers to frequently asked questions, and lots of advice for finding online volunteering opportunities. The projects offered by VVP range from online mentoring to helping maintain a not-for-profit organization's Web site to contributing ideas for an original musical benefiting youth. This site is a great reminder that opportunities for volunteering are everywhere!

Make a Difference Day

Make a Difference Day was created by *USA Weekend* in partnership with the Points of Light Foundation and is recognized on the fourth Saturday in October. It's a day to celebrate our neighbors, communities, and how each person can make a difference. For more information, call 1-800-416-3824.

National Youth Service Day

The third Tuesday of every April is National Youth Service Day. This is the largest volunteer event in the world, and it recognizes youth volunteer work. For more information, check out *www.youthserve.net*.

Service-Learning

In 1993, the National Service Act went into effect, which brought volunteering into the school curriculum through "service-learning." According to the Act, service-learning is a method that combines knowledge of a particular subject and community outreach. Students involved in service-learning work directly with community members in a project-based setting. For example, students might help clean up a polluted pond as part of a science class.

Service-learning—based on educator John Dewey's idea of "learning by doing"—is popular among high school students because they're given the opportunity to spend classroom time in a non-classroom setting. They often get to choose their own project and may work singly or in groups. Reflection on the experience is an important component of service-learning. Students discuss their project with their teacher or class—as a way to share information, ask and answer questions, bring up problems, brainstorm solutions, and reflect on what the experience has meant to each student and the community. These discussions usually take place before, during, and after the project. Many teens say that talking about their volunteering experiences once they return to the classroom helps them better understand the work they've just done.

Service-learning and community service requirements aren't one in the same. Service-learning is specifically designed to create a link between what the students are learning, a service provided to the community, and reflection on the entire process. Some high schools have mandatory service-learning requirements—find out if yours does. If you have questions, talk to a teacher, a guidance counselor, or your principal. The president of your school's service club may also be of help.

"I worked with the National Youth Leadership Council during my junior year of high school. I was on their Youth Project Team and the board of directors. Promoting service-learning was our main goal. At both the National Service-Learning Conference in Orlando and the President's Summit for America's Future in Philadelphia, I spoke about the positive aspects of service-learning. Students retain more when they have the opportunity to apply their learning in a practical way. Plus, the community benefits as well."—**Aisha**

Many high school students have found that service-learning enhances what they're learning in the classroom. Their work in the community helps them feel as if they're part of something bigger than their school. This feeling motivates many of them to succeed academically where they had struggled before, because what they learn finally can be applied to the real world. Another benefit: service-learning fosters a sense of caring, connection, and community. This enriches students and community members alike.

5 Ways to Celebrate Your Service-Learning Achievements

1. Invite a community member who's involved in your service project to take part in a classroom discussion.

2. Organize a student panel to talk about what you've learned in your service project. Find out if you can hold the panel during an assembly, so all students may attend.

3. Start a newsletter for your school and other schools involved in service-learning. Write articles about students who have really made a difference in other people's lives.

4. Put together a class journal or a photography exhibit that showcases your service project. Display it at a local community center.

5. Throw a party for everyone involved in your service-learning project. Celebrate what you've accomplished and have fun hanging out together in a laid-back setting.

Volunteering Abroad

F. Y. I.

Applying to college? Your volunteering experience will give you something unique to talk about in the essay portion of your application. Write about what volunteering has meant to you and all that you've learned from it.

Volunteering in your community is rewarding, but there's even more you can do. Have you ever considered volunteering in another country? When you volunteer overseas, you have the chance to get to know young people from all over the world and work with them to meet a common goal. Along the way, you have opportunities to mix with the locals, get to know their culture, learn a new language and way of life, and do something genuinely unique. How many teens can say they spent the summer building a sewer in Tanzania or vaccinating children in Chile? Now *there's* some interesting material for a back-to-school essay entitled "What I Did on My Summer Vacation"!

Volunteering abroad can take the form of participating in an archaeological dig, teaching children English, or working as an intern at a company or business that interests you. Some volunteer programs are organized as "work camps" in which you and other students work together on projects like digging latrines, building dams, or doing other community-building activities. You don't need any experience or special skills, because you'll be trained on the job. Most of these programs are offered in the summer, but sometimes year- or semester-long programs are available. Housing and meal costs are usually covered.

If you're interested in volunteering outside your state or abroad but you don't have much travel experience, take a look at Chapter 7, "Go to Camp, Go on an Adventure, Go Overseas," to learn more about the benefits of hitting the road or heading overseas. It's a *big* decision to travel as a teen, so you'll want to be sure you're ready. Part 2 of this book is filled with advice on getting prepared and making the most of your experience.

"I went to Paraguay to do a construction job through a work camp. Even though I didn't know anything about construction before I left, the people there taught me everything I needed to know, from how to hammer nails to how to read a floor plan. I learned so much."

—Manuel

FIND OUT MORE

Alternatives to the Peace Corps: A Directory of Third World and U.S. Volunteer Opportunities by Filomena Giese, Marilyn Borchardt, and Martha Fernandez (Oakland, CA: Food First Books, 1999). This book guides readers who would like to volunteer outside of their local community. It includes helpful information such as a list of expenses related to each opportunity and Web sites for contacting many of the organizations.

The International Directory of Voluntary Work, 7th Edition by Louise Whetter and Victoria Pybus (Oxford, England: Vacation Work, 2000). This essential handbook to traveling the world while volunteering is conveniently divided into two sections. The first lists opportunities by area of the world, the second by type of work. The authors include a lot of important information including what expenses are covered by each organization. If you're looking for a way to travel without being a tourist, this is the book for you!

The Peace Corps and More: 175 Ways to Work, Study, and Travel at Home and Abroad by Medea Benjamin and Miya Rodolfo-Sioson (Santa Ana, CA: Seven Locks Press, 1997). This book will show you how to check out your options for working in developing countries, including study and volunteer opportunities, and socially responsible travel.

So You Want to Join the Peace Corps: What to Know Before You Go by Dillon Banerjee (Berkeley, CA: Ten Speed Press, 2000). If you're thinking about the long-term commitment of the Peace Corps, this is a helpful question-and-answer book. It provides a ton of information including tips on strengthening your application, choosing what to pack, and dealing with loneliness. This easy-to-read guide will give you a glimpse into what to expect from the Peace Corps and help you decide if it's the right experience for you.

Volunteer Vacations: Short-Term Adventures That Will Benefit You and Others by Bill McMillon and Edward Asner (Chicago: Chicago Review, 1999). If you're looking for an alternative way to see the world, add this book to your reading list. It covers many types of volunteerism for people of all levels of experience. Besides containing information on agencies seeking volunteers, the book also has a detailed cross-referenced index that allows you to choose an adventure that matches your interests, schedule, and budget.

American Farm School
1133 Broadway, Suite 1625
New York, NY 10010
(212) 463-8434
www.afs.edu.gr

The American Farm School is an organization that trains young men and women in Greece to become village leaders and master farmers. The school offers a program specifically for American high school students, called Greek Summer. Lasting five weeks in Thessaloniki, Greece, Greek Summer brings students to help with village projects such as building roads. Students live with a family, help with the school's summer farm work, and see the sights of Greece. The enrollment is around forty, and students must have completed tenth grade.

American Friends Service Committee Youth Programs
1501 Cherry Street
Philadelphia, PA 19102
(215) 241-7000
www.afsc.org./default.htm

This organization offers service opportunities and summer work camps in Mexico and Cuba for young adults ages eighteen to twenty-six. You must speak Spanish fluently to take part.

Amigos de las Americas
International Office
5618 Star Lane
Houston, TX 77057
1-800-231-7796
www.amigoslink.org

This organization gives high school students (those age sixteen and above who have completed their sophomore year) the opportunity to provide public health and environmental services to people in Latin America over the summer. Applicants must have studied at least two years of Spanish or Portuguese.

Council on International Educational Exchange
205 East 42nd Street
New York, NY 10017
1-800-40-STUDY (1-800-407-8839)
www.ciee.org

As the mission statement says, CIEE "helps people gain understanding, acquire knowledge, and develop skills for living in a globally interdependent and culturally diverse world." This is a great resource if you're looking into international volunteer programs.

International Partnership for Service-Learning
815 Second Avenue, Suite 315
New York, NY 10017
(212) 986-0989
www.ipsl.org

This organization combines academic study and community service in locations such as Ecuador, Israel, Scotland, and others. It's an excellent resource for those who want to volunteer abroad while also attending classes.

Volunteers for Peace
1034 Tiffany Road
Belmont, VT 05730-0202
(802) 259-2759
www.vfp.org

This organization offers international work camps in 60 countries. Volunteers spend two to three weeks per work camp, mostly during the summer months. There are 17 programs for ages 15 and up, 126 programs for ages 16 and up, and 271 programs for ages 17 and up. If you're 18 or older, almost every program is open to you.

"Volunteering provides teens with an opportunity to see outside themselves and build self-esteem through helping others. It helps instill compassion and empathy for all beings. And it inspires a sense of connection."

**Melynda DuVal, Volunteer Coordinator
People for the Ethical Treatment of Animals**

If you're itching to experience the real world, become a volunteer. Volunteering can add excitement to your life and give you an education that you won't receive in any civics class. You'll discover how fascinating it can be to spot real-world problems and come up with ways to fix them. You'll know you're part of the solution, and that's a great feeling. Instead of reading textbooks and doing research on what other people have accomplished, you'll be creating your own history because of the actions you take. Along the way, you'll enrich your community and your education. The bottom line is this: In the process of helping others, you'll help yourself!

Chapter 2

Take Courses Outside the High School Classroom

"Jumping at several small opportunities may get us there more quickly than waiting for one big one to come along."

Hugh Allen

- Are you interested in a class that your school doesn't offer, like nineteenth-century art history or Japanese?
- Do you find that the work in your classes is too easy?
- Do you want to be surrounded by older students, who may place more importance on academics than many of your peers do?
- Do you want to take nonacademic courses that your school doesn't offer (such as archery, printmaking, or computer programming)?
- Do you want to know what a college campus and class-room are really like?
- Do you want to get a head start on your college education?
- Do you want to do more independent work?
- Have you already taken all the classes that challenge you—and do you want more options?

If you answered yes to several of these questions, you're probably wishing your high school had more to offer. And if you're like many smart teens, you crave a deeper level of thinking than what might be experienced in high school-level classes. Maybe you want to participate in more intense discussions or cover more material than what's offered. Perhaps you're interested in subjects like sociology or anthropology, and they aren't offered in the course list. Or perhaps you want to try something completely off the beaten path, but you can't find a class that answers this need.

There's a point of frustration that many high school students reach when they realize that (1) their school's course offerings are limited or (2) they've taken all the advanced classes and are coasting through the others. Do you ever feel that many of your classmates aren't as interested in academics as you are? Or that your teachers don't have the time to find ways to further challenge you? If so, you may be ready to do college-level work and sample the college experience. And that's where taking classes at a local university or college comes in.

Dual Enrollment—What Does It Mean?

Maybe you've been sitting in ceramics class, daydreaming about learning more about sculpture and modern art. Or perhaps you yearn to speak Italian but your school concentrates on French and Spanish. If your high school isn't satisfying your growing intellectual curiosity, consider searching elsewhere for learning alternatives.

One option is to register for a class at a local university or a community college, while still attending high school. This option, known in some states as *dual enrollment,* is a good choice if you live near a college or university and have reliable transportation. Many high school students have found that dual enrollment is a great way to reap the intellectual benefits and variety of college life, while still staying close to home and participating in the familiar high school social scene.

"I had taken every single course that was advanced or looked at all interesting. At the same time, I didn't want to leave high school and become a college student. Dual enrollment was the happy medium."—**Bill**

Taking a class at a college or university isn't the same as being a full-time college student, but it's a nice opportunity to see higher-level education firsthand. You may relish the academic challenges that await: longer lectures, more advanced textbooks, heavier assignments, deeper discussions, greater independence, more learned peers. At the same time, you may fear that you won't fit in socially because you're younger than the other students and won't be part of dormitory life. Before deciding whether taking college courses is the right option for you, ask yourself the following questions:

1. Am I ready to form new friendships with people older than me?

2. Can I handle being "just another face in the crowd" in lectures or on the college campus?

3. Am I ready to work more independently—without reminders from my professor to stay on top of my work and prepare for exams?

4. Will my high school friends accept my decision to take the class (and is their acceptance important to me)?

5. Will I have less time for my friends, and if so, how will I handle this?

6. Are my parents supportive of my choice to pursue educational opportunities outside of high school?

7. Am I comfortable with the workload ahead of me?

8. Do I care whether I fit into the college social scene?

9. Do I understand the expectations of the course I'm interested in?

Write your answers in a notebook or journal, so you can spend time thinking them over. Take a look at them: Do you think you'll have the support of family and friends? Do you feel comfortable blending in with older students and having a heavier workload? If not, you may want to wait a few months or a year and then ask yourself the same questions. It's important to be ready intellectually *and* emotionally.

One major benefit of dual enrollment is that you'll get a head start on college. Seventeen-year-old Cherry took a college math course while still in high school. She had this to say: "I'm glad I did it. I realized that I was ready to do more in-depth work, and now I know what to expect from college math professors." Many high school students agree that taking classes at a college or university gives them more realistic expectations about higher education. It can help you figure out if the "college track" is really right for you.

Besides, you may even be able to get high school and/or college credit. What does this mean? Depending on the course, you could earn credits that (1) are counted toward your high school graduation requirements, or (2) will be added to your college transcript—if the credits are accepted by the college you decide to attend. Either way, you come out ahead because you've already completed some of your graduation requirements. To find out more about credit requirements, talk to your school guidance counselor. If you have an idea about which college or university you'd like to attend full-time in the future, contact its dean to ask about the school's policies on college credit.

More good news: your state may pay for your college-level classes! Different states and schools have different procedures for dual-enrollment students. In Minnesota, for example, high school juniors and seniors have a "post-secondary enrollment option" that allows them to take classes at many colleges and universities—private and public—across the state for free. What's the best way to learn about the options in your state? Call some local universities and colleges directly; ask for the "advanced high school admissions" or the "post-secondary education" office. Inquire about dual enrollment and find out whether high school students receive help paying the costs. (Some state universities refer to high school students who take courses as "non-degree students," "concurrent enrollers," or "precollege students" instead of using the term "dual enrollment." Once you begin talking to various schools, you'll get a better feel for the terminology they use.)

SPOTLIGHT ON

Rebecca Neel
Watertown High School
Watertown, Massachusetts

In the middle of my senior year of high school, I decided to drop a course that just wasn't working out. But soon the "Senior Slump" began to kick in, and my lighter course load only made it easier for me to slack off. I needed something to keep me going. The challenge and depth of a college course appealed to me, so I enrolled in "The Makers of Modern Poetry."

One reason I chose this class was that I found poetry to be pretty frightening—as though the poet was deliberately trying to baffle and frustrate me. I wanted to tackle this behemoth that I had always feared. Another reason was that I was planning to take the Advanced Placement English exam in the spring, to see if I could enroll in upper-level English classes. More exposure to English and writing could increase my chances of passing.

As it turned out, the poetry course was wonderful. The professor was skilled at engaging the class—she gesticulated like crazy and wore vibrant suits with bright scarves. She said that poetry can't be read like a newspaper or a novel; it must be read several times, slowly, and at least once out loud. Although "The Makers of Modern Poetry" was a lecture class of about sixty people, I felt a sense of intimacy—if not with the other students, with the poetry itself.

Taking this class helped me succeed on the Advanced Placement exam, as I'd hoped. I also received both high school and college credit. One of the most rewarding aspects of the course was the way my papers were graded. The teacher's assistant who did the grading wrote copious notes, with great attention to the quality of the writing. Ultimately, I became a lover of poetry.

I would advise any high school student who's thinking of taking a college course to consider a subject that he or she finds intimidating. This can be a chance to challenge yourself in a new area. You may just find that a subject that used to intimidate you will become one of your passions.

If you know you're ready to take a college-level course or two, talk to your school's career counselor or guidance counselor to see what opportunities are available. Ask if any other teens at your school have taken higher education courses, or are currently enrolled in them. These trailblazers can tell you what it will be like. If you still want to know more after talking to a counselor and other students, call a few of the major colleges and universities in your area and ask to speak to the office that handles high school admissions. Find out:

- how old you have to be to sign up
- what the requirements for enrollment are
- how many credits you can take
- how you register for classes
- whether you need to meet with advisors at the college or university first
- whether you need to attend an orientation session

Be sure to take notes during the call, so you have a record of what you've learned.

Before making a final decision about taking college courses, you've got a few more questions to consider:

- If your state doesn't cover the costs of dual enrollment, can your family help you pay?
- Will you need to earn money to pay for the course yourself, and if so, how will you earn it? (For ideas, see pages 209–215.)

- Is the cost worth it to you in terms of the payoff—college credit, high school credit, or the value of what you'll learn?
- Do you have reliable transportation?
- If you'll need to depend on your mom or dad to drive you, have you asked whether this will cause scheduling conflicts?
- Are you comfortable with missing out on some high school experiences as a result of your extra work?

If there's nothing stopping you, then go for it!

"By the time I graduated from high school, I had taken a total of seven classes from my community technical college and a nearby liberal arts university. When I entered college as a full-time student, I wasn't nervous about the work or the expectations. I had already gotten comfortable with the way institutions of higher learning function. I had experience with public computer labs, research papers, college bookstores, and the registrar's office. All of this reduced the element of the unknown as I started my four years at college."—**Wendy**

Managing Your Time

If you're ready to take classes outside of high school, you'll need to make sure you know how to successfully manage your time. Ask yourself if your time-management skills could use some help. For example, do you often wonder why other people seem to get more done during the day than you do—even though each person has the same number of hours to work with?

Managing your time in high school is tricky, because you have to balance homework assignments, extracurricular activities, friendships, family responsibilities, and sometimes a job, too. Add in a college-level class, and you might quickly feel overwhelmed by the amount of reading you have to do and the papers you need to complete. But if you know how to manage your time well, you can fit any kind of alternative learning experience into your already busy life. The good news is time-management skills can be learned—and practiced—just like any other skills. Here are some tips for improving your techniques:

- **Learn to depend on yourself.** Do you need constant prodding from your mom or dad to get your chores done? Do you usually wait until your teacher hounds you for that overdue homework assignment before turning it in? If so, you're relying on other people to motivate you; instead, you can rely on *yourself*. Becoming more independent and responsible is a sign of maturity.

- **Talk to someone who's productive.** This person may accomplish a lot because he or she is organized and efficient. Find out how this person stays on top of everything. Ask about work habits and tips you can try. Borrow some ideas and see if they work for you.

- **Get a calendar or daily planner**. These tools can save time and energy because everything you need to know is in one handy place. You can note your appointments, class times, sports schedule, homework assignments, test dates, and social events all in one spot. (And you won't be searching everywhere for little reminders you've written to yourself or calling a friend to see if you've missed something important.)

- **Keep a to-do list.** What are your tasks for today? What do you want to accomplish? Make daily lists that you keep with your calendar or planner. As you complete each item, cross it off your list. This can be a very satisfying process because you get to see, at a glance, just how much you've gotten done.

- **Avoid procrastination.** Do you wait until the last minute to start your projects? Do you regularly watch the sun come up as you frantically try to finish your work or cram for a test?

F. Y. I.

If you have a little time in between classes, don't let it idly slip by. Read an article, finish up some homework, or organize your class notes. This way, you make each minute of your day count.

Everyone procrastinates once in a while; some people do it a lot! Ask yourself why you put things off. Are the tasks overwhelming? (Then break them down into smaller jobs that you can do quickly and easily—they won't seem so immense anymore.) Are you so worried about doing "perfect" work that you're afraid to make a start? (There's no such thing as perfection, so give yourself a break. Tell yourself that you're going to do your best and then get started.) Understanding *why* you procrastinate is a good first step toward breaking the habit for good.

- **Get to know your personal work style.** Do you like to work on several projects at once—or do you prefer a more methodical approach, completing one task before moving on to the next? Do you work fast and furious, or slow and steady? Do you hate interruptions? Are you easily distracted? Now ask yourself what you can do to accommodate your work style. Can you give yourself more time to complete projects? Do you need a quieter work space? Would it help to take frequent breaks, so you feel more energized? Find out what works, and then stick with these techniques.

- **Reward yourself effectively.** Are you the type of person who prefers delayed gratification—meaning that you save the good stuff like seeing a movie or going out with a friend until your work is done? Or do you want instant gratification—indulging yourself now and putting off your tasks until later? Whatever your style, make it work for you. If you tend to delay gratification, give yourself fun incentives to finish your work. Choose a movie, for example, and plan to see it at a certain time; then you'll be more motivated to finish what you have to do. If you like to have fun before digging into your work, set a time limit for yourself. Do something you enjoy for an hour or so, but then sit down at your desk. These self-rewards can be a big help, if you use them to your advantage!

Summer Options

Not ready to take additional classes during the regular school year? Then how about trying out college life during your summer vacation? Find out if any local colleges or universities offer summer workshops or

> "Only you can know how much you can give to every aspect of your life. Try to decide what is the most important."
>
> **—Barbara Walters**

clinics that focus on research, writing, theater, art, music, or any other subject that interests you. Although you probably won't receive college credit for these learning experiences, they can give you a feel for what college will be like and get you out of the house during the summer. Plus, if you're not sure you can commit to extra classes during the school year or leave your friends behind, summer coursework is a great compromise. It can also give you a clearer idea of whether you may want to pursue dual enrollment the following year.

With a little know-how, you can find free or low-cost summer programs that will allow you to sample college life. For example, the Summer Scholars Program at Saint Peter's College in New Jersey allows high school students to earn college credits in biology, philosophy, and child psychology. In San Francisco, the Summer Art Experience at the Academy of Art College offers teens professional-level training in graphic design, cartooning, and more. Summer experiences like these can serve as a wonderful way to:

1. expand your interest in a particular field

2. delve into a topic that intrigues you

3. get an "insider" look at life as a college student

Not all summer programs have an academic focus. In fact, many fall under the category of volunteering, athletics, or outdoor adventure. Whether the program is academic or not, you get a chance to mix with college-age students, who are "older and wiser" than you. Many teens who've had the opportunity to learn from and hang out with older students say that this is both fun and eye-opening. You can participate in programs in your area or in other states. Housing and meal costs are usually included, so be sure to ask about this. Soon you may be living it up in the dorm and chowing down in the cafeteria—a true taste of the college experience!

If college isn't in your game plan, you can still benefit from participation in a summer program and from dual enrollment in general. These alternative learning experiences are fun, challenging, and enriching. They help you stay active and are a good alternative to more passive pastimes, like watching TV, playing video games, or surfing the Internet. Plus, a summer program is something to put on your résumé. You can show potential employers that you're serious about your field of interest and motivated to gain more experience.

FIND OUT MORE

 College Credit Without Classes by Dr. James L. Carroll (Chicago: Ferguson, 1996). Did you know you can you earn up to sixty semester credits without going to college? More than 2,500 colleges and universities in the U.S. and Canada have procedures for getting academic credit for certain life experiences, and this book explains how. Through the use of worksheets, examples, and models, you can discover if your experiences can earn you college credit.

Free (and Almost Free) Adventures for Teenagers by Gail L. Grand (New York: John Wiley & Sons, 1995). The name says it all—if you're looking for free and low-cost summer and school-year programs, look no further. This book is an excellent resource filled with all the details you need to know about an assortment and range of options. The author has included listings of activities and programs, their duration, housing facilities, application deadlines, and much more.

The Yale Daily News Guide to Summer Programs 2000 by Sara Schwebel (New York: Kaplan, 1999). This is a complete guide to more than 500 programs in a wide range of categories including academic, community service, and leadership. You'll find advice to help you decide which program best fits your interests, apply, prepare writing samples, and ace the interview. The book is compiled yearly, so make sure you get the latest edition.

SPOTLIGHT ON

Josh Aaronson
Upper Canada College
Toronto, Ontario

By the summer of 1996, after finishing twelfth grade, I had become tired of my usual summertime camping trips. While my friends searched for jobs in retail and banking, I looked for an alternative learning experience that could give me an early taste of university life and a leg up in my high school studies. In Ontario, students complete five years of high school (up to grade thirteen), unless they "fast track" and finish their studies in four years. My plan was to graduate at the age of nineteen, when I'd be a legal adult.

I soon found out that the majority of the university programs I was interested in wanted applicants to be high school graduates. Because I was a Canadian student in a province that required five years of high school, I wasn't yet a graduate. That's when a friend of my mother's encouraged me to further my two years of Spanish by applying to the Middlebury College summer language program in Vermont. No one in my high school was familiar with the program, so I had little idea of what to expect. We did know, however, that Middlebury has one of the best summer language programs in America.

I was seventeen and had never traveled. Shortly after I arrived at the school, I found out two things: (1) I was one of the youngest students (we ranged from ages seventeen to eighty-four!) and (2) everyone took a language pledge that was regarded very seriously. The pledge, which you had to sign, required students to communicate *only* in the language of study. That meant I had to speak Spanish during every class and in every social situation—even when introducing myself to people for the first time.

I'll never forget the first meal. We sat at large tables; silence reigned. Pretty soon, Spanish murmurs could be heard. I'm sure that everyone else was as nervous as I was. But after the first week, I was astounded at how fast things began to pick up. We were committed to learning the language, and everyone was very focused. Our teachers were native speakers of Spanish, and we had four hours of class each day, plus extracurricular activities. I spent the afternoons playing soccer and golf. In the evenings, we worked on group assignments or just hung out. In many ways, my routine was like that of a college student.

I think the language program was one of the most valuable summer experiences I've ever had. I met lots of great people, and I still keep in touch with many of my fellow students and my professors. It was an opportunity I'll never forget. And to this day, I firmly believe that it was my frustration at not being able to talk to people that drove me to fluency in Spanish!

Early Admission—Are You Ready?

If taking a class at a university or college sounds *great,* maybe leaving high school altogether and beginning college early will sound even better.

Some teens are ready to start their college experience early. If you're one of them, there's a unique institution you can turn to: Simon's Rock College of Bard in Great Barrington, Massachusetts—the only four-year college in the United States devoted exclusively to academically motivated younger students, who begin college after grades ten or eleven.

The college attracts talented students who find that their high schools can't provide the academic challenges they need. It's small and personal, enrolling only 350 students each year. Students take classes for the first two years in the Lower College, earning an A.A. (Associate of Arts) degree. If they choose to continue their education, the Upper College program leads to a B.A. (Bachelor of Arts) degree. Students who decide not to stay at Simon's Rock to complete their B.A. have the option of transferring to another college as a junior. Simon's Rock offers many scholarships, full and partial, to outstanding high school sophomores. To learn more, visit the college online at *www.simons-rock.edu.*

Other colleges and universities around the country sometimes accept students for early admission. This means high school students who have completed their junior year may be accepted as full-time college or university students. Usually, early admission students have high grades and standardized test scores, so you'll need to make sure you qualify. If you're not quite ready to leave home, you may be able to find a nearby college or university that will accept you as a full-time student. Find out what your options are for living at home while you pursue your degree.

F. Y. I.

High school may involve a lot of busywork, nightly assignments, and pop quizzes. But college often skips all that in favor of a few papers and exams that comprise your grade. This means you've got more freedom—but more responsibility, too!

Early admission students may not be issued a high school diploma. But if you can live with that, you'll be out of high school and into college a year early—and that means out of college and into the real world a year early as well. If you're interested, check out this option with your high school principal and the colleges or universities you're considering. You may want to ask yourself these questions first:

- Am I ready to leave my high school friends behind and become friends with slightly older peers?

- Am I ready to miss significant senior-year bonding activities like the prom and graduation?

- What are my reasons for wanting early admission?

- Can I achieve these aims in any other way (such as through dual enrollment)?

- Can I handle going from my smaller high school to a huge university campus with thousands of other students (or from a large high school or city to a small college campus)?

- Will I feel anonymous in a college atmosphere, and does this bother me?

- Do my friends support my decision for early enrollment (and is this important to me)?

- If I want to stay at home for the first year of college, am I willing to trade college independence for at-home security?

- Am I ready to be fully immersed in the college experience, from living independently in the dormitories to being away from home for long periods of time?

- How far away from home do I really want to go? What are the advantages of staying nearby? What are the advantages of leaving the nest? What are the disadvantages of each?

- If I'm not yet eighteen, will I feel intimidated by older students who can do whatever they want as legal adults, while I'm still technically under my parents' guardianship?

- Am I mature enough to handle problems on my own, even though I'm not yet an adult?

- Do I know where to go for help while I'm away if I need it?

You may not have easy answers to these questions. Take some time to think about the pros and cons of early admission; write them down so you can go back to them again and again. Talk to your family and friends to get their perspectives and advice. You may also want to speak to a teacher, your guidance counselor, your principal, or another adult you trust.

How can you make up your mind as to whether early admission or taking classes at a college or university is the best option for you? Authors and educators Judy Galbraith and Jim Delisle offer this advice: "If you asked your parents, teachers, and counselors, they would probably vote for dual enrollment over early admission. Adults believe that it's important for high school students to participate in high school social events—proms, pep rallies, yearbook committees, clubs, and the like—and they have a point. It's easier to make up for lost time in academics than in dating and other forms of social development. On the other hand, some high school students could care less about football, dances, and homecoming floats. We feel that each decision about early college entrance should be made on an individual basis."*

Think about what your parents and other adults in your life have to say, but in the end, you'll need to decide what's best for *you*.

SPOTLIGHT ON

**Katie Devine
Carleton College
Northfield, Minnesota**

When I was a junior in high school, I made the decision to enroll in college a year early. I had known since my freshman year that early enrollment would be possible for me because summer school and a college-level math class had given me enough credits to finish high school before my peers. Was early enrollment a difficult decision? Yes and no. I was excited to take harder classes, but in high school, I had close friends and clubs I loved—I was comfortable. I decided that challenge was more important to me, though.

I looked at colleges that would accept me without a diploma. Some smaller liberal arts schools will actually put a note in their admissions booklet stating their policy on this sort of thing. I was lucky because I got into Carleton College in Northfield, Minnesota—my top choice. Northfield wasn't that far from my hometown of Rochester, and the school had the academic reputation and atmosphere I was looking for. I

*From *The Gifted Kids' Survival Guide: A Teen Handbook* by Judy Galbraith, M.A., and Jim Delisle, Ph.D (Minneapolis: Free Spirit Publishing Inc., 1996). Used with permission.

had told my family that if an acceptance letter from Carleton came, I was definitely going.

I was lucky because my parents didn't try to steer my choices. They encouraged me to think things over, and they let me know that it was never too late to back out of my decision if I needed to. It made me realize how cool my parents could be! The incredible thing about my decision to leave high school early was that it was something I did completely my own. No one ever said "Do this"—it was up to me. I realized that I could decide on important issues by myself and be happy with the outcome.

Leaving high school *was* hard. I left behind senior-year activities like homecoming, school plays, and prom. Hearing about all the mischief my friends were creating as seniors made me miss high school—but I never regretted my decision. At college, I was independent, and that's what I'd hoped for. Even though I had always gotten along well with my family, I wanted to be on my own, and college gave me that chance. In fact, going to college early even improved my relationship with my parents.

College gave me my first taste of really challenging class work, allowing me to explore what I was truly interested in or good at. And my new independence taught me a lot about myself—what I value, the lifestyle I prefer to lead, the type of people I like to be friends with, and more. The confidence this gave me has carried over into other aspects of my life. I now trust my instincts and gut feelings more because I know I have the power to make the right choices for myself.

The most important bonus of leaving early was this: I knew that another year of high school would be a waste for me academically, compared to a year in college. I thought, "Why waste any time?" Life's too short for that!

Distance Learning

Maybe you're interested in taking college courses for personal enrichment or for credit, but you don't live near a university or a community college. What can you do? Consider distance learning or correspondence courses.

Although the terms *distance learning* and *correspondence courses* are often used synonymously, they're actually two different things. Correspondence courses (also known as independent study) are completed entirely through the mail or via computer. Students use snail mail or email to register for classes, buy textbooks, or turn in assignments, depending on the course. Correspondence courses don't require any form of attendance, but during exams, students may have to be supervised by a proctor who's designated by the correspondence university.

Distance learning is a little different, because of the technology involved. Students participate by logging into a chat room or "meeting" with the professor via video-conferencing. A class Web page may have a listing of the assignments; classmates may email one another as they work on projects; lectures may take place through videos. All of this technology allows for more interaction than traditional correspondence courses.

If you have access to a computer and are comfortable with technology, you may prefer distance learning over a correspondence course. But both of these alternative learning experiences offer flexibility and convenience, and they cost about the same amount. If working independently at your own pace appeals to you, look into these options— even if you *do* live near a college or university. You might enjoy the flexibility of checking your professor's assignments in the middle of the night, or sending off your homework via email before anyone else is awake.

FIND OUT MORE

Barron's Guide to Distance Learning by Pat Criscito (Hauppauge, NY: Barron's Educational Series, 1999). This book provides an excellent introduction to distance learning, including a section on figuring out if distance learning is right for you. The guide lists schools that offer distance learning courses along with contact information, costs, admission requirements, and teaching methods.

College Degrees by Mail & Internet by John Bear, Ph.D., and Mariah Bear, M.A. (Berkeley: Ten Speed Press, 2000). If you're looking for a directory of colleges and universities in the U.S. offering courses by mail, this book is for you. It discusses ways to earn credit through distance learning, including correspondence courses, equivalency exams, and foreign academic experience. You'll also find a list of accredited schools that offer degrees through home study.

Other Educational Alternatives

Have you looked into what your school has to offer in the way of alternative learning experiences? Some of them may include:

> "A wise man will make more opportunities than he finds."
>
> **Francis Bacon**

- **Advanced Placement (AP) Classes:** AP classes are considered to be at the college level. They go beyond the basics by requiring more extensive reading and critical thinking, and are geared toward students of higher aptitude. AP classes tend to have fewer students, which allows teachers to offer each one more personal attention. The classes usually last a year.

"My AP teacher was able to be more experimental. She incorporated movies, paintings, and exploration of other disciplines in my AP class."—**Becca**

- **Advanced Placement Exams:** To get college credit for your AP class, you need to complete the course successfully and take the AP exam, usually offered in May or June. The AP exam is scored from 1 (the lowest) to 5 (the highest). Colleges differ as to how they accept AP credit; some only accept scores of 4 or 5, for example. If you take lots of AP courses and do well on the exams, you have the chance to enter college with credits on your transcript already. This can be an advantage if you want to graduate early or take time off for travel during the school year. The tests cost around $75 each; most states help students cover the fees on an as-needed basis.

"In college, I was exempt from two classes because I did well on the AP exams I took in high school. This allowed me to pursue more interesting classes sooner, because I didn't have to worry about covering the basics first. Plus, the cost of the exam was a lot cheaper than the cost of college credits."—**Sean**

- **The College Level Examination Program (CLEP):** If your high school doesn't offer the AP classes you want (or doesn't offer them at all), you may want to look into the CLEP program. The purpose of CLEP exams is to give students credit for information they already know, whether they learned it in school, at home, or through life experiences. Five general exams and thirty subject-area exams take place at hundreds of testing centers across the country each year. Talk to your school guidance counselor or principal to get more information.

- **Enrichment Programs:** If you're interested in higher-level skills like creativity and problem solving, see if your school offers enrichment programs. They're designed to enrich the high school curriculum by allowing students to expand their learning through discussion, debate, or research. In the words of one student: "Enrichment classes saved me from the monotony of high school. They made me realize that every-day classes can go much further, and that discussions can take place on a much deeper level."

- **Acceleration Programs:** Through acceleration, you can pursue higher levels of learning, at a pace that matches your needs. Accelerated students are able to skip courses that they're already proficient in or advance to a higher grade level altogether.

- **Independent Projects:** Have you ever been fascinated by a topic in school when there wasn't enough class time to study it in more depth? An independent study allows you to immerse yourself in research and in-depth learning. You design the project yourself, work at your own pace, set your deadlines, and see the project through from start to finish—all of which requires initiative and persistence. Most likely, you'll work with a teacher who acts as your advisor throughout the project. You may or may not receive academic credit for your independent study, depending on your school's policies.

See what your school has to offer and take advantage of any opportunities that interest you!

FIND OUT MORE

College Board Advanced Placement Program
45 Columbus Avenue
New York, NY 10023-6992
1-800-CALL-4-AP (1-800-225-5527)
www.clep.org/ap

College Level Examination Program
Corporate Headquarters
Educational Testing Service
Rosedale Road
Princeton, NJ 08541-6600
(609) 921-9000
www.clep.org

Other Ways of Learning

Maybe you're not ready for advanced placement or dual enrollment. In fact, maybe the whole idea of prepping for college or taking university classes is the furthest thing from your mind. No problem. There are other avenues to pursue.

You don't have to "learn for college credit," if that's not what you're into. And you don't have to learn in strictly academic settings. Community centers, youth groups, faith communities, and libraries are some other places you can go for educational opportunities. Here are ideas to get you started in a different direction:

- Take an art class (painting, sculpture, collage) at a community center.

- Find out what course offerings are available at a local writing center (poetry, creative writing, storytelling, mysteries, autobiography).

- Look on the bulletin board of your local library or bookstore for upcoming events such as writer's workshops, readings, lectures, and book-club meetings. Start your own book club, if you'd like.

- Get on the mailing list at a bookstore that holds readings. Come prepared with questions for the author or poet.

- Use the library for research that you conduct on your own—just because you want to learn more about a topic that fascinates you.

- See if a local recreation center offers yoga, self-defense, karate, judo, aerobics, or swimming classes.

- Join a youth group through your faith community or another source. Activities may include social events, discussions, sports and fitness, or even trips.

- If you've got a dog, take classes in basic or advanced dog training.

- Sign up for acting classes or theater workshops.

- Join a community choir or jazz band.

- Enroll in dance classes at a local studio.

- Ask someone who knows sign language to teach it to you.

- Inquire if your local nature center offers any classes or nature walks.

- See if a local cookware store features cooking classes, or team up with a friend and start your own!

- In the summer, get into the art scene by checking out arts and crafts fairs. Talk with the artisans and find out how they started their craft and how they do it. Inquire about classes that may be available in your area.

- Plant a garden and find resources that will help you learn about different species of plants and how they grow. Nurseries can be a great place to learn more about plant care.

- Check out your local community center to find out what kind of community education programs are offered. (Foreign languages? Belly dancing? Weight lifting?)

- Write a column or article for your community newspaper or neighborhood newsletter. See how much you learn by interviewing people and trying out your writing skills.

- Get out a telescope and look at the stars, along with a reference book on astronomy. Call a planetarium for show times and test your knowledge.

- Volunteer at a local museum, or just visit one on a regular basis. Spend time learning about the history of different objects or peoples.

- If you live near a college or university, attend lectures, concerts, or seminars open to the public. This is a great way to learn more about a topic you probably never would have heard about otherwise.

"The indispensable first step to getting the things you want
out of life is this: decide what you want."

Ben Stein

Now that you're more familiar with the world of options that
awaits you, one BIG question you can ask yourself is *What do I
want to learn?* Do you know yet? This is your call to introspection. Take some time to look inward and think about this question, because knowing what you want is the first step toward
getting it. You may even need to devote some heavy-duty writing
time to this question. Get out your notebook or journal (or use a
computer) and put this question at the top of the page:

What do I want to learn?

Brainstorm as many ideas as you can. Now look over your
list. What is it trying to tell you? Are there any connections you
didn't see before but can see clearly now? Are the things you
want to learn mainly academic? Physical? Intellectual? Spiritual?
Are there any surprises there? Write down your thoughts.

Now ask yourself *why* you want to learn the things on your
list. Is it because you're truly interested—or that you feel pressured to take more and more courses so you can get into a good
college? Are you learning what *you* desire to learn—or what your
teachers, parents, and other adults say you should learn? Be sure
you know the difference and that you're following a learning
path that truly interests you. After all, it's been said that life isn't
a destination but a journey. Enjoy it every step of the way.

Chapter 3

Get a Mentor, Be a Mentor

"People who grew up in difficult circumstances and yet are successful have one thing in common: at a critical juncture in their early adolescence, they had a positive relationship with a caring adult."

President Bill Clinton

Do you have a caring adult in your life? Someone who's willing to listen to you, offer advice when you ask for it, and give you guidance when you need it? Someone who's always on your side, rooting for you to do your best? If you've got someone like this in your life, you're one of the lucky people who has what's known as a mentor. Mentors are caring adults who spend time with you one-on-one and offer their wisdom, support, and advice. Many teens have a parent, relative, neighbor, older friend, coach, or community member who serves in this capacity.

The term *mentor* calls to mind many images. Some think of a trusted friend, others think of a role model they can look up to, and still others think of someone who can help them go after their dreams and attain their goals. Some teens want their mentor to introduce them to a career and help them succeed; others are looking for academic help. Some need a confidant, while others seek someone who can encourage their personal development. Mentors can be all these things and more.

Mentor relationships fall into three general categories:

1. Informal mentoring: You and an adult spend time one-on-one, learn from each other, and have fun together. Your mentor can talk with you, help you out with problems, and guide you in reaching your fullest potential, if that's what you want out of the relationship. The two of you don't need to go through any agencies or special screenings, or follow any application procedures. Your mentor offers friendship, plain and simple. If this type of mentorship appeals to you, you can approach an adult you trust and respect, ask the person to be your mentor, and let the relationship develop from there.

2. Mentoring of at-risk youth: The term *at-risk* refers to young people who are in danger of getting into trouble with the law, abusing alcohol or drugs, or dropping out of school—often as a result of growing up in tough conditions. Studies have proven that linking young people with an adult mentor can help them learn to set goals, plan for the future, and improve their lives in many other ways. In fact, research involving the mentoring organization Big Brothers Big Sisters of America showed that young people who have mentors are 27 percent less likely to start using alcohol and 53 percent less likely to skip school. In most cases, at-risk youth are paired with a mentor through a community agency. (To learn more about this type of mentorship, see "Find Out More" on pages 72–73, where you'll find more information on Big Brothers Big Sisters and other organizations.)

3. Career mentoring: If you're interested in a specific career path, you can find a mentor through a school-based mentoring program or a community agency. Your mentor can help you explore a particular field of interest and offer advice on how to pursue a specific career. Talk to your guidance counselor to see if your school offers a career mentorship program. Usually, career mentorships involve a commitment of at least a semester.

All three types of mentoring are equally valuable. The overall goal of each one is to help you learn more about yourself and realize what you're capable of. What kind of mentorship you choose to pursue depends on your particular interests, your situation, your goals, your motivation, and your level of commitment.

Why Have a Mentor?

Think about all the celebrities you admire: athletes, actors, musicians, writers, artists, directors, and so on. How many of them would you bet had a mentor who showed them the ropes, provided words of encouragement, and guided them as they embarked on their careers? The answer: just about all of them. Many successful people, from film stars to politicians to CEOs of Fortune 500 companies, say that they couldn't have made it without a mentor.

Mentors provide young people with guidance, support, reassurance, friendship, and perspective. Although friends your own age can offer these things too, there's something special about having a connection with someone who's older and more experienced than you are. Here are some of the things an adult mentor can help you with:

- **Growing-up issues.** Spending time with your mentor lets you learn something about an adult's job, life, and hobbies. You might find that you're taking an interest in a hobby or career you hadn't considered before. In addition, it's helpful to get an adult's perspective on issues you're facing as a teen.

- **Taking risks.** Taking healthy risks means going beyond your comfort zone to try something new—like a volunteer position, a college-level course, or an internship. A risk may feel scary, but when you know there's a caring adult behind you all the way—someone who won't judge you or criticize you— you'll feel more confident about going for it. In this way, a mentor can help you assert your independence and try new things.

- **Understanding differences.** If your mentor is of a different ethnic background or culture, you have the perfect opportunity to learn about his or her heritage and to share information about yours. Mentorships can help break down stereotypes that people of different cultures, races, ages, or religious backgrounds may have of one another. If you're feeling a bit uncomfortable at first, try to look beyond the surface and figure out what you and your mentor have in common. Do you both like to see movies? Do the two of you dream of traveling to Egypt? When you start with similarities, the differences become less intimidating.

- **Setting goals.** A goal can be your greatest motivator—the thing that makes you keep getting up and trying again, no matter what the odds. Do you have goals? Do you know how to reach them? A mentor can help you identify a goal, plan your steps for reaching it, and then encourage you every step of the way.

BUILDING YOUR WEB

Did you know that you can have more than one mentor at a time? According to research by Search Institute in Minneapolis, teens need at least three adults in their lives (besides their parents) who they can go to for advice and support. If you want to succeed in life, it's a great idea to have a network of caring adults you can turn to and count on. For example, you could have one mentor who's active in a career you're interested in, another who offers you advice about the college application process, and yet another who's an adult friend you spend your free time with. You could have a mentor who shares your hobby, one who's mainly a good listener, or one who offers guidance in times of trouble. Mentors can play many different roles in your life—all of them positive. Do you already have several adults you can go to for support and advice? If not, take the initiative. Talk to an aunt or uncle, a teacher, a coach, a neighbor, a counselor, a religious leader, a grandparent, or someone else you respect and trust. Or join a community club, an organization, or a service project so you can get to know the adults working with you.

FIND OUT MORE

The Person Who Changed My Life: Prominent Americans Recall Their Mentors, edited by Matilda Raffa Cuomo (Secaucus, NJ: Carol Publishing Group, 1999). With a foreword written by Hillary Rodham Clinton, this book is exactly what the title says: famous people discussing the mentors who changed their lives. It provides encouragement for those seeking a mentor and inspiration for those who wish to become one.

How to Choose a Mentor

If you want to find a mentor but you're not sure exactly where to begin, start by identifying which type of mentoring relationship appeals to you the most. Are you looking for a more casual relationship? Do you want to go through Big Brothers Big Sisters of America and find a caring adult who can help you work through some problems? Are you more interested in a mentor who can guide you in a potential career? Take some time to think about this. You may find it helpful to write down your thoughts.

F. Y. I.

When recently asked by the Carnegie Corporation task force what they most wanted in their free time, the majority of teens who responded said they'd like to spend time talking with a trusted adult who enjoys young people and knows something about the world.

Informal Mentoring

In an informal mentoring arrangement, you choose your mentor. This person doesn't need to be a professional or have prominence in your community, unless that's important to you. Look for someone you trust—someone who's a good listener and who cares about young people. Maybe this person is someone you're already close to: a grandparent, a neighbor, an adult friend of the family. On the other hand, maybe you want to look outside your immediate circle and get to know someone new: a local business owner or a teacher you haven't had before, for example. The goal is to find an adult you feel comfortable turning to for guidance, support, and advice. You'll want someone trustworthy who will:

1. believe in you

2. care about you

3. be honest with you

Is anyone coming to mind yet?

Start making a list of adults you know or admire. Ask yourself if they fit the above criteria. If you can't come up with any names and you don't know anyone who might make a good mentor, start approaching adults who might be able to point the way: a parent, a teacher, a religious leader. Let them know you're interested in finding a mentor and ask if they can come up with some contacts for you. Another option is to become involved in a club, a service project, or a community center so you can get to know the adult leaders there.

If you're online, the National Mentoring Partnership's Web site can help you identify who might be a good mentor for you. Go to *www.mentoring.org/f_youth.html* and scroll down the page until you find the "Worksheet" button. Once you've come up with a few names, ask yourself which person you'd most like to be your mentor. Depending on how well you know the person, you may want to do something to break the ice first. You could send a friendly note, ask for some advice, or offer a compliment. Next step: ask the person to be your mentor.

Some teens prefer to do the asking face-to-face; others like to do it over the phone or by email. What are you most comfortable with? Does the thought of asking in person make you nervous? Then maybe you'll want to put your request in writing. If you need to introduce yourself to the person, then of course a face-to-face meeting is necessary. Decide what the best option is and approach your potential mentor.

Here are some easy steps to follow:

1. Be friendly and honest. You might say, "I'm interested in having a mentor, and I thought you would be the right person to ask. You're a good listener, and you really seem to care about teens." Be sure to let your potential mentor know why he or she would make a great mentor. Is it the person's sense of humor? People skills? Career expertise? Being specific will help strengthen your case.

2. Explain what kind of relationship you're looking for. What are your needs? Are you interested in career guidance? Friendship? Someone to help you with homework in a particular class? Someone who can teach you about the past? Let the person know exactly what you have in mind.

3. Ask the big question. You might simply say, "Will you be my mentor?" If the answer is no, don't take it personally. Maybe the person is too busy right now. Express your thanks and move on. If the person says yes, set up your first meeting right then and there. If your potential mentor seems hesitant and doesn't give you a definitive yes or no, suggest a trial period. The trial period could last anywhere from a week to a month or two. That way, you can both try out the mentoring relationship without a major commitment.

4. Suggest how often you'd like to meet. Consider your mentor's schedule and your own. Do you want to meet once a week? Once a month? Mainly by email? Always in person? When will you meet—during the school day or after? On weekends? Where will you meet? At the mentor's workplace? At a library? Talk about what might work for both of you.

Suppose you've found a mentor and you've set up your first meeting . . . now what?

First and foremost, show up for that initial meeting (and all the others) on time. Depending on what you think is best, you can use the meeting to (1) get to know each other, or (2) talk about your expectations for the mentorship. You may want to prepare some conversation-starters ahead of time, so you feel comfortable with what you're going to say. Be open about what you hope to gain from the relationship. Are your expectations similar? Different? Talk about ways to make the mentorship a positive experience for you both.

Be sure to think of your mentorship as a *partnership*—meaning both people involved need to contribute to make it successful. If you've never had this type of relationship with an adult, things might be a bit bumpy at first. You may not know what to say, or you may be used to the adults in your life doing all the talking. Even if you're unsure or shy at first, do your part to make the meetings interesting. Come prepared with questions or suggest an activity you can do together each time. Some teens have found that taking notes during conversations is helpful, especially if the mentor is offering advice or guidance. Other teens have discovered that the meetings are more fun if they take place in a relaxed environment—outdoors or at a coffee shop, for example. And still other teens have found that staying in touch through email, in addition to regular meetings, helps them stay close to their mentors. Find what works best for you.

THE ONLINE MENTORING ALTERNATIVE

Maybe you don't have the time or the ability to meet with a mentor face-to-face, for whatever reason. Online mentoring might be just the thing for you. One option is Hewlett-Packard International Telementoring, a Web site that connects kids and mentors online. Visit the site at *www.telementor.org/hp* to get more information. Another option is Girl Geeks, a Web site for girls and women *(www.girlgeeks.com/mentoring)*. Girl Geeks connects girls with women in the technology field. At the site, you can join a mentoring group headed by professional women in a variety of technological fields and communicate through email.

F.Y.I.

The Points of Light Foundation defines *mentor* as "Any caring adult who makes an active, positive contribution to the life of a child who is not his or her own. It's someone who has found ways to succeed in life—and cares enough to pass those lessons along."

Mentoring of At-Risk Youth

For at-risk youth, a mentor can sometimes make all the difference. A study by Philadelphia-based Public/Private Ventures showed that young people who met with a mentor three times a month for one year were:

- 52 percent less likely to skip school
- 33 percent less likely to get into fights
- 46 percent less likely to start using illegal drugs

Currently, 13.6 million youth in America have been identified as at-risk. You may be one of them, depending on your situation at home. Maybe you don't have a parent you can lean on, or any adults in your life who can be role models for you. Maybe you haven't found ways to reach out to your teachers for the help and guidance you need. Perhaps you're facing obstacles that seem overwhelming to you right now. Perhaps you're doing poorly in school and are looking for ways to feel good about yourself and your life. Does any of this sounds like what you're going through? If so, you can find a mentor—someone to guide you through the tough times and be a role model you can look up to and believe in.

Many teens have worked with mentors to:

- stay in school
- fill their free time with positive, productive activities
- cut out destructive behaviors (like using alcohol and other drugs)
- start planning for college or a career
- look at the future in a more positive light

Mentors offer the support and encouragement that troubled teens sometimes need to get back on their feet.

In 1997, President Clinton, government leaders, and General Colin Powell gathered in Philadelphia for a summit on the future of America. Mentoring was the main topic of discussion. A major aim of the summit was to encourage nonprofit agencies, schools, churches, and community organizations to launch mentoring programs or improve existing ones—to meet the goal of having two million mentors by the year 2000. Many young people and adults who got involved as a result of the summit expressed that mentoring has been one of the most positive experiences in their lives.

If you're interested in pursuing a mentorship like the ones described here, there are many ways to do so. See the "Find Out More" section on pages 72–73 for places to start.

"The group mentorship I'm in is fun, and it keeps me off the streets. The leaders have positive attitudes, let us speak, and treat us the way we want to be treated. Before this mentorship program, I didn't get along with others that well, but now I have the courage to be a better person, along with a good attitude. The mentorship has also got me thinking about my plans after high school. Right now, I'm thinking about going to a technology college."—**Frank**

Wondering what you and your mentor will do during the time you spend together? The options are endless! Here are some suggestions:

- go to the movies
- attend a sports event
- visit a museum
- take a walk in the park
- window shop
- work on some of your school assignments
- talk about a book you are both reading or have read
- cook a meal and share it
- tour your mentor's workplace
- do a community service project together
- plant a small garden
- play board games
- throw a Frisbee or ball
- just talk

You could even start a creative project together, such as working on crafts, collecting, or putting together a journal that combines writings and photos of your individual lives. Being creative and working on something that you can see and touch can make your time together even more meaningful.

SPOTLIGHT ON

Dante Merrell
Chicago Vocational Career Academy
Chicago, Illinois

I first got into 100 Black Men through the YMCA, and I've been in it for five years—since I was thirteen. 100 Black Men is a national organization; the Chicago chapter has a group mentorship program called YPALS. The group meets at Chicago State. There are about ten kids at the meetings, and about six mentors. All the mentors are great—there are two I work closely with and relate especially well to, Mr. Green and Mr. Coates. Mr. Coates is like a father. He comes to my brother's football games and drops my brother off at school sometimes.

At a typical meeting, everyone arrives at different times, and the mentors start asking us questions about how our week is going and about any problems we've encountered. They give us tips on how to deal with different situations, and I get different and better answers than I would if I asked other people for advice.

Sometimes we have homework from the group, and other times we go on trips. When we take a trip, often we'll have to write down what we learned or did. One trip we took was to Detroit. There we went to a food festival. We also attended a black-tie fund-raising gala in Chicago where we met lots of celebrities. All of these events were free to us. We've also learned mealtime etiquette by going to an elegant restaurant called the Pump Room.

Through 100 Black Men, I've experienced lots of things I wouldn't have otherwise, like going out of town by myself for the first time. Being in 100 Black Men has shown me how to be strong and dependable, live right, and keep religion in my life. It's shown me how to be a real man and how to raise a family right. My mom and grandmother love that I'm in the group—they see how much it's changed my life.

100 Black Men has changed the way I view things, and has given me different perspectives on life. Now I look at things a lot more sensitively and in a more manly way. We also talk about careers and life after high school in the group—some of the kids want to be in the NFL, but we talk about more realistic career options. I plan on going into the Navy and being a computer network designer. My mentors have offered advice about this and shown me the different types of classes I'll have to take to prepare.

FIND OUT MORE

Big Brothers Big Sisters of America
National Office
230 North 13th Street
Philadelphia, PA 19107
(215) 567-7000
www.bbbsa.org

Big Brothers Big Sisters has programs nationwide that match at-risk youth with caring adult mentors. Contact the national office or visit the Big Brothers Big Sisters Web site to find out what's available in your area.

Communities in Schools
277 South Washington Street, Suite 210
Alexandria, VA 22314
1-800-CIS-4-KIDS (1-800-247-4543)
www.cisnet.org/index.html

This organization helps schools connect with community resources to guide youth to stay in school, prepare for life, and learn. As part of this commitment, Communities in Schools matches up teens with mentors. Check out the Web site or contact the organization directly to find out what programs are offered in your area.

Save the Children
54 Wilton Road
Westport, CT 06880
1-877-BE-A-MENTOR (1-877-232-6368)
www.savethechildren.org

One of the many programs offered by this global organization matches adult mentors with youth. By calling the number above, you can access the names and phone numbers of mentoring organizations in your area.

100 Black Men of America
141 Auburn Avenue
Atlanta, GA 30303
(404) 688-5100
www.100blackmen.org

This organization is a national alliance of leading black men who share their skills and resources with African-American youth. The organization's mission is to improve the quality of life for young people by empowering them through various initiatives, one of which is mentoring. Local chapters have mentoring programs that meet weekly and sponsor speakers, outings, and participation by teens in various work environments. Check out the national headquarters or find a chapter near you.

YMCA of the USA
101 North Wacker Drive
Chicago, IL 60606
1-800-872-9622
www.ymca.net

YWCA of the USA
Empire State Building
350 Fifth Avenue, Suite 301
New York, NY 10118
(212) 273-7800
www.ywca.org

The YMCA and YWCA are two national organizations that partner youth with mentors. Each "Y" offers different programs, so visit the Web sites to find out more about what's available in your area.

Career Mentoring

- Have you exhausted all of your school's resources relating to your field of interest?

- Do you have a clear idea for a job or career and feel ready to learn more about it?

- Are you looking for a way to develop and sharpen your job skills?

- Are you interested in beefing up your résumé, so you can get out there and find the job of your dreams?

"You know, when you're young and curious, people love to teach you."
—**Dede Allen**

- Are you in search of advanced training, guidance, support, and encouragement in your potential career?
- Do you want specialized attention and a one-on-one relationship with an adult who's already in your field?
- Are you ready to commit to a long-term relationship with a career mentor who can show you the ropes?

If you answered yes to all or most of these questions, career mentoring may be for you. A career mentorship links a teen who's very serious about a specific interest—academic, medical, industrial, or business-related—with a professional in that field. If you decide to pursue this type of arrangement, you'd work closely with a scholar, an expert, or a professional. You'd probably be assigned a project that's designed to both strengthen your knowledge and skills *and* offer assistance to your mentor. A career mentorship not only helps you get more familiar with the work environment but also gives you valuable job experience and career contacts for the future.

Here are examples of what you might do in a career mentorship:

- work with a biologist who's monitoring the effects of pollution on marine life
- study under a published poet
- observe and record elephant behavior at the local zoo
- work under the supervision of a physics professor at a university
- conduct AIDS research under the direction of a medical expert
- help a history scholar gather research for a book

Justin, for example, was a sophomore who had been interested in paleontology since kindergarten. When he found out about a unique career mentoring program in his area, he decided to talk to the coordinator and brought with him a five-subject notebook of dinosaur information he had been compiling over several years. Justin was admitted to the program during his junior year; he went through a preparation process that included weekly meetings at a community college focusing on verbal communication skills, interviewing techniques, etiquette, and more. Next, he was paired with a two mentors at a local science museum: the Curator of Vertebrate Paleontology and a research associate and writer.

Justin's mentors educated him about fossils and gave him a true taste of the field of paleontology. One of his more memorable moments was when he was given the task of sorting boxes of bones to come up with a complete *Thescelosaurus* skeleton. His mentors showed him how to catalogue museum stock, scrutinize data, and take samples—things he never could have learned from books alone. During the mentorship, Justin was also required to complete ten hours of individual work and independent study on related projects each week. The entire experience lasted two years, but as the people closest to Justin remarked, the changes they saw in him happened almost overnight. He had always been on the quiet side, but after joining this mentorship program, he became much more outgoing and confident. Later, Justin used his mentorship connections to put together a research paper on fossil *foraminifera* (single-celled microscopic oceanic organisms that are like amoebae with shells), which he entered in an Intel Science Talent Search. Although he didn't win, he was a semifinalist!

Mentorships of any kind require time and effort. But *career* mentorships like Justin's are more demanding because you're expected to enter into the arrangement with some knowledge of your field and to perform specific duties while on the job. Career mentorships usually last for at least a semester, and possibly a year or two, so there's more of a commitment. You're expected to prepare ahead of time and to work very hard for your mentor(s). Plus, you're often graded on your performance.

What do you get in return? Lots! Here are some of the benefits of career mentorships:

- You get firsthand experience in your chosen career.

- You increase your skills and knowledge, which leads to greater confidence.

- You have the opportunity to work with adults in a professional setting, and to be treated as a professional yourself.

- You become more aware of the various positions that are available in your field of interest, which is an advantage when you're ready to find your first real job.

- You gain insights beyond what's offered in the classroom or in textbooks.

- You learn more about yourself, your interests, your strengths and weaknesses, your capabilities, your work ethic, and your dreams for the future.

- You get to spend school hours doing something you're passionate about (and perhaps get high school credit for it, too).

Career mentorships are usually arranged through your school or an organization that works with your school or district to match up students with professional mentors. So, in other words, these mentorships aren't for dabblers—you'll need to have an established interest in a specific field. Sometimes it's hard to decide if your interest is something you're 100 percent committed to, or just a passing phase. Have you already explored your interest in other ways, such as through classes in or outside of school, or through independent study and extracurricular projects? Have you mastered the basic skills in your field, and do you have a solid foundation of knowledge in it? Have you gone beyond the basics by making use of all the resources your school has to offer, including teacher guidance, library materials, and lab or computer equipment? Do you have questions that only a professional mentor can answer—or needs that can best be met through one-on-one work?

If you feel you're ready for a career mentorship, talk to your school guidance counselor to find out what your options are and if you're qualified. Many school-based career mentorship programs have a rigorous application process, requiring students to document their interest and skills. Some programs take into account your grades, extracurricular activities, and standardized test scores, too. And some even require nomination by teachers or guidance counselors. Screening ensures that only serious students are selected, which contributes to a more successful learning experience for everyone involved.

When you talk to your counselor, find out whether there are any special screenings to match you to your mentor (usually there are). Useful questions to ask include: Is there an application process for both parties? How are mentors selected? Is there a pool of established mentors from which students choose? Do students have a choice at all? Can students make a special request for a mentor and have the high school fulfill it?

F. Y. I.

Don't let poor grades or test scores stop you from applying; most career mentorship programs consider many other factors, including a demonstrated interest in or passion for the field.

If you're accepted for a career mentorship, you'll probably be required to take a class (before or during your mentorship) that teaches communication and research skills. You and your mentor will go over your project, so you understand the duties involved, and you'll meet on a regular basis to assess your progress. At the end of the project, you may be expected to write a paper or present a lecture as a way to reflect on the experience.

Career mentorships are popular, and one reason is that high schools aren't designed to allow students to focus on a specific interest, whether it be boat building or chemistry. Students usually don't graduate with the skills needed to enter the world of business or to find a job in their field of interest either. In addition, few

F. Y. I.

According to a Louis Harris poll of 400 high school juniors and seniors who participated in a national mentoring program called Career Beginnings: 59% of mentored teens got better grades, 73% raised their goals higher, and 87% went directly to college or planned to attend college within one year of graduating from high school.

teachers have the time to nurture students' career goals or foster their talents. Career mentorships serve as an excellent way to supplement what's taught in the classroom, let students explore a field of study that isn't available in school, and prepare them for the future.

MENTORSHIPS ARE A TWO-WAY STREET

You may be wondering why adults who have busy jobs would volunteer to be career mentors. What do they get out of it? Plenty! For one thing, the learning goes in both directions—it's a two-way street. Here are some positive things that career mentors have to say about the experience:

- Working with young people offers new ideas and fresh perspectives.

- Enthusiastic teens are fun and inspiring to be around.

- It's gratifying to teach young people new skills.

- Mentoring offers a chance to "give something back" to the world, and to carry on the traditions our own mentors left us.

- Sharpening young people's skills and knowledge of the field ensures that the quality of people entering the profession stays high.

FIND OUT MORE

National Mentoring Partnership
1600 Duke Street, Suite 300
Alexandria, VA 22314
(703) 224-2200
www.mentoring.org

The National Mentoring Partnership's mission is to bring mentoring into the lives of people nationwide. Each local partnership is committed to making it easier for mentoring to occur, helping adults and youth connect, bringing innovative approaches to mentoring, and ensuring good coordination of mentoring efforts. Check out NMP's Web site—you'll see tips on finding and being a mentor, state and community mentoring resources, and helpful advice on the mentoring process.

You can also contact a wide variety of mentoring providers in your city, including faith-based organizations, schools, businesses, community organizations, and mentoring agencies. The following is a list of the National Mentoring Partnership's local associations. You can contact the one in your state and ask about what mentoring opportunities are available near you. If your state isn't listed here, go to an online search engine and type in your state name and the word *mentoring.*

CALIFORNIA:
California Mentor Foundation • 100 Main Street • Tiburon, CA 94920 • (415) 789-1007 • *www.calmentor.org*

CONNECTICUT:
Connecticut Mentoring Partnership • 30 Arbor Street • Hartford, CT 06106 • (860) 231-8831 • *www.ctdhe.commnet.edu/dheweb/mentoring.htm*

DELAWARE:
Delaware Mentoring Council • University of Delaware • College of Human Resources, Education, & Public Policy • 015 Willard Hall • Newark, DE 19716 • (302) 831-0520 • *www.udel.edu/mentoring*

FLORIDA:
Governor's Mentoring Initiative • 50 North Laura Street • Suite 1938 • Jacksonville, FL 32202 • 1-800-825-3786 • *www.flmentoring.org*

MAINE:
The Maine Mentoring Partnership • c/o Communities for Children • 170 State House Station • Augusta, ME 04333-0170 • 1-888-387-8755 • *www.mainementoring.org*

MASSACHUSETTS:

The Mass Mentoring Partnership • 105 Chauncy Street • Suite 300 • Boston, MA 02111 • (617) 695-2430

MINNESOTA:

Mentoring Partnership of Minnesota • 81 South 9th Street • Suite 200 • Minneapolis, MN 55402 • (612) 370-9162 • *www.mentoringworks.org*

NORTH CAROLINA:

North Carolina Promise, Office of the Governor • The NC Commission on Volunteerism and Community Service • 116 West Jones Street • Raleigh, NC 27603 • 1-877-SERVE-NC • (1-877-737-8362) • *serve.nc.state.nc.us*

OREGON:

Oregon Mentoring Initiative • c/o Volunteer Works • 2145 NW Overton Place • Portland, OR 97210 • (503) 413-8905

TEXAS:

Governor's Mentor Initiative • P.O. Box 13385 • Austin, TX 78711-3385 • (512) 463-1814 • *www.governor.state.tx.us*

UTAH:

Utah Mentor Network • 120 North 200 West • Suite 419 • Salt Lake City, UT 84103 • (801) 468-2191 • *www.utah-mentor-network.org*

VIRGINIA:

Virginia One to One: The Mentoring Partnership • P.O. Box 843066 • Richmond, VA 23225 • (804) 828-1536 • *www.vcu.edu/ocp/ocpdocs /mentor.html*

WASHINGTON:

Washington State Mentoring Partnership • P.O. Box 45330 • Olympia, WA 98504 • 1-877-301-4557

SkillsUSA-VICA
P.O. Box 3000
Leesburg, VA 20177-0300
(703) 777-8810
www.skillsusa.org

If you're interested in learning more about trade, health, industrial, and technical occupations, this is a helpful organization. SkillsUSA-VICA can give you information about these careers, offer mentoring and partnerships, and help you post your résumé online.

SPOTLIGHT ON

Lindsay Bell Wolff
Mahtomedi High School
Mahtomedi, Minnesota

When I was a junior, I joined our school's debate team on a whim. After my first meet, I discovered that I loved the research and argument involved. I wanted to expand this interest into a career, and law was the obvious choice. But having no experience with law other than watching a few episodes of *Ally McBeal* and *The Practice*, I wasn't sure if I would enjoy being an attorney. I mentioned this to my counselor, and she suggested I try Mentor Connection, a program for students who want to experience real-life work environments through a mentorship. I enrolled my senior year and loved it.

The program was set up to allow students a lot of freedom. We attended class once a week during the first semester and were required to spend a total of ten hours a week on Mentor Connection activities. Because the study was so independent, we could complete our hours whenever we wanted—on weekends, at night, or right after school. This arrangement was perfect for me, because I didn't have to put in my hours right after school each day. I'm a figure skater and I enjoyed the opportunity to skate in the afternoons, rather than before school.

The first half of the year was designed to prepare us for our mentorship. We were taught how to properly shake hands, how to stand when talking, and how to ask good questions. My class felt really silly the day we formed a line and took turns shaking each other's hands, but the way you greet someone creates an impression. I can't think of anywhere else I could have learned this skill.

Outside of class I spent most of my time reading. I borrowed books on a wide range of topics, including the history and evolution of law, the lives of the Supreme Court Justices, and court procedures. I discovered that the philosophy and development of law is fascinating! I also visited our government center and spent an afternoon with a judge in his court. This initial preparation was very important—not because I memorized what belongs in a summons or a petition, but because I learned very important things about myself, such as my interest in the history of law and my ability to work productively without rigid guidelines.

My mentorship was fabulous. I was placed with a family law attorney in an office converted from a small white house. The filing and copying were done in the slightly remodeled kitchen, and I worked upstairs in an old attic bedroom. I had—and still have—a great relationship with my mentor. She discussed cases with me as though I were another attorney. And I was poised and confident enough to converse intelligently with her (thanks to my preparation classes). This relationship was one of the best parts of my mentorship. It wasn't one of a student and teacher; instead, it was peer-to-peer, friend-to-friend.

My work at the office was mostly the work that no one else wanted or had time to do. I filed and researched and drafted documents—nothing like the flashy images of lawyers in the movies. I think that some part of me had a misguided notion that I would be standing up in court and arguing a case. That wasn't going to happen, so I made a commitment to learn from the "grunt work." I read the documents as I filed or drafted them and, consequently, I became familiar with many laws and legal documents. My favorite thing to do was to help with the research. I really liked to dig into a case and find supporting evidence. I also got the opportunity to sit in on client meetings, hearings, and oral arguments. It was great to listen and know exactly what was going on. My mentorship gave me intimate knowledge about the world of law that I couldn't have gotten any other way.

Poise, confidence, and the ability to interact as a peer with adults were some of the most important skills that I took away from the experience. I also became a better, more inquisitive listener and learned how to discuss a wide range of ideas with assurance. I believe that mentorships are a great alternative to traditional school classes, even if you don't know what you want to do with your life. They will give you the tools you need to succeed no matter what you become.

The teens I've spoken with have said that successful career mentorships depend mainly on:

Mentors who . . .

- take the time to answer questions
- assign meaningful work
- talk about new advancements and research in the field
- respect teens and expect them to do good work
- help with goal setting and planning
- treat the arrangement seriously
- remain committed to the arranged times and dates
- are trusting and trustworthy
- create a supportive atmosphere where strong relationships can be built

Teens who . . .

- ask questions
- show their eagerness to learn
- keep a journal of their learning experiences during the mentorship
- ask for a list of recommended readings
- treat the arrangement as seriously as they would a job
- develop a trusting relationship with the mentor

Like any good relationship, a mentorship requires work on the part of both people involved. Good communication is the key.

Do your best to be open and communicative, honest and direct—otherwise, communication problems or misunderstandings may occur. For example, fourteen-year-old Karen began a mentorship with her neighbor, a man who raised dogs and shared her interest in caring for animals. The two of them met once a week. Karen was naturally quiet and reserved, and for the first few meetings, she was nervous about opening up or talking about her life. Her mentor got the impression that Karen preferred privacy, and he didn't want to pry by asking questions about school, her family, or her friends. Although Karen wanted very much to talk about the problems she was having in school, she didn't know how to bring up the subject. As the mentorship progressed, Karen and her neighbor had conversations only about animals, though both longed to talk about more. After several months, Karen summoned her courage and explained to her mentor about her poor school performance. To her relief, he was enthusiastic about helping her study for tests, and the two devoted one session every other week to her schoolwork. They were able to work through their initial obstacles, and the mentorship turned out to be a rewarding experience for both of them.

But what happens if the mentorship doesn't turn out as you expected? What if you and your mentor don't seem to get along or simply aren't making much progress? You and your mentor may have too many differences, difficulties, or disagreements. The best course of action is to try to resolve the problems by talking things over. If this approach doesn't work, if you can honestly say that you've given it your best shot and that you stuck it out for a sufficient amount of time, then tell your mentor how you feel. Let your mentor know that you no longer want to continue the relationship; be sure to thank the person for the time you spent together nevertheless. If your mentorship was arranged through school or an organization, you may wish to talk to your guidance counselor or the director of the program. Once the mentorship is over—whether it ends on a positive note or not—send your mentor a thank-you note as a token of goodwill.

Making the Most of Your Mentorship

No matter what type of mentorship you decide to pursue, there are some important steps you can take to make the experience as rewarding as it can be. Here are some suggestions to try:

- **Set goals for your mentorship.** At your first meeting, you may want to take the lead and let your mentor know what you hope to accomplish. Do you want help with your French? Do you want to learn about your mentor's career? Do you need help preparing your college application? Do you just want to talk about life?

F. Y. I.

Make sure you honor your mentor's time. If you're going to be late or if you'll have to miss a session, be sure to call ahead of time. Treat your mentorship like a job or an important appointment, and you'll be treated as an adult accordingly.

- **Show up for your appointments.** Mentors are busy people, just like you. They're taking time out from their schedules to meet with you, so be sure to respect that.

- **Be assertive.** Practice talking and asking questions in a direct, straightforward way. Don't ask vague questions or make your mentor try to guess what you want or need.

- **Practice your conversation skills.** Avoid answering questions with *yeah* and *uh-huh*. Instead, offer as much information as you can and be sure to ask questions that will show interest in your mentor.

- **Listen actively.** Pay attention to what your mentor is saying; avoid letting your mind wander. Nod your head to show that you understand.

- **Keep an open mind.** If your mentor suggests an activity that you've never tried or you don't think you'll like, give it a try anyway. What's the worst that can happen? Next time, you can suggest an activity you'd enjoy more. Be open to new experiences—you just may be surprised about what you learn!

- **Be persistent.** Don't give up on your mentorship if things aren't as you imagined right away. Like all worthwhile pursuits, mentorships require time and effort. If the mentorship isn't working out in the beginning, stick it out for a few more meetings and talk to your mentor about how to improve the relationship. Be sure to give it your all before even thinking about calling it quits.

- **Be appreciative.** Let your mentor know how much the time you spend together means to you. Every so often, write your mentor a note of appreciation or send a thank-you card.

Touch Someone's Life: Be a Mentor

Perhaps you've already been involved in a mentoring relationship, and you want to give something back to other young people who might benefit from mentoring, too. Or maybe you simply want to make a difference in a young person's life. Either way, becoming a mentor is a great opportunity to feel a sense of connection and to give back to your community. Many teens have discovered the rewards of building a trusting, giving relationship with a child.

Teaching a younger person about life and offering advice on growing up can lead to a feeling of accomplishment and pride. You may really enjoy sharing your own hobbies and skills with someone younger than you. Plus, you'll enrich your life with a new friendship.

Perhaps you've considered mentoring, but you didn't think you could fit it in with your busy schedule. Ask yourself if you could squeeze just one hour out of your week. Do you have a free hour one day after school or on the weekends? Making room for this learning experience is definitely worth the effort.

How do you become a mentor? First, there are several questions to ask yourself:

- What age group am I interested in? Elementary school? Middle school? Kindergarten?

- How much time do I have available to commit? One hour a week? A few hours a month?

- How long can I commit? (Most mentoring programs will require at least a six-month commitment.)

- Where can I meet with the child I mentor? Do I have the transportation to meet in a variety of places? How will the child get there?

- Are there any special skills I bring to the mentoring relationship? Can I help with homework assignments? Work on a special project with the child?

- What kind of mentoring relationship am I interested in? Working with at-risk youth? Being a friend?

- How many children do I want to work with? One? Two? A whole group?

Once you've decided on some of the specifics, you have a couple of options. The first one is mentoring through an organization. However, many mentoring organizations have a minimum age requirement of eighteen. There *are* exceptions to these rules. For example, although you have to be nineteen to be a Big Brother or Big Sister, Big Brothers Big Sisters of America has a program especially for teens who'd like to be mentors, or as they're known at the organization, "Bigs." The "Big Buddy" program is designed for high school students who want to mentor children ages seven to eleven. The mentoring activities often include studying, going to movies, and playing sports. See "Find Out More" on page 72 for contact information for Big Brothers Big Sisters.

If you'd prefer not to work through an agency, there are plenty of ways you can get involved with mentoring:

- Help coach a Little League team.
- Sponsor an after-school workshop for elementary school kids.
- Tutor a child in a subject you enjoy.
- Become a youth group leader or scouting volunteer.
- Volunteer in the nursery at your place of worship.
- Get a young pen pal or email buddy who you can correspond with.
- Find a young person you'd like to help—in your apartment or neighborhood, through your place of worship, or through a community center. Talk to the child's parents to see if you could become his or her mentor.

Even if you can only give a little bit of your time, you're acting as a role model for a child—and that's doing a lot. You may want to keep a journal of your mentoring experience, and take photos of your time together, so you have a record to look back on someday.

FIND OUT MORE

Mentoring: A Practical Guide by Gordon F. Shea (Menlo Park, CA: Crisp Publications, 1997). If you're thinking about becoming a mentor, this is a good guide to start with. The book discusses many aspects of mentoring that can help you determine if a mentoring role is right for you. The guide is written in workbook format, so there's space to reflect on and respond to the thoughts and ideas presented. It also develops scenarios and questions to help prepare a first-time mentor.

Mentorship: The Essential Guide for Schools and Business by Jill M. Reilly (Dayton, OH: Ohio Psychology Press, 1992). This book is a gold mine of information on mentorships for students, teachers, guidance counselors, and prospective and current mentors. It includes information on what a mentorship is, the screening process for students applying to become mentors, resources for finding mentors, and how to build a mentorship program at your school.

Boy Scouts of America
1325 Walnut Hill Lane
P.O. Box 152079
Irving, TX 75015-2079
(972) 580-2000
www.bsa.scouting.org

The Exploring Division of the Boy Scouts of America has posts that are organized around careers and jobs, plus ways you can participate in mentorships. Check out your local headquarters or contact the national organization to find out what's available in your area.

Camp Fire, Inc.
4601 Madison Avenue
Kansas City, MO 64112-1278
(816) 756-1950
www.campfire.org

This organization offers volunteers the opportunity to mentor small groups of students in grades K–12. Whether you're looking for a mentor or want to become one, you can contact Camp Fire for information.

Girl Scouts of the USA
420 5th Avenue
New York, NY 10018-2798
1-800-GS-USA-4U (1-800-478-7248)

While you might know about Girl Scout meetings (and Girl Scout cookies), many people don't realize that Girl Scouts of the USA also offers mentorships where adults work with girls in both short-term and long-term arrangements. Contact your local Girl Scout office or the national headquarters listed above.

eteen
www.e-teen.net/index.htm

If you're a community-minded teen and you're interested in becoming a mentor, there's a Web site especially for you. Eteen is created by and for teens who want to contribute to their communities, have fun, volunteer, and get involved in social issues. The Web site shares ideas about mentoring, volunteering, activism, and more.

"Your future depends on many things, but mostly on you."

Frank Tyger

Mentoring is an alternative learning experience that doesn't necessarily have a certain timeline or stopping point. You may find that your relationship with a special mentor lasts much longer than you ever expected, simply because you both enjoy it. For example, some teens have a mentor in high school whom they stay in touch with throughout their college years and beyond. If you use what you've learned from your mentoring experience to become a mentor to someone else, you're carrying on an important tradition of guidance and giving. In fact, you may decide to mentor well into your adult years if you enjoy it. In this way, mentoring is a learning experience that can last a lifetime.

Chapter 4

Job Shadow a Professional

"We learn through experience and experiencing. . . . This is as true for the infant moving from kicking to crawling to walking as it is for the scientist with his equations. If the environment permits it, anyone can learn whatever he chooses to learn; and if the individual permits it, the environment will teach him everything it has to teach."

Viola Spolin

Has anyone asked you lately what you plan to do with your life? If so, you're aware that with hundreds of thousands of career possibilities, it's not easy to figure out exactly what you want to do or be. After all, you're in high school, and with the exception of observing teachers, your principal, and various administrative staff, you probably haven't had the opportunity to check out many professionals in their work environments. Maybe "astronaut" or "rock star" sounded like a pretty good career when you were a kid, but now you might be considering other, more realistic possibilities. Many teens say that they want to learn about specific jobs and what they're actually like, but they don't know where to start.

Are you curious about careers? Itching for new experiences? In search of new environments to explore? Are you interested in getting a head start on your future after high school? And do you want to get a taste of the job world—*without* having a real job yet? Then shadowing is the answer. In fact, it's the single best thing you can do to start "test-driving" different careers.

You probably wouldn't buy a car without test-driving it first. So why commit yourself to a career without trying it out to see if it suits your needs and lives up to your expectations? Shadowing a professional in your field of interest is a quick and easy way to put the job to the test. Plus, it's a fun opportunity to introduce yourself to the work environment, meet new people, and experience life outside the classroom.

When you shadow a professional, you spend a workday with the person (your host)—following him or her around, observing, learning, and asking questions. You don't actually have to perform any tasks, unless you've arranged to do so ahead of time. Instead, you watch and form opinions. You determine whether the job interests you and whether you might be good at it. You get a firsthand look at the workplace, the responsibilities, and the skills required to do the job well. Think of a job shadowing experience as a smorgasbord: you get to taste a little of this, a little of that, without committing to anything specific just yet.

Wondering what the difference is between job shadowing and some of the other options you've got, such as career mentorships, internships, or apprenticeships? Here's a breakdown of what each learning experience includes:

Job Shadowing

- observation of host
- no work assignments (unless you've requested one)
- a short-term commitment of one day or a few hours

Career Mentoring

- one-on-one work with a mentor who's a professional in the field

- active participation in research, a project, or specific job duties
- a short-term to long-term commitment (a few months to a year)

Internships

- paid or unpaid work under the direction of a supervisor who assigns your duties and reviews your progress
- a short-term to long-term commitment of a few weeks to a few months

Apprenticeships

- one-on-one, paid work with a supervisor who's an expert in a trade
- hands-on participation in the trade, to increase your skills and knowledge
- a long-term commitment of several months to several years

Job shadowing is like a reality check. You have the chance to see what a particular job is *really* like—not how it's portrayed on TV, in books, or in the movies. Not how your mom or dad may describe it. And not how you probably imagine it in your own mind. This will give you a better sense of what the "daily grind" is all about.

Sixteen-year-old Alisha observed an auto mechanic for a day because she was interested in cars and how they work. She wondered if her interest could lead to a possible career, so when a friend asked if she wanted to shadow her uncle at an auto-body shop for a day, Alisha jumped at the chance. In her own words, "I asked my host all sorts of questions at the workplace. I learned all about how to select the right trade school and which ones in my area were the best to go to." This knowledge gave her an edge when deciding on a trade school and a job. You too may find that a day of shadowing makes you more sure of a possible career path.

"As a freshman, I wanted to get a taste of a bunch of different careers—nurse, banker, real estate agent, and hairdresser. I was able to shadow them all. Actually, I discovered that I didn't want any of those jobs!"**—Ami**

On the other hand, you may discover that the job you thought you were interested in isn't right for you after all. Jason was fifteen when he shadowed a dentist for a day. Although he had been considering a career in dentistry, Jason realized that the daily routines at the dentist's office weren't fun for him—an important discovery. He could have spent years pursuing an education in a field that wasn't ultimately his passion. Realizing early on that, as he put it, "teeth don't really excite me," Jason decided to follow a different path than he originally had envisioned. Similarly, seventeen-year-old Tonya found that shadowing a bank teller was a useful experience: "I realized how boring it would be for me to work with numbers day in and day out. I decided then and there that it was definitely *not* the job for me." No day of shadowing goes to waste—even (or especially) if you find that you're changing your mind about a possible career.

What many teens learn during shadowing is that most jobs have both fun and not-so-fun parts. Even the so-called "glamorous" careers aren't exciting every moment of every day. Most working people have to make routine phone calls, attend long meetings, fill out paperwork, or complete tasks that don't interest them much. Seeing this firsthand can help you understand the realities of life on the job; plus, you get to watch how professionals motivate themselves to accomplish some of their least-favorite duties. In the words of a freshman named Demond, "When you shadow someone who has the job you want, that person will tell you both good and bad things about it. If you still want to do the job after hearing all this, then you should definitely pursue it." Not sure you want to find out that your dream job as a reporter includes hours of fact-checking and detailed proofreading? Think of it this way: it's better to find out *now* than later!

What if you have no clue what you'd like to do for a career? Shadowing is perfect for you! By sampling several different jobs through shadowing, you may be able to pinpoint an area of interest. This brings you a few steps closer to finding out what you might want to do with your life—or at least what you *don't* want to do. Start the process by making a list of the school subjects you like and dislike. Next to each subject write down a related career. If you need help coming up with ideas, ask a parent or a teacher for suggestions. Here's an example from a student named Brad:

Like . . .

- Art—artist, graphic designer, cartoonist

- History—museum curator, historical journal editor, history professor

- Chemistry—chemist, doctor, forensic pathologist

Dislike . . .

- Phys Ed—gym teacher, trainer, martial arts instructor

- English—writer, editor, journalist

Brad discovered that one of his options, historical journal editor, was similar to a job on his "dislike" list: editor. He decided to narrow his list by crossing off both options, at least for now. Next, he determined that graphic designer and curator were careers worth checking out through job shadowing. Try this exercise yourself to see what careers you may find intriguing.

Another way you can start brainstorming possible jobs is by making a list of everything you loved to do as a child: drawing pictures, reading, spending time outdoors, inventing, cooking, dressing up, or whatever. These may be clues to interests you still have. Ask yourself if any of these activities appeal to you today. Can you link them to a possible career?

"Most high-schoolers don't know what they want to do in the future. If you have even a remote interest, you can get a better idea by spending time with a professional. It's never too late to begin shadowing, even if it's your senior year."—**Maria**

Ready to Shadow?

The great thing about shadowing is that there are no limits. You don't have to confine yourself to a day at work with mom or dad (although this can be a fun experience, too). And you don't need to restrict yourself to careers in the business world, even if that's where you see yourself someday. Perhaps you're curious about many different fields, and you'd like to know more about them. For example, maybe your hobby is photography, and you'd love to see a professional shutterbug in action. Why not job shadow a pro photographer for a day? If you enjoy drama, you could observe a stage director, set designer, or lighting expert. If you're into working out, you could shadow a fitness expert or a personal trainer. There are so many jobs to explore—open yourself up to the possibilities. Thinking outside the box will help you identify some of the many fascinating careers to shadow.

In high school, I shadowed a journalist at an alternative newspaper for a day. At the time, I was also doing an internship at a suburban newspaper, so it was especially eye-opening to see the differences between the two publications. While job shadowing, I listened to my host interview people by phone, observed him writing and editing stories, and talked to him about what a typical day for a journalist was like. In college, I continued to job shadow professionals in a variety of fields, including an obstetrician and an eye surgeon. I watched the doctors interact with patients, observed medical exams, and even sat in during surgeries. These learning experiences are ones I'll never forget!

Shadowing Through Your School

Suppose you've identified some careers you're interested in and you're ready to shadow someone. Where do you begin? An easy place to start is at school. Find out if your high school has a shadowing program; if it does, check it out. You can make an appointment to meet with your guidance counselor to learn more about the programs offered. Find out what types of professionals you can hook up with and when you can start.

The guidance counselor will most likely ask you to fill out a survey of your interests. This helps the school determine what type of shadowing experience may be right for you. The school will then match you with a host who's in a field you want to explore. (NOTE: Sometimes it isn't possible to match students with their exact preference. If you want to shadow a firefighter but you get placed with an emergency medical technician, for example, make the best of the situation. You can still learn a lot, and you may even discover a new interest.)

After you're matched up, you'll probably be required to participate in an orientation program to polish your professional manners and to learn what kinds of questions to ask your host. You may be taught how to shake hands correctly, use proper body language to express interest and enthusiasm, and make good eye contact. Depending on the type of shadowing experience you're going for, you may also need to learn about safety on the job or how to handle emotional stress at work (for example, if you're shadowing a doctor in a hospital or a social worker who helps abused children).

After the orientation, you'll most likely be asked to bring home a release form to get a parent's signature. You'll also need to call your host to arrange a shadowing date. When you make this call, you may want to ask for some background reading materials that can help prepare you for your day of shadowing.

Your school's program may require you to fill out an evaluation of your experience or write a paper about it. If you know this is the case, take plenty of notes as you shadow.

Shadowing on Your Own

If you plan to arrange the shadowing experience yourself, you've got some choices. First, you could find out if other students are interested. If they are, approach your principal as a group to see if you can get some school backing or support. Perhaps there's schoolwide interest in a shadowing program; working together, you may be able to create a wider pool of contacts from which to choose hosts.

If you prefer to go it alone, start by talking to adults who can suggest potential job shadowing hosts. Your mom or dad, a teacher, a guidance counselor, an aunt or uncle, or the parent of a friend could be a good source of ideas. Interested in medicine, accounting, law, or dentistry? Perhaps your family doctor or dentist, or a relative's accountant or lawyer, could be your host. Start with contacts you already have.

Another option is to call schools in your area (for example, medical, law, trade, business, art, or beauty schools) to see if they can recommend a contact for you. If you explain that you're a high school student interested in a career or a particular field, the school may be willing to give you the names of some recent graduates to contact in your area.

THE ALUMNI CONNECTION

Another great way to find someone to shadow is to contact your school's alumni. If your school has a guidance office or career center, start there. If you're in a private school, the development office may have alumni contact information. (You could also talk to older siblings of your friends, if they attended your school, and see if they'd let you shadow them.) Once you have some addresses, write letters to "alums" asking whether they'd be willing to act as your host for a day of job shadowing. The good news is that most alumni will be delighted to talk to a young person from the same school who's interested in the same career. And most will go out of their way to host you and share their expertise.

Once you've gotten the names of some professionals in your field of interest, you can make a phone call or write a letter introducing yourself. Begin by telling the person that you're a high school student who's seeking a job shadowing experience. Be sure to mention the name of the person or the school that served as your connec-

F. Y. I.

Organizations that offer internships to teens can be a good resource when searching for a host to job shadow. The internship directories listed in "Find Out More" on pages 127–128 are a good starting point.

tion to the professional you've contacted—this gives you an "in." Politely request an opportunity to shadow the professional you're speaking with. Explain that you'd like to spend one day observing and asking questions, so you can get a better feel for what the job entails. If you're contacting the person through mail or email, make sure that you provide your address and phone number. If you're using the phone and you have to leave a message, state your name clearly and provide your home number for a return call. (Say the number slowly, so the person doesn't have to keep replaying your message.)

Now that you've made contact, the ball is in the other person's court. If he or she turns you down, don't take it personally; move on to the next professional on your list as soon as possible, so you keep your momentum. If the person says yes, immediately set a day and time for your job shadowing experience.

How to Prepare Yourself for the Big Day

A good shadowing experience starts with preparation. You've got a few logistics to figure out first: How will you get to your host's work site? How will you get home? Do you need special permission to get a day off from school? Is your release form (if you have one) signed, and have you turned it in?

As the day of shadowing draws closer, think of some questions you'd like to ask your host. Here's a list of possibilities:

- What are your job duties?

- What do you like best about your job?

- What do you like least?

- Is the work environment here casual and relaxed, or more formal?

- How does someone in your job advance to higher levels? How long does it take to be promoted?

- Is this a competitive field to be in? Why or why not?

- What kind of lifestyle do people in this occupation lead? Do they have to put in lots of extra hours? Are there opportunities for travel?

- What's your educational background?

- Did you need any special training for your current position?

- Can you tell me about your typical workday?

- What are the pros and cons of this job?
- How did you go about finding your job?
- Did you do any internships when you were my age or during college? What were they like?
- Did you have many contacts in this field before you got your job?
- How are new employees recruited here? Through college recruitment? Job fairs?
- What kind of educational background would I need for this particular position? A college degree? Advanced degrees? What course of study would be best for me?
- Do you have any advice for someone just starting out in this career?
- Are there opportunities for me to get a volunteer position, an internship, or a job here?
- What are some of the changes and advancements being made in this field?
- Would you be willing to give me the names of other people I can contact to learn more about this career?

Next, consider what you hope to gain from this experience. Do you want to make some career contacts while you're shadowing? If so, plan to ask whether your host can introduce you to other employees. (Remember to collect business cards, so you don't forget the names and titles of the people you meet.) Do you hope to someday get an informational interview at the place where your host works? Then make a point of asking your host how to set one up. It may be helpful to write down all of your questions beforehand in a notebook that you bring with you. This way, you can record the answers, write down people's names, and store business cards in a handy place. Be sure to remember a pen, so you don't have to ask for one.

F. Y. I.

The informational interview is exactly what it sounds like—an interview to get information about a certain career, business, or field. It's a good way to practice your interview skills, network, and even have your résumé critiqued.

You may want to do a little extra "homework" before you job shadow to make a good impression on your host. For example, you could do some reading about the job you're shadowing, so you can ask very specific questions. Or you could familiarize yourself with your host's work—has he or she written any articles? Developed a product? Made advancements in the field? Won awards? You can do your research through the organization itself, on the Internet, or at the library, depending on what you're trying to find out. Sixteen-year-old Andy planned to spend the day shadowing a chiropractor; beforehand, he went to the library to see if the chiropractor had published any articles—which she had. According to Andy, "When I asked my host questions based on her article, she was way impressed!" This kind of extra preparation can be well worth the effort.

Here are some more tips for putting your best foot forward:

- **Greet your host professionally.** Look the person in the eye, smile, extend your hand, and offer a firm handshake. (You may want to practice your handshake with a parent or friend, so you feel comfortable.) You could say, "Nice to meet you, Ms. _____," or "I'm happy to meet you, Professor _____." Make sure to call your host by his or her last name and title, unless you're invited to do otherwise. This is proper business etiquette and is more impressive than giving a casual "What's up?" or a brief wave.

- **Use direct eye contact.** This skill is important in any business or work situation. When you look people in the eye while listening or speaking, you come across as focused, eager, and attentive. A comfortable level of eye contact involves a relaxed gaze, but not a stare. If you have trouble looking people right in the eye, a trick is to look at their forehead instead, which still gives the impression of good eye contact.

- **Go for a neat and professional look.** If you're a guy, you may want to wear dress pants and a tie; if you're a girl, wear a skirt, a dress, or dressy pants. Avoid jeans and sneakers, unless you're shadowing someone outdoors or you're sure that you'll get messy while on the job. Above all, wear something you're comfortable in, so you appear relaxed.

- **Show up on time.** Arrange your transportation beforehand, and be sure to give yourself extra time in case you get lost or have trouble finding a parking space. You may want to plan on arriving ten minutes early, so you can stop in the bathroom if you need to.

- **Bring money for lunch.** Your host may decide to treat you to lunch—or you may offer to treat as a way to say thank you. On the other hand, you could find yourself with no one to hang out with during the lunch hour, depending on how busy your host is that day. Be sure to bring along enough cash to buy lunch and snacks. (A growling stomach is a distraction you don't need!)

- **Be prepared for downtime.** Your host may not be able to attend to you the entire day, for whatever reason. Unexpected deadlines and emergency situations may arise, so be prepared. If you've got your notebook or a book to read, you won't have to sit around with nothing to do during downtime.

Have a backup plan in place. If your host gets too busy or has an unexpected conflict at work, be ready to deal with it. Ask if you can shadow a colleague or offer to come back another day. Make sure you have transportation home if you need to leave earlier than you'd planned. Your host will appreciate your flexibility.

- **Be friendly.** Most likely, you'll be meeting lots of new people as you follow your host around. If you're left alone periodically during the day, introduce yourself to others so they know who you are and why you're there. Offer a friendly hello and a handshake to everyone you meet.

- **Be a good conversationalist.** When talking with professionals, try to minimize your use of slang or filler words such as *uh-huh, yeah, um, I dunno, like,* and *ya know.* To see how often you speak like this, tape record yourself talking at the dinner table with your family. Are your conversation skills in need of a little work? If so, ask your mom or dad to help you role-play your job shadow experience. Practice greeting your host, asking questions, and offering answers to questions asked of you. Tape record this session if you'd like to figure out when you tend to use slang or filler words the most. When you're nervous? Excited? Unsure of yourself?

- **Ask for what you need.** If you're curious about a certain task or technique, let your host know. Feel free to be direct about what you hope to learn. Your job shadow host isn't a mind reader!

- **Be a good listener.** Ask questions to show that you're interested. Be sure to nod your head to indicate that you understand what your host is saying. Take notes, if you want to. Your host will appreciate your attentiveness.

- **Share information about yourself.** Just as you're interested in finding out more about your host, he or she wants to know about you. Be open and friendly. Talk about why you're interested in this career.

- **Imagine yourself in the work environment.** Can you see yourself doing this job day after day for a number of years? Does this career opportunity excite you? Intimidate you? Bore you? Are you intrigued by some of the responsibilities but not others? Is there a related field that may be of more interest to you? Spend some time mulling over these questions. If you're alone during the lunch hour, you could keep busy by writing your thoughts in your notebook.

- **Say thank you and put it in writing.** At the end of the day, thank your host and shake hands. Send a thank-you note afterward as well, expressing your appreciation for his or her time and the experience in general. This is a great way to leave your host with a lasting impression.

SPOTLIGHT ON

Paul Abosh
Garden City Collegiate
Winnipeg, Manitoba

I had such a great time in metal shop in high school that I was considering a career that would allow me to work with metal. But I wanted to know more about my options and what working with metal in a professional setting would specifically entail. My mom helped put me in touch with a sheet metal business owner, and he said he would be more than willing to take me under his wing for a day. The business he owned manufactured metal trim to be turned into pipes and gutters.

I wasn't quite sure what to expect when I first got there, but my initial impression was that the place was warm and friendly. While job shadowing, I saw a little bit of everything. I watched the foreman with his roll of sheet metal, which looked like a big roll of newspaper held up by a forklift. He unrolled the metal and cut it into sheets and strips. Then I watched as other workers inserted the long, flat sheets of metal into other machines, to shape the metal into pipes and gutters. I liked the way everyone talked and joked as they worked, and the way the owner would come down and ask everyone how their day was going. I thought it would be great to work in a place that had so much camaraderie.

During the day, I also observed other aspects of the business (like working with vendors, dealing with customers, and overseeing the entire operation). I sat with the owner in his office, listening to him talk on the phone and asking him questions when I could. I also asked questions of the employees, in an attempt to learn about selling these products wholesale to home-improvement retailers.

Overall, my job shadowing experience was positive. I felt that I had a much better sense of what working with metal would be like, which is much more than I would have gained from reading a book or talking to my metal shop instructor. I also felt proud that I was able to ask important questions and have them taken seriously by the metal workers. One of the best parts of the day was getting to have lunch with the owner. We went to a little hamburger place, and I got to pick his brain and ask all sorts of other questions about the business.

One day afterward, I did an informational interview at the business. Because I had shadowed, I was able to ask intelligent and informed questions. I found out how much physical labor is involved in the work, how much vacation time employees receive, what the job outlook for certain positions is, and what kind of training is required for some of the more technical assignments. I felt like I had a much better handle on what working at a sheet metal manufacturer was like. Because my job shadowing experience was so successful, I still maintain a great relationship with the business owner today.

If you're fascinated by what you see and one day just isn't enough, ask your host whether a follow-up session would be possible. Some teens have found that subsequent shadowings are a great way to further explore the work environment and job duties. Because they've already been through all the introductions and know their host, many teens feel more at ease the second time around. If a follow-up day isn't possible, you may be able to communicate with your host through email or a phone call. Find out whether it's okay to stay in touch if new questions occur to you down the road.

You may also want to request an informational interview with your host after the shadowing experience. Perhaps he or she would be willing to offer tips on strengthening your interview skills or improving your résumé—or even give your résumé to the human resources department to keep on file.

Shadowing Is More Than a Day Off from School

As with any other alternative learning experience, you'll get as much out of shadowing as you put into it. If you make an extra effort to research your host and his or her workplace, ask plenty of questions, take notes during the session or once

you've returned home, and then spend time reflecting on the experience, job shadowing will be of greater value to you. In fact, shadowing can be a real eye-opener and an important learning experience on many levels. Not only do you gain knowledge about a career you may have one day, but you also discover more about your own likes and dislikes and your dreams for your future. Plus, you get to practice meeting new people and handling yourself in unfamiliar situations.

You can extend the experience by sharing what you've learned. Get the word out by trying one (or more) of the following ideas:

- Create your own job shadowing evaluation to give to your guidance counselor. He or she can post it on a bulletin board for other students to read.

- Write an article about the experience for your school or community newspaper.

- Organize a panel of students who have shadowed. Together, you can talk about your experiences and share what you learned. Find out if you can hold the panel during a school assembly.

- Propose a "shadowing fair" at school. Gather a panel of professionals who have been shadowed or are willing to let students shadow them. Invite these professionals to speak to your class or the student body about what they do for a living, so that other teens may feel inspired to give shadowing a try.

So, how many people should you shadow? As many as you have time for. It's a terrific way to build a network of contacts that you can turn to a few years from now, when you're looking for a real job. At that point, all those shadowing experiences will come in handy—especially if you reconnect with your hosts to see if their companies are hiring. Even when interviewing at other places of employment, you can mention your shadowing experiences to show that you have a varied background and plenty of initiative.

Shadowing is just a one-day commitment, so why not live it up? Get out there and experience as much as you can. Shadow a doctor, a painter, a carpenter, an accountant, a piano tuner, a producer, and a zoologist all in one year (or month). If nothing else, you'll encounter interesting people and places . . . and have some exciting stories to tell your friends.

FIND OUT MORE

Adventure Careers by Alex Hiam and Susan Angle (Franklin Lakes, NJ: Career Press, 1995). This book will give you all you need to know to start thinking about careers off the beaten path. The authors discuss topics like planning your future, job search strategies, resources for different career paths, and more. If you're thinking about a career in politics, the arts, the environment, entrepreneurship, or some other "adventure," this book will help you make it happen.

Career Choices: A Guide for Teens and Young Adults by Mindy Bingham and Sandy Stryker (Santa Barbara, CA: Academic Innovations, 1990). This book will assist you as you explore your interests and talents to see how they relate to potential careers. The first part of the book helps you figure out who you are, the second part asks you to think about what you want, and the third helps you set a plan to get what you want. You'll learn about setting goals and getting experience—including job shadowing. Plenty of worksheets, surveys, and checklists make this a truly interactive book.

Free and Inexpensive Career Materials: A Resource Directory, edited by Elizabeth H. Oakes (Chicago: Ferguson, 1998). This directory lists over 800 sources of free or inexpensive career information materials. A complete index and guide to resources provides quick and easy access to data in over 300 occupational categories.

Jobs for the Future
One Bowdoin Square, 11th Floor
Boston, MA 02114
(617) 742-5995
www.jff.org

This organization focuses on building effective partnerships between schools and the workforce and creating successful School-to-Work transitions for teens and young adults. Jobs for the Future has several initiatives that might be right for you. Call, write, or visit the Web site to find out more.

Junior Achievement
One Education Way
Colorado Springs, CO 80906
(719) 540-8000
www.ja.org

If you're interested in free enterprise, business, or economics, check out Junior Achievement, which offers many programs for high schoolers including setting up job shadowing experiences.

The Job Shadowing Handbook
www.state.nj.us/njded/voc/shadow.htm

Looking for more information on job shadowing specifically? Check out this online document created by the New Jersey School-to-Career Partnership. Although written for adults who are planning to provide job shadowing experiences, it answers a lot of questions students might have too—plus it gives you an idea of what you can expect.

Groundhog Job Shadow Day
Groundhog Job Shadow Day is celebrated in early February with the goal of building partnerships between businesses and schools. The Web site will help you find the School-to-Work contact people in your state, who in turn can help you set up a job shadowing experience. For more information, call (202) 452-9468 or visit *www.jobshadow.org.*

Job Shadowing Month
February is Job Shadowing Month. If you're finding it difficult to shadow a professional because of transportation, time constraints, or other reasons, check out virtual job shadowing. For the entire month of February, you can shadow a variety of career mentors online at *www.jobshadow.monster.com.*

Take Our Daughters to Work® Day

The fourth Thursday of every April is Take Our Daughters to Work Day. This day celebrates the idea that girls are the next generation of future leaders and can benefit from exposure to the world of work. Take Our Daughters to Work Day has been in existence since 1993, giving millions of girls ages nine to fifteen the opportunity to see what careers are all about and stay focused on their futures. For more information, contact the Ms. Foundation for Women at 1-800-676-7780 or visit *www.takeourdaughterstowork.org.*

SPOTLIGHT ON

Aisha Bierma
Mounds View High School
Shoreview, Minnesota

During my freshman year, our school had a "shadow day" where students got to spend a day with a professional in a field they were interested in. I shadowed a lawyer at a firm in Minneapolis. My host, Jay Quam (he told me to call him Jay), set up a great day for me. I met attorneys from different specialty areas who told me lots of interesting things about law school, various types of law, and what it's really like to work in a law office. I also went to lunch with my host and some other people from the firm. That was a lot of fun, and it gave me a chance to ask questions and learn more about the legal profession.

After lunch, Jay took me to sit in on a few trials so I could see firsthand what goes on in a courtroom. By the end of the day, I had a much better idea than before of what it would be like to practice law. My shadow day also helped confirm my plans to attend law school. Of course, I couldn't see every aspect of an attorney's job in a day. Still, I felt the lawyers were very honest with me about the pros and cons of their profession, and I learned a lot. Jay invited me to come again, and I was so impressed with my experience that I went back to shadow him on several other occasions.

Sitting in on different trials was especially interesting because it gave me an important insight into the life of a lawyer. Sometimes the law can be exciting and even inspirational, but it can also be boring, frustrating, and bureaucratic. Every lawyer I talked to at the firm warned me that the job isn't completely glamorous, and they were right. I went to quite a few trials that were painstakingly dull, either because of the topic (such as a business merger) or because of the minutely detailed information being discussed. (I found out that expert witnesses can sometimes make even murder cases dull.)

However, there were intriguing moments, too. The most memorable was when a lawyer objected that it was an "outrage" for a female witness to accuse his client of pulling down his pants in front of her; the attorney asked to have the visitors leave the courtroom. The judge was clearly not very happy with the objection since the trial was open to the public and the lawyer knew it.

While some moments were amusing, others were sad or horrifying, and many were just generally interesting. It might sound corny, but one of the best parts of shadowing was watching trials where it was obvious that justice was being done. The law may not always be perfect, but it does serve an important purpose.

I'd encourage any student who has the chance to go on a shadow day to take full advantage of the situation. Ask your host if you can talk to other people in the workplace, especially if their jobs have a slightly different focus than your host's. It's useful to get different perspectives. And while it helps to hear people talk about their jobs, you'll learn a lot more by watching a professional "in action," like I did when I visited courtrooms. If you have a good experience and feel like there's still more to see, ask your host if you can come back. The more you get to see and hear, the better. Shadowing will definitely teach you things you can't learn sitting in your desk at school.

"Choose a job you love,
and you will never have to work a day in your life."
Confucius

As you'll find out, job shadowing helps you determine what you might enjoy as a career—by making you ask yourself questions like *What do I like to do?* or *Do I like to do this?* Figuring out what inspires and challenges you is an essential career goal, because when you love your work, it doesn't seem so much like *work* anymore. You're not too young to have goals and a plan for your future. In fact, now is a great time to be thinking about what you want to do in life. Knowing this early on helps you make the most of your education—the time you spend both in and out of school.

Once you've begun to figure out what you want to do, your learning path will become clearer, your steps surer. You can start asking yourself other important questions—*Do I want to go directly to college? What kind of college or university should I attend? Do I want to get a job after high school and delay college for a year or two? Is a trade school in my future? What can I be doing now to improve life for myself later on?* And then you can go digging for the answers.

Chapter 5

Find an Internship

"One thing about experience is that when you
don't have very much you're apt to get a lot."

Franklin P. Jones

Maya was a junior at a high school in New Mexico. Like many
other students her age, she wondered what she was going to do
after graduation, which was only a year-and-a-half away. She felt
a bit anxious and unprepared for what lay ahead. Should she go
to college? Enter the workforce right away? Work while attending
college courses in the evenings? Travel? Take a year off while
mulling over her choices? Maya wasn't sure what she'd like to do
or what her options were. She'd had a few summer jobs working
as a waitress, but she knew this wasn't the career for her. She
realized she needed an alternative experience—something that
offered more responsibility and greater challenge.

After learning about an internship opportunity with a company that provided tours of her city, she applied and was
accepted. Maya enjoyed giving tours and answering questions
about the people and places around her; she realized that she
wouldn't mind doing this kind of job for a few more years.
Although she didn't need to make any decisions about her future
just yet, she felt more confident about her skills and her ability
to make choices regarding the kind of career she might go after
someday. Her increased confidence helped her look at graduation
with excitement, instead of worry.

Maybe you and Maya have something in common. See if any of the following statements apply to you:

- You don't know what you want to do with your life yet, but you're interested in finding out.
- School doesn't provide you with the hands-on experience you want and need.
- You've had summer jobs before, but they didn't let you see into the day-to-day operations of the business. Plus, the duties were kind of dull.
- You're a hard worker, and you need greater challenges.
- You'd like to get more skills and experience.

If you answered yes to any of these questions, you're a good candidate for an internship.

"I was a freshman, and I had never even held a job before. I couldn't think of a single job-related quality that would make me a good candidate for an internship. I talked about this problem with my mom, and together we came up with a list of positive characteristics I have that would help me get an internship, like my skills with animals and my responsibilities around our family's farm. Because I was applying for an internship with a vet, these skills really helped me out."—Janice

An internship can be a wonderful opportunity to test yourself and try something out of the ordinary. You don't have to be a junior or a senior to get one, either. These days, more and more younger high school students are seeking internships to enrich their education, explore potential careers, and get experience that can enhance a résumé or a college application. Just think: Instead of spending the summer mowing lawns or watching someone's kids, you could be working with professional adults who are willing to share their knowledge and expertise. And if you intern during the school year, you may have a chance to leave class on certain days of the week to work with your supervisor one-on-one in an environment you're curious about and interested in. This can be a welcome change from the routines of the school day.

If you think interning means being the gofer who fetches coffee, baby-sits the copy machine, and brings back lunches for the whole office—think again. Contrary to what you may have heard, internships aren't just "grunt work." Plenty of teens have been involved in fascinating internships that include lots of variety and responsibility.

Here are some examples of what you might do as an intern:

- assist a group of athletes at the Special Olympics
- help crunch numbers at an accounting firm
- work at a major tourist attraction like the Space Needle in Seattle
- become a production assistant at a children's theater company
- help out a cartoonist, a set designer, a special effects wizard, or another artist
- aid a researcher in a health-care advocacy organization

- work in the design department of a toy manufacturer
- organize the photo archives at an art gallery
- fact-check press releases for a public relations company
- learn about corporate finance at a bank
- lead hikes and nature talks at an environmental learning center

SPOTLIGHT ON

Beth Scott
Westdale High School
Omaha, Nebraska

During eighth grade, I became involved in the Explorers program at the Omaha Henry Doorly Zoo. (Explorers is through the Boys Scouts, but it's for both girls and boys.) After going through this program and learning about how the zoo functions, I applied to be a ZooAide, which is the teen internship program at the zoo. There were three open spots that year, and probably over 100 applicants, so I felt lucky when I got accepted. I don't think I've ever been so excited about anything! And the experience over the next four years truly did change my life.

The internship was year-round and had two parts: education hours and animal hours. Education hours included helping at birthday parties and classes and at campouts where groups of kids would spend the night in one of the zoo's education buildings. We did activities with the campers and then took them on a night hike to see all the nocturnal animals. That was fun!

After you completed so many education hours, you could apply to work in an animal area. My dream was to work in the aquarium—Omaha's is one of the best in the country and it had just been renovated. At the time, only one ZooAide was needed. I was a certified scuba diver (trained for diving with an oxygen tank), which meant I could assist with cleaning the tanks, and I think that helped me get the position.

On one of my first days working at the aquarium, something pretty funny happened: I fell into one of the tanks! The tank had harmless fish, so I wasn't hurt, but I was really embarrassed. I could only imagine what the people walking by the tank in the viewing area must have thought when all of a sudden a person came crashing down into the water. The other crew members teased me about it for weeks.

I worked with the aquarium fish for the first two years of my internship. During the school year, I worked every Saturday and Sunday from 7 A.M. till sometime in the afternoon. Often there'd be a campout in the evening as well. In the summer, I worked much more often. I would prep food for the animals, take readings from the tanks to make sure the water was stable, feed the animals, and clean, clean, clean! There was always work to be done.

After a couple of years, my sister became a ZooAide as well. She worked with the aquarium birds, and soon I started working there with her. The responsibilities were still pretty much the same, except now I was working with all sorts of penguins and puffins. It was always wintertime in the penguin enclosures, and the snowmakers would make fresh piles of snow each morning. It was strange to be freezing when outside it was over 90 degrees. Contrary to popular belief, penguins are *not* the cutesy animals people think they are. There were a few that liked to chase my sister around and bite her on the rear end!

I spent four years interning as a ZooAide. That experience led me to even more interesting opportunities, including an internship in marine biology research in the Bimini Islands, which I did the summer before entering college. I'm glad I pursued my dreams in high school. Instead of just fantasizing about being a marine biologist, I actually participated in it. I wouldn't trade those experiences for anything.

What's an Internship—and What Can It Do for You?

In general, an internship is a temporary agreement with a professional person, a company, or a for-profit or nonprofit organization. In exchange for your time and labor, you get actual on-the-job experience, plus the guidance of the supervisor who's in charge of you. You may work for a few weeks or several months, and the job may be paid or unpaid. You can do an internship while you're in school, over the summer, or during your time off (a winter or spring break, for example).

WHY DO COMPANIES WANT INTERNS ANYWAY?

You may wonder why employers would ever hire young and inexperienced interns. Being young and inexperienced has its benefits. Teens are often full of enthusiasm and eager to learn; their youthful perspective is a nice change of pace. Plus, it doesn't hurt that teens can be a source of cheap or free labor. Nonprofit organizations often rely on the work of interns, because there's not always enough money to hire more experienced help. Other companies depend on interns to help out with tasks that paid employees don't have time to do, especially during busy seasons. Some start-up companies use interns because they can't afford to hire employees. Interns who prove themselves sometimes get employment offers from the company or organization they worked for. This saves the employer time and money in recruiting— another benefit of sponsoring internships.

Suppose you were to intern at a book publishing house. Your duties might include filing correspondence from authors, assisting an editor with administrative tasks, and photocopying manuscripts. While these responsibilities may not sound super-challenging, they're definitely useful—and anyone who's going to work in an office day after day needs to master them. You could make the most of the situation by taking a look at the letters and manuscripts to see what you might learn from them. Knowing you're seeking valuable learning experiences, your supervisor might even offer you a long-term assignment to complete as time allows and hand in for an evaluation. For example, you may be asked to read a manuscript and make comments about its content—or even have the chance to test your editing abilities. This personalized attention can go a long way toward building your confidence and sharpening your skills.

Here are some more benefits of becoming an intern:

- **You'll have fun learning new information.** In the classroom, you're usually told what you need to know. But in an internship, the learning is up to you. You'll feel energized when finding out about what goes on in the work environment and making new discoveries about yourself.

- **You'll make professional contacts.** Adults in your field of interest can be a good resource for you—perhaps one might even become your mentor (read more about this in Chapter 3, "Get a Mentor, Be a Mentor"). When you observe these adults, ask them questions, and get their advice, you'll learn more about the job world and what the future may hold in store for you. Plus, you might get to meet and talk with the owner of the business or the chief executive officer, which can be a fascinating experience. Talk to everyone you can on the job— you never know who might have something important to share with you.

- **You'll get more responsibility.** Maybe you don't feel challenged enough at this point in your life. As an intern, you'll have the chance to show people how reliable you can be and to practice taking on more responsibility. This can be an asset when job hunting or applying to college—or even convincing your parents to let you do something you've never done before.

- **You'll get job experience.** It's well known that you can't get a job without any experience—and that you can't get any experience without a job. An internship helps solve this age-old problem. When you have some experience, potential employers will take you more seriously.

- **You'll learn to use new tools and equipment.** Is your internship at a print shop? In a lab? At an Internet start-up? Whether you're surrounded by machinery or technical equipment, you'll need to become familiar with how to use it—another bit of experience you'll gain while interning.

- **You'll have more to put on your résumé.** The responsibilities of an internship give you something to add to your résumé or college application. (Plus, you'll stand out from other teens who only have "waiter" or "cashier" on theirs.) If you're considering jumping right into the workforce instead of going to college after high school, an internship will not only look good on your résumé but also will give you something to discuss in-depth with interviewers.

- **You'll be able to make more well-informed choices.** It's not easy to know what you want to do with your life. What if you feel overwhelmed by the tons of job possibilities out there? An internship is your opportunity to "try before you buy"—meaning you get to sample what it would be like to work in a certain field, without committing yourself to it. In fact, doing several internships while you're still in high school is a great way to find out whatever you can about your career interests.

THE LETTERS-OF-REFERENCE BENEFIT

Letters of reference can be important tools in both a job search or the college-application process. Most potential employers will ask for three references—people who can vouch for your character and offer insights about the kind of worker you are. Toward the end of your internship, you can ask your supervisor if he or she might provide you with a letter of reference. This letter could include information about what you accomplished during the internship, what it was like to work with you, and what your unique personal qualities are. Sometimes, intern supervisors will agree to write the letter and then ask you what you'd like it to say. You can then request that they tailor the letter to meet a specific need or make it more general so you can use it in different circumstances. A glowing recommendation on company letterhead—with the signature of your internship supervisor—can be a powerful tool when you're competing for a job or enrollment in a college or university.

"I think everybody needs office skills—how to write a business letter, how to fold it up and put it into an envelope, how to answer a phone call at a company, and so on. As an office intern, you learn all this—plus how to make the coffee."—**Scott**

Where to Start

If you're considering becoming an intern, begin by asking yourself what your goals are. It's not enough to have goals like these:

- I need to pad my résumé.
- I want to make my parents happy.
- My best friend got an internship, so I'd better get one, too.

Instead, you'll want to spend time thinking about what you really hope to get out of an experience like this. Do you want to make career contacts? Explore a certain kind of job or work environment? Find something you're really interested in? Figure out what you're capable of? Hang out with more adults, so you can learn from them? All of the above?

Get a piece of paper and write what your main goals are (save this list; you'll need it later). Your list may include:

1. Learn more about a specific industry.

2. Apply what I've learned in the classroom to real-life situations.

3. Work on my communications skills.

4. Explore what it's like to be in an actual workplace, with adults who can show me what to do.

5. Gain skills directly related to a career.

The more specific you are about your goals, the easier it will be to evaluate potential internships. It's fine to have lots of different goals, because a high-quality internship will satisfy many of them at once.

Next, consider what field, work environment, or activity most interests you. Here are a few categories to get you thinking:

Care Facilities

- hospitals/clinics
- hospices
- eldercare/rehabilitation

Education

- schools
- tutoring centers
- mentoring organizations

Computers/Internet

- technical support
- computer animation
- graphic design
- Web site design

Environment

- national parks
- environmental agencies
- nonprofits concerned with the environment

Government/Politics

- local, state, or national government
- political groups/ activism
- campaigning

Science/Research

- labs and research companies
- space and astronomy centers
- museums

Media

- television stations
- radio stations
- newspapers
- magazines

Visual/Performing Arts

- arts organizations
- art schools
- theaters
- orchestra halls

Internships exist in a variety of fields and careers. Almost any organization or company you can think of probably offers an internship—from huge corporations to a local bank. Once you've pinpointed a field of interest and your goals for your internship, you're well on your way to finding something that will match your needs.

You may be thinking, "Interning sounds great, but I don't know any CEOs, and none of my mom or dad's friends have jobs I'm interested in. So there's no way I can find a cool internship on my own, right?" Wrong. Although there's no denying that contacts help, plenty of high school students locate internships on their own, without the benefit of knowing any influential people. A very good place to start is at school.

If your high school offers an internship program, check it out. The program will either match you up with an employer in a field that interests you or assist you with locating an internship yourself—in other words, much of the up-front work is done for you. Depending on what your school has to offer, you may get help from a guidance counselor or an "internship coordinator."

Ask this person questions like:

- Will I be arranging my own internship, or does the school arrange it for me?

- Is there a listing of internships I can look at? Is it organized by fields of interest, so I can find something that's right for me?

- Will the internship involve some sort of learning contract—a document that spells out certain objectives for the experience?

- Does the internship program include preparatory classes or independent work?

- Do I need to complete a set number of internship hours?

- Will someone evaluate my internship performance? Who? How will this person conduct the evaluation?

- Will I automatically receive academic credit or a grade for my internship? If not, what options do I have for arranging to get credit or a grade? Do I need to talk to the principal?

- Will a teacher or school administrator visit me at my internship to check my progress?

- Will I have assignments, presentations, or projects to complete during the internship or afterward?

- Do I need to make my own transportation arrangements?

- Will I need to sign a waiver releasing the school from responsibility if something happens to me while on the job?

- How will this internship fit in with my school schedule?

- What kind of payment will I receive, if any?

F. Y. I.

Some internships offer stipends (pay) of minimum wage or a few hundred dollars per week. But the reality is that most are *un*paid. Keep in mind that the experience you'll get makes up for the fact that you won't receive wages.

SPOTLIGHT ON

Kate Van Gundy
Friends' Central School
Swarthmore, Pennsylvania

I did an internship that was built into my senior year curriculum. We could choose where to intern, and I worked at my community's weekly paper. I really like creative writing, and I thought this would allow me to experience a different kind of writing. It was such a small newspaper that they let me pick my own subjects, set my own itineraries, and go from there. Other people in my class did "gofer" work at their internships. I did, too, but I also got to do much more. The editors gave me a lot of freedom—I was surprised at all they let me do.

My daily work at the paper was varied, and I think that was the quality I liked most about the internship. Many days I summarized passages for press releases; I frequently organized some of the archives, which I especially enjoyed because I could see the development of the paper and community over the years. At other times, I was sent to photograph events in town or to attend town meetings.

I wrote two extensive articles for the paper completely independently. One was a piece in response to the violence at Columbine High School in Colorado. I tried to put a local perspective on youth violence. I interviewed school principals, psychologists, and counselors and wrote an article about their reactions to the event and the measures local schools were taking to address violence.

I also wrote an article about the relationship between Swarthmore (my hometown) and Chester (a neighboring town). The two towns are hugely different in terms of their cultural and socioeconomic makeup. I interviewed people about how the two towns had interacted across many decades in a variety of different areas from political activism in the 1960s to housing improvements in the 1970s to educational and artistic collaborations in the 1990s. I compiled all of my interviews into one large piece that painted a picture of cooperation between two distinct communities.

Gofer work can be repetitive and boring, but it's still an important part of an internship. You have to gain a complete understanding of the workplace, and gofer work is usually an integral part of that. At the paper, this often meant going through the archives, and I learned how to have fun with that. I also got to know a lot about what was going on in Swarthmore by summarizing press releases.

Internships give you real-life experience—skills besides those learned in school. In general, I loved my internship and think that working at a smaller operation gave me exposure to a whole business rather than just one tiny department. I liked the paper's locale, too. Being in a familiar place allowed me to relate more closely to the news and to feel more passion and interest in the pieces I wrote.

If your school doesn't have an internship program, you can pursue an internship on your own. Many enterprising teens have found their own internships by simply making "cold calls." This means they found a business or an organization they were interested in, and then phoned to ask if an internship might be available. Try this yourself: you may be pleasantly surprised at the positive responses you get—even from organizations that haven't ever had an intern before. I found all three of my internships by making cold calls and sending out résumés and cover letters to places that weren't even advertising. Doors often open when you say you'll work for free!

Other teens have used the career office of a local college or university as a resource. These offices usually contain plenty of internship listings and may be willing to let you browse, if you explain that you're a high school student and make an appointment ahead of time.

Library and bookstore shelves are filled with directories containing a wealth of choices for anyone looking for an internship. Most of them include listings of internships open to high school students (some internships are designed for college students only). If you use one of these resources, it's likely that the internships will be presented in alphabetical order by the name of the sponsoring company or organization, or by the geographical location. Some directories focus on specialized internships, such as those available in the arts or the media. For suggestions on which directories to look at, see "Find Out More" on this page and the next.

If you feel overwhelmed by all of the choices, narrow the possibilities by focusing on a specific field or a particular kind of internship (paid or unpaid; short-term or long-term). Once you've identified some internships that you're interested in, you can call or write for more information. Internship directories usually provide the name of a contact person, along with an address or a phone number. When you write or call, introduce yourself as a high school student who's looking for an internship and find out if the one you're interested in is available. If you're told that an intern has already been hired or that the internship is no longer open to students, you can move on to the next possibility on your list. When you find an internship that's currently open, you're ready to apply. See "Applying for an Internship—What Does It Take?" on pages 129–141 for what you need to know.

 ## FIND OUT MORE

To find an internship, take a look at some internship directories, which are indexed by field of interest, perks, age requirements, and other categories. The following are examples of some of the directories you can find at a high school or university career center, or at your local library. Many directories are updated yearly, so make sure you grab a current edition.

America's Top Internships, 2000 Edition by Mark Oldman and Samer Hamadeh (Princeton, NJ: Princeton Review, 1999).

The Internship Bible by Mark Oldman and Samer Hamadeh (New York: Random House, 2000).

National Directory of Internships by Gina Gulati (Raleigh, NC: National Society for Internships and Experiential Education, 1998).

Peterson's 2001 Internships: The Largest Source of Internships Available (Princeton, NJ: Peterson's Guides, 2000).

The Yale Daily News Guide to Internships 2000 by John Anslem (New York: Kaplan, 1999).

If you have an unusual internship in mind and don't find it in one of the general directories just listed, you can look at some of the more specialized internship directories such as the following:

The Internship, Practicum, and Field Placement Handbook: A Guide for the Helping Professions by Brian N. Baird (Upper Saddle River, NJ: Prentice Hall, 1998).

National Directory of Arts Internships by Warren Christensen (Valencia, CA: California Institute of the Arts, 1998).

Other fun and helpful resources include the following:

The Back Door Guide to Short Term Job Adventures by Michael Landes (Berkeley, CA: Ten Speed Press, 2000). Looking for an extraordinary interning experience? Then you need this newly revised and updated guide. Inside, you'll find hundreds of options to learn something new, do something different, or even change your life. This comprehensive guide includes internships, seasonal jobs, volunteering, and more. It features tips, inspiring quotes, and advice to help you determine what you want in the way of adventure.

Career Exploration on the Internet, edited by Laura R. Gabler (Chicago: Ferguson, 2000). The Internet is a great source for career information, but it's easy to be overwhelmed by all the sites. This book outlines some of the best and most useful sites while covering critical steps in finding possible career paths. The CD-ROM version has the complete text of the book plus hotlinks that will take you directly to all the sites mentioned.

InternshipPrograms.com
www.internshipprograms.com

Visit this site and find out what it's like to intern at specific companies by reading program reviews written by interns themselves. Also search a huge database of internships by category, company name, or U.S. city and state.

Rising Star Internships
www.rsinternships.com

Check out this site and search for the internship of your dreams or post your résumé online.

Applying for an Internship— What Does It Take?

So, you're ready to apply for an internship . . . what's the next step? If you're pursuing the internship through a school program, you'll probably need to talk with the guidance counselor or internship coordinator and fill out some kind of application. If you're finding an internship on your own, you've got a bit more work ahead of you.

The first thing you'll need to do is to put together a résumé, so you can introduce yourself (on paper) to your potential employer. Maybe you've thought about doing a résumé but just haven't gotten around to it yet. Maybe you have one, but

F. Y. I.

Résumé is the French word for summary. One of the keys to a résumé is its brief length. Your résumé should serve as an at-a-glance summary of what you've accomplished so far.

you're not sure it's up to par. Or maybe you've been avoiding résumés altogether, because you're convinced you don't have anything to put on yours. The truth is, you can create a great résumé, and an accompanying cover letter, even if your only work experience is baby-sitting or delivering newspapers.

Basically, a résumé is a one-page document that lists your credentials, qualifications, and experience. The accompanying cover letter is one page as well; it explains who you are and why you want an internship at this particular place. Because these two items make your first impression on a potential employer, it's important that they're professional and easy to read.

You might think that since you're only applying for an internship and not an actual job, you don't really need a résumé. It's true that some internships don't require a résumé, but others do. Putting together a résumé isn't as painful as it may seem, and it's a good idea to have one—you never know when you might need it. (After all, your internship supervisor may invite you to apply for part-time work after the internship ends. And you may need a résumé if you're putting together a college application or trying to find an after-school job.) Look at creating a résumé as a way to consider everything you've achieved and put it on paper. Once you've finished it, all you have to do is update it periodically.

Building Your Résumé Step-by-Step

Step #1: Your first step is to make a list that includes information about your education, work experience, service projects, extracurricular or academic activities, clubs, hobbies, and interests. Write down anything and everything—you can always pare down the list later. If you've never held a job of any kind, focus on the other stuff: awards, honors, independent studies, job shadowing experiences, or computer knowledge, for example.

Yvonne wanted to apply for a journalism internship but was worried that she didn't have enough related experience—or any job experience at all. After she finished writing down her education, accomplishments, and activities, her list looked like this:

- Junior, Washington High School, 3.2 Grade Point Average (GPA)
- Sports Editor, Washington High School newspaper
- Forward, Washington High School junior varsity girls' soccer team
- Member of synagogue youth group
- Proficient in QuarkXPress, Microsoft Word, Excel
- Play the oboe
- Love to cook dinners for my family
- Painter/artist

Step #2: Your next task is to write down all of your responsibilities for each major activity, and the skills you learned. If you were a cashier at a toy store, for instance, you may have been responsible for taking inventory once a week, talking with customers, and learning how the computer system worked. If you ran the concession stand at a movie theater, your duties may have included cleaning the equipment, making popcorn, and serving customers.

Ask yourself what you've gained from your work experiences and extracurricular activities: Leadership abilities? Time-management skills? A commitment to teamwork? Now try to relate your skills to the internship you're applying for. What qualities make you a good candidate?

Yvonne thought about her responsibilities and what they had taught her. Her modified list looked like this:

- Sports Editor, Washington High School newspaper—researched and wrote weekly articles; conducted interviews; responsible for layout and design of sports page.

- Forward, Washington High School junior varsity girls' soccer team—played in every game last season; voted Most Valuable Player.

- Member of synagogue youth group—coordinated a number of special events; member of the youth group's board of directors.

- Skills: good writer, team player, know how to interview people by phone, able to juggle lots of activities.

Step #3: Next, think about the work you've done in your classes. Have you gained any specific skills, such as computer know-how, writing competency, or the ability to speak a foreign language?

Yvonne thought about her relevant classes and what they'd taught her. She had taken a keyboarding course and a creative writing class, and had attended a journalism camp the previous summer. She added the following information to her list:

- Keyboarding class ninth grade—can type 70 words per minute.

- Creative writing, tenth grade elective—wrote several stories that were published in the school literary magazine.

- Journalism camp—took writing and editing classes.

Step #4: Now decide on a format for your résumé. The right format can highlight your experience and skills, instead of emphasizing your weaker areas. There are two major résumé formats that you can try: *chronological* and *functional.*

Using a chronological format, you list your most recent activities and qualifications first. This format is the simplest way to organize your information and works well if you have little experience.

Using a functional format, you emphasize how your skills and knowledge relate to the position you're seeking. This format works best when you have a lot of experience and expertise in a particular area.

Step #5: Begin to organize your information into a sequence. Here are the basics you'll need to include:

- Your contact information (name, address, phone number, email address)

- Your education, work experience, skills, achievements, and qualifications

The format you choose will dictate the order in which the information appears. If you're presenting the information chronologically, you'll need to start with your education, followed by your experience, skills, and so on. If you're using a functional format, you'll begin with the contact information and focus on your qualifications and skills that relate to the internship. You have the option of including an *objective* in either format. An objective is basically your goal, or the position you want to attain.

Using Yvonne as an example, her résumé might look like either of the following:

Chronological format

Yvonne N. Jackson
111 Third Avenue
Washington, D.C. 20000
(201) 555-1234 • *yvonne@speedymail.com*

OBJECTIVE

To find an internship that uses my writing and editing skills.

EDUCATION

Washington High School, expected graduation 2001. GPA: 3.2.
Coursework in English, creative writing, and keyboarding.

EXPERIENCE

Washington High School

Sports Editor, Weekly Telegram. Researched and wrote weekly articles;
conducted interviews; responsible for layout and design of sports page.
1998–present

Forward, junior varsity girls' soccer team. Played in every game last
season; voted Most Valuable Player.
1997–1998

Georgetown University
Student, journalism camp. Completed a writing and editing class.
Summer, 1998

Mount Zion Temple
Youth group member. Coordinated a number of special events;
member of the youth group's board of directors.
1996–present

SKILLS

Proficient in QuarkXPress, Microsoft Word, Excel.

ACTIVITIES AND INTERESTS

Painting, oboe, cooking.

References Available Upon Request.

Functional format

Yvonne N. Jackson
111 Third Avenue
Washington, D.C. 20000
(201) 555-1234 • *yvonne@speedymail.com*

OBJECTIVE

To find an internship that uses my writing and editing skills.

EDUCATION

Washington High School, expected graduation 2001. GPA: 3.2.
Related coursework: English, creative writing, and keyboarding.

WRITING EXPERIENCE

Washington High School
Sports Editor, Weekly Telegram. Researched and wrote weekly articles;
conducted interviews; responsible for layout and design of sports page.
1998–present

Georgetown University
Student, journalism camp. Completed a writing and editing class.
Summer, 1998

LEADERSHIP EXPERIENCE

Washington High School
Forward, junior varsity girls' soccer team. Played in every game
last season; voted Most Valuable Player. 1997–1998

Mount Zion Temple
Youth group member. Coordinated a number of special events; member of
the youth group's board of directors. 1996–present

SKILLS

Proficient in QuarkXPress, Microsoft Word, Excel.

ACTIVITIES AND INTERESTS

Painting, oboe, cooking.

References Available Upon Request.

Creating a First Draft

Now you're officially ready to put together your first draft. If you don't have a computer at home, use one at your school's media center or at your local library. Include the following information, in the format you prefer:

- **Contact information:** Put your name at the top of your résumé. Use your given name, and your middle name or initial (for a more formal look), and your last name. Include your complete address and phone number, and an email address, if applicable.

- **Objective:** State your goal in a succinct way. Example: "To obtain an internship in biomedical research."

- **Education:** List your high school(s) and any honors and awards you've received. Include your GPA if it's 3.0 or higher. Leave out your middle school experiences, unless you're a freshman or short on material.

- **Experience:** Mention any relevant employment, including summer jobs, volunteer work, and previous internships. In general, you should list your job title, the place of employment, and the dates you were employed. Describe your duties, using active verbs (for more about this, see "Make Your Words Count" on page 136).

- **Skills:** List any special skills or abilities. You may also include any awards or honors you've received in school, clubs, or outside activities.

- **Interests:** You may want to list activities that will highlight your diverse interests (weaving, choir, intramural basketball).

You can add the phrase "References Available Upon Request" at the end of your résumé, if you choose to. This line indicates that you have at least three references—people who can comment on your work experience, skills, abilities, and personal qualities. (Your family members and close relatives may have wonderful things to say about you, but it's best not to use them as references. Instead, talk to former employers, teachers, coaches, mentors, and other adults who know you well.) Be sure to contact your potential references ahead of time to find out whether they're willing to speak with employers who may be interested in hiring you. If they agree to serve as references, get all of their contact information (phone number at home and at work, address, email address) right away and keep it on file, so it's handy when you need it.

Even if you don't use the phrase "References Available Upon Request," you'll want to find people who can act as references for you. You can include their names, addresses, and phone numbers on a separate sheet attached to your résumé; simply put the title "References" at the top.

MAKE YOUR WORDS COUNT

Résumés are brief, so when writing about your experience and activities, be as specific as possible. Don't say, "Helped out in the kitchen" when you can say, "Operated dish-washing equipment." Use active verbs to give your résumé punch. Choose verbs from the list below.

accomplished	demonstrated	implemented	reorganized
achieved	designed	improved	repaired
attained	edited	learned	reported
cared for	established	motivated	researched
collaborated	evaluated	observed	served
communicated	expressed	operated	simplified
compared	facilitated	organized	supported
compiled	gathered	performed	tested
completed	generated	planned	trained
coordinated	guided	prepared	traveled
created	helped	processed	used
delivered	identified	published	wrote

Your résumé will be circulating among professionals. It represents who you are and is a reflection of you. Make sure your résumé is accurate, organized, and neat. Techniques like underlining, using bold print and italics, and varying the fonts can give your résumé greater impact—or make it much harder to read. It may be helpful to look at sample résumés, so you get a better idea of the different formats and looks you could try. You can find sample résumés in job-hunting books or at your school's career center or guidance counselor's office. See "Find Out More" on page 139 for further suggestions.

Keep these helpful hints in mind when doing your résumé:

> **F. Y. I.**
>
> Although your English teacher may groan, your résumé should use incomplete sentences. Instead of, "I raised funds for the local humane society" you'd say, "Raised funds for local humane society." Leave out the "I" in every description.

- **Don't rush it.** Leave yourself plenty of time before your interview date to put the document together. Rushing can lead to mistakes.

- **Keep it short.** One page is the maximum length. If you have a lot of information to include, try a smaller font to make it fit. (Don't go too small, however, as the words will be harder to read.)

- **Edit and revise.** Read through your first draft and figure out what you might do to improve it. Have you highlighted your accomplishments clearly and concisely? Will it be easy for a potential employer to see how your skills match the internship opening? Show your résumé to your mom or dad, your guidance counselor, a teacher, or another adult who can offer some words of advice.

- **Check for spelling and punctuation errors.** Run a spell-check to catch any obvious misspellings. Then read it over carefully to find any errors. Ask a detail-oriented adult to proofread your résumé to look for mistakes you may have missed.

- **Make corrections on the computer.** Never hand-correct your résumé and send it out. This looks unprofessional and makes a negative impression.

- **Use a laser printer and letter-quality paper.** If the computer you're using doesn't have a laser printer, save your résumé on disk and take it to a copy shop for printing. Look for a paper stock of moderate weight that has matching envelopes, if you'd like a more formal look. Choose a color that's not too dark (this could make it hard to read) or too bright (go for neutral tones). You may want to print out a bunch of copies at once, so you don't have to keep running to the copy shop.

> "The one piece of advice I give to everyone about their résumé is: Show it to people, show it to people, show it to people. Before you ever send out a résumé, show it to at least a dozen people."
>
> —Cate Talbot Ashton

- **Keep it current.** Update your résumé whenever any of your contact information changes or when you have new experiences to add.

POSTING YOUR RÉSUMÉ ONLINE

These days, lots of teens are posting their résumés online. If you're interested in doing this too, you can post your résumé on your own Web site (if you have one); that way, potential employers can simply print it and keep a copy. Or, if you're searching internship databases online, you may find that most of them feature a section for posting résumés. You can add yours by either typing the information into the form that's provided on-screen or sending it via email. The main benefits of online résumés are (1) convenience and (2) broad exposure. The main drawback is the security issue. When you post your contact information online, *anyone* can see it. If you don't feel safe posting your home address, you can use your name and email address only, and then add the phrase "Official Résumé Available Upon Request" at the end. Potential employers can follow up if they're interested in you. For a Web site that will give you the lowdown on posting your résumé online, visit *titan.iwu.edu/~ccenter/resume/*.

FIND OUT MORE

The Everything Résumé Book by Steven Graber (Holbrook, MA: Adams Media Corp., 2000). This book is useful because it shows you résumé makeovers—the "before" and "after" of the same document—so you can spot areas of your own résumé that may need help. The book contains a huge section full of sample résumés, provides information about electronic résumés, and gives excellent advice about punctuation.

Your First Résumé, 4th Edition by Ronald W. Fry (Franklin Lakes, NJ: Career Press, 1996). This informative book shows you how to create a great résumé, even if you've only had a part-time job or two. It also provides worksheet space where you can list hobbies, extracurricular activities, and other interests in preparation for writing your own résumé and to help you take stock of your achievements. Learn how to transform even a modest work and activity history into an impressive résumé.

Writing Your Cover Letter

No résumé is complete without a cover letter. Like peanut butter and jelly, the two are meant to go together. Anytime you send out a résumé, include a cover letter that introduces you to your potential employer.

The cover letter complements your résumé—instead of rehashing everything on it. In the letter, you can express why you're interested in this particular internship; what special skills, personal qualities, or expertise you'll bring to it; and what you hope to accomplish in your work at the company or organization. While résumés are brief and to the point, cover letters offer the chance to go into more detail about specific experiences or accomplishments.

Your cover letter should follow the standard business letter format, (see the example on page 140). This includes the use of a colon after the addressee's name, and single-spacing throughout.

1234 First Street
Columbus, Ohio 43081

May 10, 2000

Ms. Jane Doe, Editor
Fitness Magazine
555 Sixth Avenue
Columbus, Ohio 43212

Dear Ms. Doe:

I was very excited to see that *Fitness Magazine* is seeking interns this summer. I subscribe to the magazine and am a fitness buff myself. As you'll see on my résumé, I am a member of my high school's swim team and track team. I assist with teaching swimming lessons at the YMCA, and I love to mountain bike as well.

Currently, I am a sophomore at Mills High School with a 3.8 GPA. I joined the debate team this year, and I have been a member of the chess| club since freshman year. My work on the debate team has increased my confidence and made me comfortable with public speaking.

I took a marketing course at South Community College last semester, which led me to seek an internship in your marketing department. I believe that my enthusiasm, people skills, and background in sports and fitness help make me a good candidate for this internship. The possibility of working at such a well-known magazine is exciting! I hope to get a firsthand look at how your sales and marketing departments operate. I believe I would be an excellent assistant to your marketing staff.

I am available for a phone interview during after-school hours. I will call your office next week to further discuss this opportunity.

Thank you for your time and interest.

Sincerely,

Juan Garcia

Juan Garcia

Enclosures: résumé, references

The key is to personalize the cover letter. State clearly why you've chosen this particular internship to apply for and why you belive you're the right person for the position. What makes you stand out? What will you contribute? Your letter should be formal yet friendly. (Remember to use active verbs from the list in "Make Your Words Count" on page 136.) It's a good idea to read your cover letter aloud when it's finished to see if it flows well.

If you're applying for several internships at the same time, you still need to personalize each letter. Be sure you use the contact person's name, instead of something like "Dear Human Resources Director." Double-check that you've correctly spelled the person's name, as well as the name of the company or organization.

A couple of don'ts to remember: *Don't* photocopy a generalized cover letter and send the copies out to different places. You could come across as someone who's not willing to put in extra effort. The personal touch shows that you care and are sincerely interested in the position. *Don't* create a form letter where you leave a blank space to handwrite the contact name, the company name, and the name of the position each time. Your letter will look extremely unprofessional if you try this and most likely won't be given a second glance.

It may be helpful to keep your cover letters on your computer hard drive or on a disk, so you can refer to the old ones each time you need to create a new one. This will save you time and effort.

FIND OUT MORE

Cover Letters They Don't Forget by Eric R. Martin and Karyn E. Langhorne (Lincolnwood, IL: VGM Career Horizons, 1993). This book is all about writing cover letters that stand out. It has plenty of examples for people in all sorts of jobs or life situations, and includes topics such as how to make the most of your credentials.

Winning Cover Letters by Robin Ryan (New York: John Wiley & Sons, 1997). The author takes you through all the basics and pinpoints exactly what you should and shouldn't do to create powerful, attention-grabbing letters. You'll find tips from managers and human resources personnel on common mistakes to avoid, plus successful cover letter samples and exercises to help you assess your skills and accomplishments. The book also includes charts and special sections with advice for new graduates, volunteers, and others.

Acing Your Interview

When people hear the word *interview,* they have mixed feelings. Some people get nervous; others feel a sense of dread. (They may see the interview as a "grill session" or even an interrogation.) And still others actually look forward to their interview because they're excited to find out more about the position. No matter how you feel, it's best to approach the interview with a positive attitude. Think of it as a chance to make a good impression and decide whether this is truly the internship you want.

Interviews can take place in person or by phone. Phone interviews are usually used to screen a candidate before inviting him or her in for a face-to-face meeting. Interviewing for an internship is much like interviewing for a job. The employer will expect you to be professional, discuss your experience and skills, show that you're familiar with the company or organization, and ask pertinent questions.

To prepare yourself for the interview, make a list of questions that you can ask about the company or organization, the internship you're seeking, the work environment, and the field in general. Having appropriate questions ready shows that you're both enthusiastic and serious about the position. If the company or organization has a Web site (and most do these days), take some time to get familiar with it. Read its mission statement and learn about any recent projects, awards, or important clients.

Here are a few questions you may want to ask your interviewer:

- What kind of orientation or training do interns receive?
- Can you describe the work that interns here do?
- Are there any special projects that you need help with right now?
- Do interns work closely with one supervisor, or more than one?
- Are there any particular qualifications you're looking for in a candidate?

- Have you hired many interns in the past, or is this a new position?

One of the best things you can do before an interview is to try to anticipate the questions you may be asked. Maybe you've heard some interview "horror stories," where the interviewer asked bizarre questions to take the applicant by surprise. This kind of thing does happen, but it's not the norm. Some interviewers simply like to test job candidates to see how they might perform under pressure. For example, a teen named Sean went to an interview and was told by his potential employer, "Here's a pen. Try to sell it to me." Instead of freaking out about this unexpected tactic, Sean paused to think about the pen's unique features; he then launched into an interesting commentary about how useful the pen was. He kept his cool and used his sense of humor to wow his interviewer.

Most employers have conducted plenty of interviews before. So, they often have a list of standard questions that they can refer to each time. Chances are, their questions will include some of the following:

- Why do you want to work here?
- Why do you think we should we choose you over another applicant?
- What is your experience in the field?
- What are your strengths?
- What are your weaknesses?
- How would you describe yourself?
- What kind of supervisor would you most get along with? Least get along with?
- How would you deal with a problem in the workplace? Or, if you have issues with your coworkers, how would you try to resolve them?
- What are your long-range goals?
- Where do you see yourself in five years?

Spend some time thinking over possible answers to these questions before your interview. Write down your best answers and commit them to memory, so you're ready if these questions come up. What if your interviewer asks you a question that you aren't prepared for? Take a moment to collect your thoughts. If you don't know what to say, just admit it. You could say, "Good question. I'm not sure if I have a good answer to it, though." You could even steer the conversation to a related topic that you *do* know—interviewers like to see if you can think on your feet.

F. Y. I.

Feeling tense and restless while waiting for the interview to start? Take a few minutes to breathe deeply. This will bring oxygen to your brain (which allows you to think better) and will help calm you down. If you're offered something to drink, opt for water. The caffeine in coffee or tea may make you more nervous, and water will help if you have a dry mouth. When your name is called, you'll feel a rush of adrenaline as you're led to the interview room. Nervousness is normal and will keep you on your toes.

You can ask friends or family members to pretend to be your interviewer. This type of role-playing will help you figure out what to say and how to say it. Ask them to read your body language. Do you appear friendly and professional? Did you give a firm handshake? Are you making good eye contact? Are you sitting up straight? Do you fidget or do anything else that might distract your interviewer? What could you do to appear more professional? Be open to feedback and constructive criticism—the tips you get just might help you land the internship of your dreams.

Following are some more hints for doing your best in an interview and making a lasting impression on a potential employer.

Before the interview:

- **Keep your cool.** On the day of your interview, avoid stressful situations. Focus on staying calm. If possible, get some exercise beforehand or take a long, hot shower. You'll feel and look more relaxed.

- **Prep yourself.** Re-read your cover letter, résumé, application, and any other materials connected to the internship (always keep a copy of everything you send out). This way, all of the information will be fresh in your mind. Prepare a list of questions to bring to the interview, too.

Which one do you think got the job?

- **Wear professional attire.** A suit is a nice touch, but if you don't have one, you can get by with dress pants and a nice shirt (if you're a guy), or a skirt and dressy top (if you're a girl). Make sure that whatever you wear is clean, ironed, and well fitting. Above all, dress comfortably.

- **Plan ahead.** If you'll take public transportation to get to your interview, figure out ahead of time the route, where you'll have to transfer, and how much time you'll need. If you need to go by car but don't drive, find someone who can take you to your interview. Whether you're the one driving or not, be sure you have clear, accurate directions so you know where to go. If possible, bring along a cell phone in case you get lost or run into traffic. Showing up on time is essential when interviewing, but if you're unavoidably late, explain what happened and apologize. (Be sure to turn the cell phone off when you arrive—you don't want it to ring during your interview!)

- **Get there early.** Arriving ten minutes early allows time for a bathroom break, if you need one, and gives you a chance to compose yourself. Just don't show up *too* early, as you might seem overeager.

During the interview:

- **Make a good first impression.** When meeting your interviewer, stand up, make eye contact, and shake his or her hand. There's a chance you may be meeting with more than one interviewer at the same time, but don't let that throw you off. Just be sure to talk to each person equally.

- **Maintain eye contact.** Think of how uncomfortable you feel when people keep shifting their gaze away from yours. You wonder if what you're saying is boring, or if the person has a short attention span. Show your potential employer that you're enthusiastic and attentive by meeting his or her gaze and wearing a pleasant, interested expression on your face.

- **Ask questions.** Don't make your interviewer do all the work. Ask questions throughout the interview, and especially at the very end if your potential employer says, "Do you have any questions for me?"

- **Check the place out.** Instead of dwelling too much on whether you look okay or how nervous you are, focus your attention outward. Is this a work environment you'd like to be a part of? Is the atmosphere friendly? Do the people who work there look interesting? Does the internship sound fun and challenging?

- **Take notes, if you'd like.** If you're comfortable writing while listening, feel free to jot down questions and important points during the interview. (Bring your own notepad and pen, so you don't have to ask for these materials.)

- **Show samples of your work.** If you're a writer, an artist, or a musician, for example, and you're applying for an internship in your field of interest, you may want to bring along a portfolio of your work. This will give your potential employer a better sense of your abilities.

- **Sell your strong qualities, but don't overdo it.** Be honest about your skills and don't be afraid to describe yourself as creative, hardworking, or detail-oriented (as long as what you're saying is true). Now isn't the time to be modest! On the other hand, be frank about your areas of weakness. If you don't have a lot of experience, admit it and let the interviewer know that you hope the internship will provide you with the experience you're looking for.

After the interview:

- **Write a thank-you note.** You have the option of using the format of a business letter or purchasing a thank-you card and including a few handwritten words of appreciation. An emailed thank you is better than no thank you at all—but a letter or card is much more personal.

SPOTLIGHT ON
Scott Schwartz
Lakeland High School
Yorktown, New York

I interviewed for an internship at a huge technology company. Because I didn't know anything about what an interview entailed, I didn't prepare any questions ahead of time to ask my interviewers, and I didn't rehearse answers to questions I thought they might ask me. Now I realize I should have done some of this, but at the time I thought I'd just breeze through it.

I'd planned to arrive fifteen minutes early, but there was a lot of traffic and so I was actually ten minutes late. Luckily, the person who was interviewing me arrived late, too. I sat in the waiting room, eyeing all the other prospective interns. There were a couple of guys in suits and ties who looked about my age—at the time I didn't own a suit, so I'd worn slacks and a button-down shirt. I was the only one dressed that casually. This worried me, but there was nothing I could do about it, so I focused on talking to some of the other students after they were interviewed to hear about the questions I might be asked.

When my name was called, adrenaline rushed through my body. I was taken to a room and asked a bunch of questions which I don't think I answered very well. There were a few awkward silences. I know I mumbled a lot, too. The interviewer asked some questions I didn't know how to answer, and instead of taking time to show him how I thought through a problem, I just said that I didn't know.

The one area where I did excel, though, was in telling about myself and what my hopes were for the internship. I really wanted the internship, and I guess I made a pretty good case for myself, because the interviewer seemed impressed—I could tell by the way he nodded encouragingly.

Well, I got the position and was very happy. I worked after school several days a week. My duties included gathering and filing laser-print jobs and loading tape machines— not very interesting work, and I picked it up quickly. When I had downtime, I tried to speak to my supervisors and coworkers to learn more about the company. Some people were friendly and answered openly; others seemed to find my questions annoying.

While working at this company, I noticed a lot of procedures that weren't very efficient, and I spoke up directly about this, stating what I felt was ineffective and how I thought it could be improved. In hindsight, I can see that I should have been more diplomatic. This experience inside "corporate America" surprised me a little. I learned that even a large, successful company can at times be run ineffectively and have some closed-minded people on staff. I also realized that I could have approached my internship in a different way and been less pushy and stubborn.

If I had to do it over again, I would have prepared better for my interview and found out a little more about the company I was applying to. On the job, I would have tried to deal with my coworkers in a less demanding way. But an internship is meant to be a learning experience, and I definitely learned firsthand some things I couldn't have understood just by taking a business class.

FIND OUT MORE

The Unofficial Guide to Acing the Interview by Michelle Tullier (New York: Macmillan USA, 1999). If you want to ace your interview, check out this book. It provides all the information you could ever need on this topic, including guidelines for what to wear and information about the psychology of interviewing. You'll also find tips on the power of smiling and how to prepare for tricky interview questions. It's a great reference book with lots of helpful tips and advice—including "insider" information.

Your First Interview by Ronald W. Fry (Franklin Lakes, NJ: Career Press, 1996). This book will take you through everything you need to know to do well on your first interview. Learn how to make contacts, answer hard questions gracefully, and identify your strengths and weaknesses. The book also lists "The 75 Favorite Interview Questions of All Time." If you're unsure of how to present yourself in an interview situation, this book can help. It's full of examples and advice from people who've been there.

Making the Most of Your Internship

You've heard the words you were waiting for: "We'd like to offer you the internship." Congratulations (you've earned it)! What do you do now? Accept right away and arrange a starting date? Possibly. Are you currently considering other offers? Are you sure all of the pieces are in place for taking this internship?

Ask yourself these questions before making your final decision:

- Do you have transportation to and from the workplace? Will you ride a bus or have a parent drop you off? Is your transportation reliable?

- Do you have time to meet all the requirements of this internship: preparatory courses, the workload itself, special projects, long-term assignments, and so on?

- Is the timing right? Does the internship coincide with a particularly heavy course load? How will you handle this?

- Will your family obligations make it difficult to do an internship? If so, can you come up with arrangements that will make the internship possible anyway?

- Can you afford to do your internship, if it's unpaid? Will it take away from time you need to spend earning money for your family or college tuition?

- Will the internship make it difficult for you to focus on homework or extracurricular activities? If so, can you handle that?

- Is there another internship you've applied for that you want more than this one?

If you've decided you're ready to go for it, let the employer know and finalize the details about your starting date, finishing date, work hours, and compensation (if any). Be sure to thank him or her for this opportunity you've been given.

It's important to make sure you and your supervisor have similar expectations for the internship. Remember that goal list you made back when you were considering the type of internship you might want? Find the list and review it. Do your goals still pertain? Are there any new ones you'd like to add, now that you know more about the internship you've found? Talk to your supervisor about your goals. Is it possible to meet all of them during your time at the company or organization? Sometimes interns and their supervisors create a learning contract that outlines their mutual goals and expectations. It may be possible for you and your supervisor to do this, or you may just want to talk about the goals informally.

Your first day on the job will most likely include meeting everyone at the work site, getting familiar with the daily routine, learning to use the office equipment, and perhaps starting your first assignment. First days can be nerve-racking for anyone— even seasoned professionals who've had lots of work experience! Feeling nervous is perfectly normal. Most likely, the people you meet will understand and try to put you at ease. One way to deal with the first-day jitters is to keep things in perspective. You're there to gain experience and to learn. No one expects you to come in knowing exactly what to do or to complete every task perfectly. Try to relax and get to know your coworkers; after a few days, you'll feel more comfortable on the job.

Internships are learning experiences, so show everyone how eager you are to learn new things. Observe your coworkers; ask them questions; talk to them when they have a spare moment. This will help you discover more about the field. When you show that you're willing to learn and are enthusiastic about seeking new experiences, your efforts will be noticed.

"The social workers I worked with at the homeless shelter were really good about talking to me about how to get into the field of social work, and whether that was something I'd really be interested in doing. Their stories and wisdom made a big difference in my life."—**Ken**

Even though you're spending lots of time learning and observing, you'll still need to stay on top of the tasks you're assigned. It may help to get a daily planner, so you can organize your day and keep checklists of your duties. If you're unsure of how a certain task should be done, talk to your supervisor or ask another staff member—even if someone has already gone over the task with you before. You'll want to make sure you're doing the job right, and that might mean asking for help more than once.

Employers admire certain qualities in their interns, including flexibility, dependability, curiosity, enthusiasm, efficiency, adaptability, initiative, and the ability to follow directions. So, even if you don't have much experience in the field, you still have a chance to impress your supervisor and the other people you work with. Keep all of these positive traits in mind for an outstanding job performance. You may even want to write them down somewhere in your daily planner, so you can refer to them often.

F. Y. I.

Treat your internship like a job, making sure you're professional and punctual. If you're going to be late, let your supervisor know by phone—not by email. If you're ill and need to stay home one day, call your supervisor as early as possible.

As your internship progresses, you may find that you're ready to take on more responsibility. If so, it's up to you to seek greater challenges—don't wait for your supervisor to notice that you need more work. Keenan was a freshman who had an internship at an advertising firm; one of his main duties was answering phones. This wasn't enough to keep him busy, though, so he began to ask other employees if there was anything he could help them with. Most of them jumped at his offer and gave him jobs like filing and faxing. To his delight, Keenan also got to assist with advertising projects that required more skill. As a result of this experience, he realized the importance of speaking up and being flexible. If you find yourself in a similar situation, feel free to talk to your supervisor. Express that you enjoy what you're doing but you're excited for even more responsibility. Ask what more you can do.

An important discovery that many teen interns make is that internships—and the real world—are very different from school. In the classroom, you've got a textbook to follow, tests that help track your progress, and a teacher who tells you what you need to learn and reminds you about assignments. During an internship, however, you don't have textbooks that explain what you need to know. You're expected to work independently and figure out what you need to learn—and then find a way to learn it. If you want to know how you're doing, it's up to you to talk to your supervisor and come up with checkpoints to measure your progress. This newfound independence can be thrilling yet daunting. After a while, you'll get more used to relying on yourself—an important lesson to learn.

What if the worst happens: you don't like your internship as much as you expected to? Unfortunately, some teens have found themselves in this situation. If you're bored during your internship or you don't seem to get along with the people you work with, talk to someone about it: your guidance counselor, your mom or dad, a teacher, your mentor. Get some advice about how to handle the situation. Although you may be tempted to quit, this probably isn't the best solution. Other alternatives include (1) talking to your supervisor directly and letting him or her know about your frustration, or (2) if your school set up the internship for you, talking to the coordinator to see what your options are. Consider how long the internship is—if it's short-term (a few weeks), you don't have much to lose by sticking it out until you've finished what you agreed to do. If you're in a long-term internship, you may be able to talk to your supervisor about changing some of your duties or switching to a different department. Make the best of the situation before giving up on it. If you've tried everything and the internship still isn't working out, give your two-weeks notice to your supervisor. Do your best to make a graceful exit.

Most teens say that their internships were great learning experiences—especially if they made the most of the opportunities they had. Besides learning as much as they could while on the job, many of these teens found other ways to get the most out of their internships. Nadia, who interned for a photographer, kept a portfolio of the photos she took as well as the techniques she used to shoot them. Ben interned at a senator's office and kept a journal of his experiences there. In it, he collected information from the people he interviewed at the office and even recorded their quotes. Later, when he was writing his college application essay, he went back to his internship journal for ideas and information. You may find that keeping a portfolio, journal, or log of your work has many positive benefits. Another idea is to ask your supervisor for a recommended reading list, so you can continue learning about the field after the internship ends.

SPOTLIGHT ON

Kristen VonGruben
Lafayette High School
St. Louis, Missouri

For two summers I was an intern at a large chemical research company. I was lucky because I started out with a supervisor who was willing to teach me. There's a lot to learn in a science internship! Even if you were the best student in your advanced placement chemistry or biology class, that's really just the barest introduction to the subject. Most companies are doing research on a much higher level, and giving a project to a high school student is like giving Shakespeare to a kindergartner who just learned how to read.

The first summer, my supervisor was a chemical engineer. His specialty was in designing safer and faster sampling methods for chemical manufacturing plants. (Sampling is a process in which a small amount of chemical mixture is withdrawn and tested. It's similiar to testing a spoonful from a large pot of soup to see if the seasoning is correct.) A chemical reaction rarely happens instantly and perfectly, especially when there's enough of the chemical mixture to fill a swimming pool. It usually happens gradually, and this means that engineers have to keep testing and retesting the mixtures to tell when a reaction is done. To use another food analogy, you could compare it to baking a cake. The baking process is a series of chemical reactions, and you check to see that the cake is ready (meaning all the reactions are done) by sticking a toothpick in the cake's center to see if it comes out clean and dry. There are two problems: First, the engineer often has to sample the mixture by hand, which can be dangerous. Second, the tests can take hours or even a day to run. Imagine going to a baker and saying, "I'll just take this toothpick back to my lab to get a good look at it. I'll let you know in an hour or two whether the cake is done." On a larger scale, this was the problem my supervisor had in the chemical tests he was doing. My job was to try out faster tests in the lab to see if they seemed to work—or it they failed miserably. Based on my results, the company *might* assign an experienced chemist to take months or a year studying the idea in more depth.

In my work, I was using the same equipment that an experienced chemist would use. Some of the instruments cost several hundred thousand dollars. I certainly hadn't seen instruments like these in high school. My supervisor would teach me how to use an instrument and would design a study for me to run. Then he'd usually leave for a few days to visit one of the manufacturing plants. This was quite frightening at first. I wasn't in the plant alone, but I *was* the only one in the lab working on that particular project. At first, I didn't understand why or how the instrument worked—I just knew how to push buttons. The company had a library, though, so I read the manuals and some books about theory while I waited for a test to finish. Occasionally, I'd run into problems I couldn't solve from the manual, but there was always someone around who could help me.

That summer, I learned as much chemistry as I had in a semester in high school, picked up some statistics, and was almost never bored. Each project took two or three weeks; then I'd move on to something new. Looking back, I shouldn't have been so intimidated and nervous about asking questions. My supervisor understood how much chemistry I knew, and he wouldn't have let me work for him if he hadn't had confidence in my ability and been willing to help me.

No two internships are ever the same, even in labs two doors apart. I returned for a second summer and had a much different experience. I was now working for an analytical chemist who ran very accurate tests and answered questions for the synthetic chemists developing new products. I never had a project of my own that summer. Instead I ran tests for a large experiment, changed the process slightly, and ran them again, over and over. Every day, a box of vials would show up at my desk, and every day I would run twenty or so tests. It was always the exact same test every time, every day, for three months. Once in a while, there wouldn't be any samples. Then I'd be asked to file or check inventory. It wasn't worth training me to do something else because there'd only be a day or two before more samples showed up.

Over the two summers, I experienced some very different aspects of chemical research. I also learned that one of the unspoken reasons behind an internship for a large corporation is for people in the company to get a preview of you as a prospective employee, even several years before you get out of school. Initiative and enthusiasm are qualities that interest them. If you believe you're capable of doing anything they explain to you, let that attitude show a little.

Before my internships, I thought a chemist worked much like a clerk in a store: get an order, fill it as quickly as possible, then get another order. There are really many other aspects to a chemist's job. I probably spent only about half of my time doing actual lab work or "wet" chemistry. I had to analyze data and write reports and fill out logs. There were also meetings to attend, manuals I had to read, and chemicals to order. The company held lunches for the interns and brought in speakers so we could learn about other types of jobs. I toured several of the plants where chemicals are produced. All of these things took time. I never would have guessed the large part that the company structure plays in a job. I went on to college and caught up on all of that chemistry, but school never taught me about what it really means to work for a large research corporation.

FIND OUT MORE

Internship Success: Real-World, Step-by-Step Advice on Getting the Most Out of Internships by Marianne Ehrlich Green. (Lincolnwood, IL: VGM Career Horizons, 1997). This guide shares how to find and get the most out of a good internship. Its pros-and-cons approach also includes case studies of real teens who have completed internships, as well as a wealth of interactive exercises.

"What we learn with pleasure we never forget."

Alfred Mercier

You may go into an internship with very little experience and much trepidation. *What will it be like? Will I know what I'm doing? Will I get along with the people there?* But what you get out of it can make all the difference in your future: new skills, more knowledge, greater confidence, and EXPERIENCE! The sooner you start doing internships, the earlier you'll be able to move on to better-paid, more interesting internships. Who knows, maybe you'll even decide to intern abroad someday! (If this sounds like an adventure worth looking into, see Chapter 7, "Go to Camp, Go on an Adventure, Go Overseas.")

Chapter 6

Become a Youth Apprentice

"Don't just learn the tricks of the trade. Learn the trade."

James Bennis

When you think of the word *apprentice* what comes to mind? Life in ancient Egypt or medieval Europe? Work that became obsolete after the introduction of the assembly line? Well, here's a modern-day definition of an apprenticeship:

Apprenticeship: (noun) a paid position that involves working closely with a supervisor, journeyman, technician, or master craftsman, who trains you to learn a trade or skill; a formal method of training for a skilled occupation.

F. Y. I.

Apprentice: a beginner learning a trade

Journeyman: a skilled worker (male or female) who has completed an apprenticeship

Master craftsman: a worker who's an expert in his or her field

Essentially, an apprenticeship is a major step in a specific career path. When you apprentice, you receive on-the-job training from an experienced supervisor who's skilled in a particular trade or craft. You're considered a part-time employee, and you're paid for your work. Often, your paid position is supplemented by classwork that teaches you about your field of interest. The classes—which may take place at a vocational school, training center, community college, or work site—are usually offered in the evenings or on weekends. This way, apprentices can still participate in high school and fulfill their regular graduation requirements.

Maybe you've heard of apprenticeships before and thought they were reserved for people eighteen or older. That's true: *regular* apprenticeships sponsored by the Department of Labor, along with state and local employment agencies, usually require that participants be above eighteen. However, *youth* apprenticeships (also sponsored by the Department of Labor) have different specifications. In compliance with child labor laws, you have to be sixteen years old before getting a youth apprenticeship. Most youth apprentices begin their program in their junior year of high school.

Suppose you were to apprentice under an electrician starting in your junior year. Your schedule might involve high school classes in the mornings, on-the-job training during the afternoons, and apprenticeship courses two nights per week. During these classes, you'd most likely learn about circuits and electrical theory. On the job, you'd actually do wiring.

After high school graduation, a youth apprenticeship may or may not be over. You may still have many more hours to put into it, depending on the arrangement you originally entered into and the amount of hours you've already completed. In other words, the idea behind a youth apprenticeship is that you're in high school when you start it. Depending on the trade or skill you're learning, you may still need to complete several courses or stay involved in your part-time on-the-job training.

Youth apprenticeships are becoming more popular, as the need for skilled workers in the U.S. rises each year. Most people assume that apprenticeships are for people interested mainly in woodworking, metalsmithing, and other trades. But apprenticeships are available in a variety of fields, including:

- cooking
- graphic design
- appliance repair
- welding
- blacksmithing
- furniture repair and restoration
- wine production

- fashion design
- pet grooming
- computer programming
- auto mechanics

- video and film
- midwifery
- making musical instruments

Employers who hire apprentices benefit from the arrangement because they get to recruit and train young people to become the skilled workers of the future—and pass on the skills from one generation to the next. These employers also have the opportunity to identify the skills needed in a particular occupation, determine the type of classwork that may be required, and ensure that well-trained people are entering their trade. Plus, many employers and supervisors welcome the idea of teaching an eager young person and "giving something back" to the working community (especially if they once were apprentices themselves).

Apprenticeships are an exciting way to gain skills that just can't be practiced in a classroom setting. Apprenticeships also provide:

- hands-on experience
- job training
- technical knowledge and know-how
- the opportunity for one-on-one work with an adult who can explain concepts in-depth
- long-term guidance from an expert
- contact with other skilled adult workers
- immersion in a work environment
- greater marketability when entering the workforce
- a chance to see what "real life" is like
- a way to link school and work
- payment for your labor (your wages may even increase as the apprenticeship progresses)

Besides, when else in your life might you get the opportunity to carve marionettes with a puppeteer or perfect your printmaking skills with an artist? Apprenticeships can offer the chance to try something off the beaten path, if that's what interests you.

Many high school students choose the trades as an alternative to attending a four-year college. Have you been wondering if a four-year college is right for you? Are you considering whether you might be better off getting a job directly after high school instead? Maybe you're curious about vocational schools, technical colleges, or community colleges and what they

F. Y. I.

At the end of your apprenticeship, you get a certificate of Occupational Proficiency, which shows that you've participated in an apprenticeship program and corresponding classroom training, and that you've acquired a particular set of skills. This certificate is recognized by the Secretary of Labor.

have to offer. And just possibly, you've been given the impression that, without four years at a private college or a state university, your future looks bleak.

There are so many alternatives open to you—don't ever feel that you have to follow a path that other people say is "the right one" or "more promising" than the one you're interested in. If you want to pursue a trade, craft, or skill, you have options. A one- or two-year program at a vocational school can provide the training you need in a specific job. A technical college can lead to certification or an associate degree in an area of technical expertise. Community (or junior) colleges offer educational benefits or job training, depending on the program you pursue. You can look into schools in your area to see what type of programs they offer.

In the meantime, apprenticing can enhance your plans—whatever they may be—in a number of ways:

1. If you're not planning on going to a four-year college, being a youth apprentice can help you learn the skills of a particular trade. This early career training will give you a jump-start into a well-paying occupation after graduating from high school.

2. Because youth apprenticeships require a classroom component, you may have the opportunity to take courses at a vocational school, technical or community college, or training center. This will help you decide whether you want to further your education.

3. You get to embark on a career path while you're still in high school. This can help you feel more energized about the classes you're taking and how they relate to your future occupation.

4. You have an added source of income. You can put it toward tuition, use it as start-up money for your own business, or save it. No matter what you do with it, earning your own money can give you a sense of satisfaction and accomplishment.

Even if you *are* planning to go to a four-year college after high school, apprenticeship programs can still be an attractive option. Many youth apprentices use their apprenticeship as a jumping-off point to careers that do require a four-year degree. For instance, a carpentry apprentice could use the skills he or she has gained to pursue a degree in architecture.

How to Get an Apprenticeship

An apprenticeship is a real commitment—the first step to a career goal of becoming a trained master. The arrangement may last from several months to several years, so it's important to be sure that you've chosen something you're truly interested in and committed to. If you have any doubts about whether an apprenticeship is right for you, it's a good idea to spend some time job shadowing a master in your field of interest. (For more about shadowing, see Chapter 4, "Job Shadow a Professional.") Ask yourself if the trade or skill is something you can imagine yourself doing now and in the future. If you're still interested, you can take steps toward getting an apprenticeship.

Many teens participate in youth apprenticeships either formally, as part of their high school curriculum, or informally, by apprenticing under a parent, a neighbor, or a family friend who's skilled in a particular area. Both kinds of arrangements can be positive experiences.

Formal Programs

If you decide to enter into an apprenticeship through school, you'll most likely become part of a program originally known as School-to-Work. School-to-Work included government-subsidized programs that aimed to teach high school students the skills they needed to succeed on the job. In fact, youth apprenticeships, job shadowing, and career mentorships were some of the program initiatives of the School-to-Work Act of 1994. In 1999, the School-to-Work Act took another name, the Work Force Investment Act, which is designed to allow each state to use federal funds to develop training projects between schools and places of employment. In other words, each state's governor now has a say about the apprenticeship programs offered in public schools.

Over the years, people have debated about the advantages and disadvantages of youth apprenticeships and other School-to-Work programs. Some say the programs force students to decide too early as to what career they may want to pursue—narrowing their options for the future. Others say that these programs are beneficial because they introduce students to a career early on—*expanding* their options for the future. What do you think about this controversy? Are there pros and cons to making a choice regarding your career while you're still in high school? What are the positives and negatives? You may want to spend some time thinking about this issue, or even writing about it in a journal or notebook.

In some high school programs, the first year of the apprenticeship is spent job shadowing a person in your field of interest, as well as being paired with a skilled worker who will provide job training. The second year may involve entering into a full-fledged apprenticeship arrangement with an employer; you'll be treated as an employee who gets hands-on training at work. Generally, youth apprentices work about ten to fifteen hours per week in their apprenticeship, earning minimum wage and receiving worker's compensation insurance.

If the idea of doing a school-based apprenticeship sounds good to you, talk to your principal or guidance counselor. Find out what kinds of apprenticeship programs are available at your school. Another option is to contact your state's School-to-Work coordinator, whom you can find online. There's a link at the site *www.jobshadow.org* where you'll see a state-by-state directory of these coordinators. (Click on the "Find Your Contact" link to get to the directory.) School-based apprenticeships usually involve a significant time commitment—from two to four semesters.

Some youth apprenticeships are administered from a local vocational/career center, which may serve a number of high schools in the area. Vocational/career centers usually offer a "tech prep" program, which provides an alternative to the traditional college preparatory curriculum of many high schools. Students in the tech prep program have the option of either enrolling in a youth apprenticeship or taking classes that will later count as credit at a community college or vocational school. (For example, a high school student interested in flying could take aviation courses that would be recognized by a vocational school; he or she would then be on the way toward a certificate in aviation.) Apprenticeships and tech prep programs were created to encourage more teens not only to continue their education but also to successfully make the connection from school to work.

CO-OP PROGRAMS

Co-op programs—a cousin to apprenticeships—are usually less structured than an apprentice arrangement. In a co-op program, high school juniors and seniors are generally placed in a year-long, part-time job for pay. This on-the-job training gives students the opportunity to learn vocational skills that may relate to what they're studying in the classroom. To find out more, visit the National Commission for Cooperative Education online at *www.co-op.edu* or call this number: (617) 373-3770.

When talking to your principal or guidance counselor about an apprenticeship, ask the following questions:

- What are the eligibility requirements for this program?
- As a student, do I receive school credit for an apprenticeship?
- How are supervisors selected by the school?
- Are there any eligibility requirements or screenings to help match a student to a supervisor?
- Is there an application process for both parties?
- Is there a pool of established supervisors from which students may choose? Or can students make a request for a certain supervisor and have the high school help fulfill it?
- Is there a lot of contact between the apprentice and the supervisor? How is this facilitated?
- What is the duration of this apprenticeship?
- What kinds of classes will I take as part of this apprenticeship? Where will the classes be held?
- Will I need to arrange my own transportation to classes and to work? Or does the school help out with this?
- Does the school help to assess how the apprenticeship is going?
- What happens if there are problems between the supervisor and the apprentice? Can the school help resolve issues that come up?
- What happens when the apprenticeship requirements are fulfilled? What do I do then?

Be sure to take notes during the meeting, so you remember everything you've learned.

Formal apprenticeship programs often require that you fill out an application and may even include an essay portion. Be sure to fill it out as thoughtfully as you would a job application and write any required essays with care. Most likely, you'll be asked to describe exactly what you're interested in doing and how you'll benefit from the experience. Think carefully about these questions because your answers will determine what type of apprenticeship you're placed in. Apprenticeship programs *can* be competitive. Ensure that your application stands out—be neat and be specific about your goals and expectations.

You may also need to have an interview, so your potential supervisor can determine whether you're truly interested in and committed to the apprenticeship. This meeting will help you both see if you're compatible and could work well together. For tips on preparing for an interview and doing your best, see pages 142–149.

If you're accepted, congratulations! Next step? Sign on the dotted line. For an apprenticeship to be legally recognized, it needs to be recorded in a written agreement or contract called an *indenture.* The indenture covers the terms and conditions for your training, as well as specifies the standards of training your supervisor must adhere to. If you have questions about this kind of contract, talk to your guidance counselor or principal.

If you're not accepted as an apprentice, you can talk to your guidance counselor about reapplying, finding another program, or trying out a more casual agreement with a supervisor. Don't give up yet!

SPOTLIGHT ON

Tammy Thomas
Weber High School
North Ogden, Utah

As a senior, I was taking only one class (AP Calculus) at school to finish up my high school graduation requirements, since I'd already satisfied the rest of my credits. I decided to take some additional classes at the Ogden/Weber Applied Technology Center (ATC), which is a local trade/technical school. I had my AP Calculus class first period, so I went to the trade school for the rest of the day. During the first semester, I took lots of drafting classes; second semester, I decided to switch to machinist classes because I enjoyed working with my hands.

During the second semester, one of my ATC teachers told me that a local company that made airplane parts was hiring seniors to be youth machinist apprentices. I thought this was something I should try, so I decided to apply for the apprenticeship. The application process involved putting together a portfolio that included an application, a list of any awards I'd won throughout the year, a parent recommendation letter, and two other letters of recommendation, which I got from two of my teachers (one at my high school and one at ATC). When I applied for the position, there were around ten applicants but only four openings. I was interviewed by a group of about seven people that was made up of the apprentice steering committee from the company's workforce, which helps set up apprenticeship programs for the company; a youth apprentice; and Kent Westergard, my current boss, who's team leader for the piston unit.

When I found out that I was chosen for the youth apprenticeship, I was so excited! I started the program a week after I graduated from high school. At the apprenticeship, we have a journeyman's guide that we follow; it lists the different rules for the company and states that we have to continue taking classes at ATC—a total of 570 in-school hours, plus 8,000 hours of on-the-job training. It will take me four years to meet these requirements.

So far, I've been an apprentice for a year. I'm treated like one of the regular workers, and I help build airplanes. Machinist apprentices spend a certain amount of hours at specific areas—like the computer numerical controls lathe (the name of a machine), the manual engine lathe, and the grind area—and then rotate to the next area. There are a total of fifteen areas. Right now, I'm in the computer numerical controls area, where I'll ultimately spend 1,400 hours. Here, one of my main tasks is to build pistons for the airplanes.

My supervisor lets me run the machines, now that I've been in this area for a while. There's a lot of problem-solving involved, like how to make the parts run faster and better.

My apprenticeship has been a wonderful learning experience. Once I complete it, I'll get a raise in salary and a journeyman's certificate. This is definitely a career I want to stay in.

Informal Programs

If you're considering finding an apprentice supervisor on your own instead of through your school, one thing you should know is that you may have to take charge of arranging coursework to go along with the apprenticeship. Some students choose not to do this, as they're more interested in the on-the-job aspect of apprenticeships. On the other hand, some students say that having an academic component really helps them relate theory to actual hands-on experience. If you want to take a class related to your field of interest, you have the option of contacting vocational schools or technical colleges to see what may be available to you as a high school student.

In the early stages of your search for an apprenticeship, spend some time outlining (on paper) your career and personal goals. Why do you want an apprenticeship, and what kind do you want? Are you interested in doing several apprenticeships to try out a range of trades, or is there one particular trade you'd like to seriously focus on? Are you willing to put in the time it takes to reach the goal of becoming a journeyman or master? Knowing this now will help you determine what kind of arrangement is right for you.

You can do an informal apprenticeship with anyone who's willing to take you on. Finding someone requires a bit of resourcefulness. A good place to start is with contacts you already have, or ones you can make quickly. For example, if you want to apprentice under a sculptor, you could consider whether family members, relatives, friends, or teachers may have a contact in the arts field. Suppose your dad knows someone at work who's married to an artist—now you have a starting point. Can you speak to that person to see if he or she could point you toward a local sculptor? Neighbors, members of your faith community, and friends of the family are all resources for you—even if they can't help, they may be able to guide you to someone who can.

Some teens who are looking for an apprenticeship successfully use the process of networking—talking to people in the field and asking for recommendations of other people to contact—to locate a potential supervisor. For your sculpting apprenticeship, you could make contacts by signing up for a sculpture class at a local arts or community center and talking with the instructor about a possible apprenticeship. Would he or she be interested in this arrangement? If not, are there any colleagues the instructor might recommend to you? Another option would be to contact the administrative offices of a few community centers to see if you can get the names of local artists. Or call vocational schools or community colleges in your area to see if they have any contacts or suggestions for you.

In the "Find Out More" resources on pages 173–174, you'll find information about the Apprenticeship Training Employer Labor Services—which may be of help in locating an apprenticeship. You can contact an office in your region or get in touch with the national headquarters.

Another alternative is to look for apprenticeship contacts in the Yellow Pages—but this can be a hit-or-miss process. To give it a try, simply choose the category you're interested in (Upholstery, Dog Grooming, Auto Repair) and look for a listing of companies or professional names to call. Start with any that are close to home, so transportation won't be a problem. When you make the call, explain that you're a high school student who's interested in the field and that you'd like to get some hands-on experience through an apprenticeship. If the person you speak to sounds open to the idea, suggest that you meet one-on-one to talk about the possibility of a trial period of working together (three weeks on a part-time basis, for example). You may have to make lots of phone calls before you find someone who's willing to take a chance on you. That's just part of the challenge!

Next, determine how long you want to do your apprenticeship. Again, anywhere from a few months to a year is a possibility if you're finding one on your own. Take into account your schedule for the period of time when you expect to do the apprenticeship. Is this a particularly busy school year for you? Will you have out-of-school commitments you'll need to attend to? How will you balance all of your responsibilities? You may want to talk to your mom or dad to get some advice about the arrangements.

To get ready for your meeting with your potential supervisor, you can put together a proposal that will outline your ideas about the apprenticeship (but this isn't required). The purpose of the proposal is to gather all of your plans and expectations in writing, so you have a handy reference point—*and* to show your potential employer how serious you are about the arrangement.

To write a proposal, simply follow these steps:

1. Give it a title.

2. State who the proposal is *to* (your potential employer's name) and *from* (your name).

3. Specify the project or experience that you're proposing.

4. Describe step-by-step how you plan to carry it out.

5. List any equipment or services you may need.

6. Let the potential employer know whether you can pay for any needed equipment or services yourself.

7. Describe your background and contacts, and offer some information about your work style or personal qualities.

8. Include the dates when your apprenticeship could start and end.

9. Provide your contact information.

Your proposal might look something like this:

Proposal for a guitar-building apprenticeship

To: Ms. Arlene Harris, guitar builder
From: Celeste Rodriguez, junior at Albuquerque High School
Date: October 7, 2000

Description: I am seeking an apprenticeship that will allow me to learn the basics of guitar building using traditional methods, to hone my wood-carving skills, and to learn from an experienced worker in the field. I would also like to learn how to string my own hand-built guitar and choose the best woods for it.

Plan for accomplishing my objective: I hope to secure an apprenticeship with Ms. Arlene Harris, noted guitar-builder and workshop leader. Because I am arranging the apprenticeship on my own and still need to attend school full-time, I would like to apprentice after school for two hours, two days per week. I would also like to attend the evening workshop session that occurs on Thursday nights. During this apprenticeship, I hope to make one fully hand-built guitar. I envision this project will take approximately six months.

Equipment and services: I will need wood-cutting and designing tools, a safety mask, guitar strings, wood, and other equipment necessary for carrying out this project. I will take the bus to and from the work site on the days of my apprenticeship, and I have arranged transportation to and from the evening workshop session as well.

Costs: I have saved money to pay for the evening workshop. My family has agreed to help pay for the tools and supplies I will need. If any other costs come up, I will not have extra money to pay for them, but I am willing to work in exchange for supplies. I can do odd jobs needed at the worksite: setup and cleanup before or after the Thursday sessions, for example.

My background: I have been a guitar player since I was in sixth grade. At school, I have taken several shop classes and have attended woodworking courses outside of school as well. On my own, I have conducted research on the history of guitar building, including reading several books on the subject. At the summer arts festival, I spoke with musicians and craftspeople who recommended your workshops to me. I am a hard worker who takes the craft very seriously.

Dates when the apprenticeship will start and end: November 1, 2000, to approximately May 1, 2001.

Celeste Rodriguez

Celeste Rodriguez
7576 Vista Del Sol Avenue, Albuquerque, NM 87190
Phone: (585) 555-0101 • ***Email:*** CelesteR@speedymail.com

To give your proposal a professional look, type it up on a computer and double check it for any errors. You may want to have someone who's a good proofreader check the proposal for any mistakes, too. Print it out and bring the proposal to your face-to-face meeting with your potential supervisor. This document will show that you're dedicated to learning about the craft and committed enough to stick with it.

You may even want to include the names and phone numbers of several people who can act as references for you—teachers, your principal, your guidance counselor, a youth group leader, or former employers. (Talk to these people first to make sure they won't mind getting a call from someone who may want to hire you as an apprentice.) Now all you have to do is wait until the potential employer says yes or no.

The person you've chosen may be too busy to take on an apprentice or may not feel comfortable with the arrangement. This can be a disappointment, but it doesn't mean you should quit. Save a copy of your proposal, in case you need to draft another one for a different potential supervisor. Then begin your search again.

One of the most important qualities you may need to have in your search for an apprenticeship is persistence. Keep at it!

"My parents' friend was a carpenter. I had had problems finding people in the phone book who would take me on as an apprentice, so I went to this guy. He felt kind of obligated to take me on, but hey—an 'in' is an in. The situation ended up working out great!"—**Tony**

If you *are* hired as an apprentice, your next step is to formalize the agreement in some way. You could ask your supervisor to sign and date your proposal, for example. Or you could create your own indenture together, by writing down your mutual plans and expectations. Talk about whether there will be any evaluations during the apprenticeship. Would these checkpoints be helpful to both of you? What might you each learn from them? How will they be conducted, and how frequently should they occur? Setting up these guidelines in advance will ensure that you both understand the terms of the relationship and the goals you hope to achieve.

FIND OUT MORE

Ferguson's Guide to Apprenticeship Programs, edited by Elizabeth H. Oakes (Chicago: Ferguson, 1998). This guide has more than 7,500 programs listed in 52 job categories. In addition to helping you locate apprenticeships and on-the-job training programs, evaluate programs of interest, and successfully apply for them, this book also includes 50 personal profiles of people who have been involved in apprenticeship programs. A job title index and state index make finding information easy. This two-book volume can be found in your high school or college career center, or at your local library.

To learn more about apprenticeships that are regulated by the Department of Labor, contact the Apprenticeship Training Employer Labor Services' regional office for your state:

Region 1 Boston Office
(including Connecticut, Maine, Massachusetts, New Hampshire, Rhode Island, and Vermont)
JFK Federal Building, Room E-370
Boston, MA 02203
(617) 565-2288

Region 1 New York Office
(including New Jersey, New York, Puerto Rico, and the Virgin Islands)
Federal Building, Room 602
201 Varick Street
New York, NY 10014
(212) 337-2313

Region 2 Office
(including Delaware, Maryland, Pennsylvania, Virginia, and West Virginia)
170 South Independence Mall, West
Suite 815-East
Philadelphia, PA 19106
(215) 861-4830

Region 3 Office
(including Alabama, Florida, Georgia, Kentucky, Mississippi, North Carolina, South Carolina, and Tennessee)
61 Forsyth Street SW, Room 6T71
Atlanta, GA 30303
(404) 562-2335

Region 4 Hub Office
(including Arkansas, Louisiana, New Mexico, Oklahoma, and Texas)
Federal Building, Room 311
525 Griffin Street
Dallas, TX 75202
(214) 767-4993

Region 4 Affiliate Office
(including Colorado, Montana, North Dakota, South Dakota, Utah, and Wyoming)
U.S. Custom House, Room 465
721 19th Street
Denver, CO 80202
(303) 844-4791

Region 5 Hub Office
(including Illinois, Indiana,
Michigan, Minnesota, Ohio,
and Wisconsin)
230 S. Dearborn Street, Room 656
Chicago, IL 60604
(312) 353-7205

Region 5 Affiliate Office
(including Iowa, Kansas,
Missouri, and Nebraska)
1100 Main Street, Suite 1040
Kansas City, MO 64105
(816) 426-3856

Region 6 Hub Office
(including Arizona, California,
Hawaii, and Nevada)
Federal Building, Room 815
71 Stevenson Street
San Francisco, CA 94105
(415) 975-4007

Region 6 Affiliate Office
(including Alaska, Idaho,
Oregon, and Washington)
1111 3rd Avenue, Room 925
Seattle, WA 98101
(206) 553-5286

Or contact the national office:

**Apprenticeship Training
Employer Labor Services**
Frances Perkins Building
200 Constitution Avenue, N.W.
Washington, D.C. 20210
(202) 219-5943
www.doleta.gov/atels

ATELS can help you find both
national programs and state apprenticeship agencies. For information
about apprenticeships and the
National Apprenticeship System,
check out the Web site listed above.

SPOTLIGHT ON

Henry Brock
Bemidji High School
Bemidji, Minnesota

One summer I became interested in blacksmithing—shaping iron. I wanted to learn how to make the kinds of things you might find in a medieval or colonial village.

Through experimentation, books from the library, and the help of equipment from neighbors, I learned quite a bit about the craft. Blacksmithing basically involves four pieces of equipment. The first, a forge, is powered by either gas or coal, and includes something like a fan or bellows to direct air flow. The other three items are a hammer (weighing about 2 1/2 to 3 1/2 pounds), an anvil to hammer on, and a pair of tongs to hold small pieces. From these tools a blacksmith can fashion any other tools he or she might need. The nice thing about this is that you can make your tools to fit the job at hand, and later modify them to fit a different job. For example, you can heat up and reshape the mouth of the tongs to hold the piece of iron you want to handle.

Armed with some basic knowledge and a little hands-on experience, I joined the Bemidji Guild of Metalsmiths and was able to learn even more. However, I thought it would be very helpful to talk and work one-on-one with a modern blacksmith who did this trade for a living. An opportunity came along the summer between ninth and tenth grade. Through a regional artist/mentor grant, I found an apprenticeship with a blacksmith named Keith Johnson.

Keith was knowledgeable and patient with me. Under his direction I created a lot of small ironwork, like ornamental twists of various designs and a fire poker. I also did some forge-welding, which involves heating two surfaces hot enough to start melting, adding flux (a substance that carries away impurities), and then pounding the surfaces together as they fuse. It took a while for me to get the basics down. Once I did, though, I was able to use the skills I'd learned to do more complicated forgings. Keith showed me how to make a ram's head out of the end of a 3/4-inch iron bar. I went on to tackle projects that required me to draw out, back up, bend uniformly, straighten, flatten, split, and forge-weld. I've now made gate latches, door handles, curtain rod holders, plant hangers, dinner bells, hooks, and most recently some iron flatware and a bowl-holder that has a circle for the bowl's base and two leaves and a vine to support the bowl.

Learning a craft on your own can be rewarding, but being an apprentice, even for a little while, can help you develop much faster. It can also help you get rid of any bad habits you've inadvertently picked up. Keith would show me a new technique, we'd talk about what was involved, and then I'd try my hand at it. We had a lot of conversation and demonstration, and I asked a lot of questions. We also talked about blacksmithing as a career—I realized it's not very feasible to be a full-time blacksmith, because there's not much demand for this now that machines do so much of the work blacksmiths once did. I'm glad I was able to figure this out, and it definitely won't stop me from pursuing black-smithing as a lifelong hobby.

If you're interested in a trade, look around. Look in the phone book—that's what I did. I didn't expect there to be a lot of blacksmiths, but there were. Talk to people, and see if they're willing to teach you. Through the apprenticeship I found out that you don't have to learn everything that inter-ests you in school alone, that it's possible to find someone in the community who's interested in working with you. I also learned that, with ample time and motivation, I could greatly increase my skill.

"Dreams and dedication are a powerful combination."
William Longgood

If an apprenticeship sounds like a great idea but you'd like to venture off the beaten path even further, how about a summer in Mexico as a jewelsmith's apprentice? Or perhaps a semester apprenticing under a mask maker in Japan? Then take a look at Part 2, where you can learn about all sorts of outside-the-box learning experiences that you can do when you're ready to leave home and travel the world. As Lao-Tzu once said, "The journey of a thousand miles begins with a single step." Read on to take that first important step.

Part 2:

What You Can Do Away from Home . . . Or Far, Far Away

Chapter 7

Go to Camp,
Go on an Adventure,
Go Overseas

"Certainly, travel is more than the seeing of sights; it is a change
that goes on, deep and permanent, in the ideas of living."

Miriam Beard

Is your life starting to feel a bit routine? The same classes day in
and day out. The same old lunches week after week. The usual
hangouts after school and on weekends. All those familiar faces
in the school hallways day after day after day. At home, are you
arguing with your mom or dad more often, especially about
wanting the freedom to make your own decisions and take control of your life? Do you sometimes feel that you just need to get
away? That you need more space? More room to grow?

Many teens feel boxed in, pent up, or stifled—ready to break
free from the confines of school and family life. Adolescence is a
time of change, as you probably already know—a time when you
begin to establish yourself as an individual with your own
unique way of looking at the world. At times, you may wish you
could live by your own rules, without always having to answer
to your parents, teachers, and other authority figures in your life.

It's perfectly natural to feel this way. You're growing up. You want to figure out who you are and take charge of your life. Once in a while (or maybe pretty often), you may feel the need to put some distance between yourself and the people closest to you.

On the other hand, maybe you get along with your family just fine and you're thriving in and out of school. Perhaps you've already tried plenty of alternative learning experiences, and you're ready to take things to the next level. If so, you may be wondering, "Where do I go from here?"

Well, either way, the answer is TRAVEL! As a teen, you can leave home on a temporary basis. Camps, adventure programs, and overseas travel offer the chance to see a bit of the world and come back with a better understanding of yourself and your place in it. These getaways expand your mind and challenge your body. They may even give you a greater appreciation for the comforts of home and the closeness that family life can offer.

Believe it or not, you're at the perfect age to travel. You're not a kid anymore, so you're old enough to take care of yourself and appreciate the many sights you'll see. But you're still young and (relatively) responsibility-free, so you can more easily pick up and go somewhere. Plus, you've got loads of energy, which can come in handy when you're trekking through the wilderness or exploring the unknown. And, as adults like to point out, you're still "young and impressionable," which is to say that you're receptive to new ideas and experiences. Travel can be an exciting way to see new faces and places—your golden opportunity to soak up all the sights, sounds, scents, tastes, and textures of an unfamiliar environment. You're not too young to take advantage of this type of alternative learning experience, so why wait?

Heading Off to Summer Camp

Does the word *camp* bring to mind hours spent out in the woods, singing around a campfire, swimming in the lake, and playing pranks on your camp counselors? Maybe you had the chance to go off to a day camp or sleep-away camp when you were a kid—and maybe you loved it (or not). Now that you're older, you've got more options if you're interested in a summer camp. As a teen, you have the choice of attending as a camper or a counselor. And you can pick a camp that has a special focus, such as the arts, foreign languages, leadership, academics, or fitness.

In the summer after ninth grade, I had the chance to be a counselor-in-training (CIT) at a day camp in my hometown. I was in charge of a group of third grade girls, most of whom spoke Russian and little or no English. As a CIT, my duties included leading games and arts-and-crafts sessions, supervising the lunch hour, assisting with swim time, and participating in other activities right along with the kids. I'd recommend this type of experience to any teen who likes working with children or wants to feel like a kid at camp again. Day camps often hire counselors-in-training, positions that may be voluntary or may pay a low wage. This can pave the way toward a higher-paying counselor position at a sleep-away camp later on, if this is something you'd like to try.

To locate a day camp in your area, you can contact your school guidance counselor or find out whether your school sponsors a "camp fair." These fairs are usually held in January or February; representatives from camps set up booths to answer questions and hand out information. You can also talk to a leader in your faith community or a local community service organization to see about summer camp opportunities. Community centers and community education programs can be great resources, too. Or look in your Yellow Pages to find a list of day camps near you.

If you're ready to get away from home and spend some time in the great outdoors, a sleep-away camp may be just what you're looking for. Sleep-away camps come in all varieties, but most have a few things in common: (1) they're designed for young people, (2) they last anywhere from a week to a few months, and (3) they offer learning experiences that usually aren't available in school. Sleep-away camps are a lot of fun, and they give you a chance to meet other teens from all over your state or from across the country, depending on the camp you choose.

One thing you should know is that summer sleep-away camps can be very expensive: Depending on the camp's specialty and the length of your stay, fees can range anywhere from free (though this is rare) to several thousand dollars and up. The fees usually include room and board, plus the cost of excursions and extra activities. Day camps tend to cost less (a few hundred dollars or in the low thousands). Some camps may offer scholarships, so once you locate a camp, you can inquire whether this is an option. For more on scholarships, financial aid, and raising money on your own, see pages 209–215.

F. Y. I.

Even if you miss your friends, you'll make plenty of new ones while you're away. The friends you make at sleep-away camp are often lifelong, and many teens go back to the same camp year after year.

Whatever your interest, there's probably a camp for you. Following are descriptions of some of the alternatives:

- **Traditional camps:** These camps include the basics: cabins, a remote location, bonding activities, a lake, and plenty of swimming, canoeing, hanging out in the woods, and sitting around a campfire. In this kind of environment, you get to discover what it's like to live with a group of "cabin mates" and be independent from your family.

- **Wilderness camps:** If learning how to survive in the wilderness appeals to you, consider a wilderness/adventure camp, where you're taught to navigate in the wild, hike properly, make a fire, appreciate the beauties of nature, and generally rough it. Some of these camps even offer the opportunity to take a solo journey into the wilderness, once you've learned how to survive there on your own. Keep in mind that some wilderness programs are a lot more rustic than others. If you like your creature comforts but still want to explore the outdoors, a traditional camp may be better for you.

- **Writing/journalism camps:** A journalism camp will allow you to explore your talents in editing, graphic design, and layout and can give you skills that you may later apply to your school newspaper or yearbook. Writing camps—specializing in nonfiction, fiction, or poetry—are usually taught by professional writers on college or university campuses. (In Chapter 2, "Take Courses Outside the High School Classroom," you can learn more about other opportunities found at colleges and universities.)

- **Art camps:** If you're the artistic type or are curious to try something new, consider attending an art camp, where you'll spend your days painting a still life, throwing a pot, or carving a block of wood. Art camps may focus on one discipline like drawing or sculpture, or they may combine several, like photography, metalwork, and oil painting. Some art camps are held at college and university campuses; others can be found at retreat centers in scenic areas.

- **Sports camps:** Looking to hone your field hockey or basketball skills? Want to try a new sport, like lacrosse or horseback riding? Then look no further than sports camps. Many of them are geared toward teen athletes who want to spend part of the summer preparing for the upcoming season, while participating in recreational activities such as movies and dances. In some cases, entire teams from high schools attend a sports camp together. To find a good sports camp, talk to your coach or physical education teacher.

- **Special interest camps:** Maybe you're interested in more scholarly pursuits, like science, research, or foreign languages. There *are* summer camps that focus on academics.

These camps provide unique educational experiences that may complement courses you've taken in school. Your guidance counselor may have information on camps like these.

> "Starting in junior high and continuing through high school, I developed an immense interest in marine biology. For two summers in a row, I attended a marine biology camp in San Diego. This camp was for junior high and high school students and involved learning about marine biology through workshops and field trips. The second summer, I became scuba certified and learned about marine biology firsthand while diving off of Catalina Island . . . truly an experience I'll never forget."—**Beth**

Watch for your local newspaper's annual camp edition, which will have a long list of summer camps. Most city newspapers print this list in late February or early March. If you don't find what you're looking for there, ask people at school about camp opportunities. Is there a camp fair at your high school or other schools in your area? Do your principal or teachers know of any camps that students have participated in and enjoyed over the years? Can any of them recommend a camp in a state other than the one you live in, if that's your interest?

When choosing a camp, keep in mind the cost. Because most programs are expensive, you'll need to consider what your budget allows. It's important to choose your camp carefully. You don't want to find out halfway through (or worse yet, right away) that the camp isn't what you expected—especially if you've paid a lot of money for the experience.

The camps you're interested in most likely will have brochures or Web sites that describe the atmosphere and provide details about the activities. You can locate camps online by typing the name of the camp into a search engine or by typing in the state you want to visit and the word *camps*. You may want to start reviewing all of the camp materials a few months in advance, so you have plenty of time to compare the alternatives. As you conduct your search, keep in mind the following questions:

- What's the level of physical activity at the camp? Is it the right pace for you?

- Will the educational/recreational activities be interesting and challenging enough for you?

- Are you looking for a camp that focuses mainly on group activities or independent ones?

- Would you prefer a camp with a religious emphasis or not?

- Do you have a disability that needs to be accommodated at the camp?

- Does the camp have a good reputation? Is it known for quality?

- Are its facilities (cabins, mess hall, activity centers) well maintained? Is the food decent?

- What are the accommodations like? (Will you be staying in a crude cabin with no indoor plumbing and be expected to take turns cleaning the outhouses every week? Or will you be staying in an air-conditioned cabin with a television and a VCR?)

- Will you be comfortable in the accommodations offered? (Be honest with yourself, especially if the camp is rustic.)

- What are the staff members like? What credentials do they have?

- Will the camp facilities make it easy for you to stay in touch with your family and friends? If not, can you handle this?

Do a thorough job of researching the camp by talking to the directors and getting the names and phone numbers of past participants, so you can ask them about their experiences. If at all possible, you may want to take an actual look at the camp before signing up.

Applying to a camp is usually a simple process. You'll receive an application in the mail asking for the basics: your name, your address, the sessions you're interested in, and any special housing or dietary needs. Some camps *may* ask you to write an essay, but only if the camp is free, highly selective, or based on a specialty such as science or

In most cases, you're responsible for getting yourself to the camp, once you're accepted. The camp may provide buses, especially if it's located in a remote area. Usually, campers catch the bus at the nearest city and ride together.

writing. The most important thing is to sign up early because the applications are processed in the order they're received. Check with the camp to find out about application deadlines.

HeLp! I'm aLReaDy HoMeSIcK

Being away from home may be a little scary, especially if you've never done it before. And *anyone* can get homesick, no matter what age. You may feel homesick just thinking about camp, or the moment you arrive, or halfway through the program, or right at the end, when you're getting ready to depart. These feelings are natural, and there are ways to deal with them. First, bring along a journal. This allows you to record your emotions, stay busy during downtime, and have a keepsake from your time at camp. Second, get out there and explore your environment and make new friends. When you're active, involved, and focused on fun, you won't have as much time to sit around feeling lonely. And last but not least, keep in touch with your family and friends back home via phone calls, letters, postcards, and email.

If you're more interested in being a counselor than a camper, there are a few things you should know. Most sleep-away camps hire college-age students to be counselors. However, in many cases, former campers who are ages seventeen or eighteen may apply for counselor-in-training positions. When looking for a CIT position, consider whether you have any special skills that may make you more hirable: Do you have training as a lifeguard? Experience in horseback riding, canoeing, or tennis? Previous training as a baby-sitter or an aide at a school? Be sure to mention these skills and experiences on your résumé. (For more about résumés, see pages 129–139.)

As a CIT at a sleep-away camp or day camp, you'll most likely have your hands full helping out the head counselors, supervising games, herding the campers from activity to activity, and periodically leading them to the bathrooms or to the first-aid tent if they get hurt. But, as a CIT at the day camp, I sometimes got to help organize sports events or arts-and-crafts activities—then I'd roll up my sleeves and get to have some real fun. At sleep-away camps, counselors and CITs usually stay in the same cabins as their assigned group of kids. At night, the camp may sponsor organized activities like dances, sing-alongs, or friendship circles for the counselors.

 ## FIND OUT MORE

The Princeton Review's Student Advantage Guide to Summer: The Best Programs, the Coolest Jobs, Travel & Adventure, and the Art of Hanging Out by Michael Freedman (New York: Random House, 1995). If summer's coming and you're looking for cool things to do, look no further than this guide, which will help you plan everything from camps to adventure programs to volunteer opportunities. Listings include program history, descriptions, costs, and more.

American Camping Association
5000 State Road 67 North
Martinsville, IN 46151
(765) 342-8456
www.acacamps.org

Want to go to camp, but not sure where? The American Camping Association (ACA) is the only not-for-profit organization that accredits all types of camps throughout the United States. ACA-accredited camps meet up to 300 standards for health, safety, and program quality. Visit the Web site and search over 2,000 accredited camps by type of camp, area, activities, and more.

Boston University's Sargent Camp
36 Sargent Camp Road
Hancock, NH 03449
(603) 525-3311
www.bu.edu/net/sargentcamp/internship/body.html

Interested in outdoor environmental education? Look no further than the Sargent Camp, where you'll receive a two-week training program in skills such as ropes course and group dynamics. You'll be working with school-children, teaching them about the outdoors. You'll also receive a small weekly stipend, plus room and board.

Center for Creative Youth (CCY)
Wesleyan University
350 High Street
Middletown, CT 06459
(860) 685-3307

If you're interested in the arts, consider applying to the Center for Creative Youth. CCY offers talented high school students five weeks of intensive study in the arts at Wesleyan University. Each class is designed to enhance problem-solving skills in music, theater, creative writing, dance, filmmaking, or visual arts. Students participate daily in intensive interdisciplinary classes, culminating in performances and exhibits. Students leave CCY with a complete evaluation to use as a college recommendation and a portfolio of their work.

Concordia Language Villages
901 8th Street South
Moorhead, MN 56562
1-800-222-4750
www.cord.edu/dept/clv/language_camp.html

Concordia Language Villages create global environments representing twelve languages and cultures. You can attend summer camps for one to four weeks, where language and culture are taught in a variety of contexts including physical surroundings, food, and activities. Concordia Language Villages also offer weekend camps during the school year as well as a unique program for college credit, designed specifically for advanced high school students studying French.

The CTY Challenge Awards Program
Johns Hopkins University Center for Talented Youth (CTY)
3400 North Charles Street
Baltimore, MD 21218-2699
(410) 516-0337

If you're a creative student who's interested in science, this free program will allow you to participate in scientific research at field stations around the country. To be eligible for the program, you must be entering grades eleven or twelve and be nominated by your school.

National Youth Science Camp (NYSC)
National Youth Science Foundation, Inc.
P.O. Box 3387
Charleston, WV 25333
(304) 342-3326
www.sciencecamp.org

If you're a graduating senior who's interested in spending three-and-a-half weeks getting exposure to science through lectures and research projects, consider NYSC. Held in a rustic camp in the eastern highlands of West Virginia, the camp is all-expenses-paid and provides plenty of free time for sports and nature activities. Each state sends two students, based on competitive selection.

Teen Tours of America
1121 Holland Drive, Suite 21
Boca Raton, FL 33487
1-888-TOUR-TTA (1-888-868-7882)
www.teentravelofamerica.com

For a a camping experience that's also a tour, try Teen Tours of America. Each trip starts in a city where all participants meet and then travel by luxury motorcoach to see the sights of many cities—staying in a combination of tents, dorms, and hotels.

Woods Hole SEA Programs
Sea Education Association, Inc.
P.O. Box 6
Woods Hole, MA 02543
1-800-552-3633, ext. 770
www.sea.edu

High school students can participate in Science at SEA or Oceanography of the Gulf of Maine, both sponsored by the Sea Education Association. Each program has a shore and a sea component; students study the marine environment from scientific, literary, and historical perspectives. Science at SEA involves studying on campus in Woods Hole, Massachusetts, for ten days, and then sailing the waters off Cape Cod for nine. Oceanography of the Gulf of Maine gives students the opportunity to experience life on an island off the coast of Maine for eight days, and then board a sailing vessel to study coastal and oceanic marine environments for nine days. Need-based financial aid is available, and a few special scholarships are offered as well.

SPOTLIGHT ON

Paul Abosh
Garden City Collegiate
Winnipeg, Manitoba

I'd been going to the same summer camp for years—B'nai Brith Jewish Community Camp in Ontario—but the summer after my freshman year was a particularly memorable one for me. That was the first year I went on a special four-week wilderness/canoe adventure, which was specifically for the older campers. B'nai Brith camp is for Jewish youth, and all the camp activities focused around a Jewish theme. Although we were planning an extended trip away from the main camp, I was still looking forward to keeping my Jewish traditions alive, even in the wilderness. Special Shabbat (Friday night Sabbath) services around a campfire, Jewish songs, and lessons on Jewish culture were all part of the trip.

Our group of ten boys had two counselors, and before we left the counselors let us know that, while they were there to guide us, we were all still responsible for looking out for each other. The night before we left, we loaded our packs with enough food and supplies to last the four-week trip, and we got our sleeping bags and canoes ready.

The next morning, we canoed away from the main camp and paddled approximately 30 miles deep into the Lake of the Woods area (the Canadian side of the Minnesota Boundary Waters), along a scenic lake surrounded by majestic islands formed out of the Canadian Shield. I marveled at the way the water looked so serene, and I thought to myself that this was going to involve a lot of hard work, but it would all be worth it to canoe through such a tranquil lake. We eased our canoes into the water and set off side by side down the lake. Along the way, I watched the birds fly by and chatted with the rest of the campers. A few nights later, after another long 30-mile canoe trip, we set up camp and our tents for the night. We ate some of the food from our packs, and that's when I started to feel sick. In fact, everyone started to feel sick. As it turned out, we all got food poisoning from that dinner, but I didn't have it as bad as the rest. Fortunately, we recovered, and the trip continued without further incident.

The wilderness part of the trip involved lengthy portages (carrying the canoes) throughout the woods, to get from one lake to the other. We usually took a break twice a day for snacks and juice to rebuild our strength and to give our sore arms and shoulders a rest. Whenever we decided to take a break, I used a pair of binoculars to try to identify the birds and plants around me. Once I found a baby bird that had fallen out of its nest, and I safely put it back in. Holding that tiny, helpless creature in my hand made me realize how fragile life is and how we should enjoy every moment that we can. I came back from the trip feeling energized and excited about all I'd seen and done—and appreciating nature more deeply than ever before.

> "Adventure can be an end in itself. Self-discovery is the secret ingredient that fuels daring."
>
> **—Grace Lichtenstein**

Getting Adventurous

Have you ever imagined yourself spelunking in a cave or bushwhacking through the jungle? Are you ready to embrace your inner adventurer? If the thought of white-water rafting down a rushing river sends your heart racing, or if climbing a mountain is your dream come true, a summer adventure program may be your calling.

How about a wilderness survival program? Or a journey that involves hiking or biking through mountains? Perhaps a scientific expedition in which you help dig up fossils or study live plants and animals? Adventures come in all shapes and sizes, but the main thing they have in common is that they require participants to be spirited, adaptable, and open to challenges of all kinds. You'll be doing something out of the ordinary—sometimes something *way* out there!

Adventure programs are usually organized by a group, a company, or an organization that specializes in extraordinary experiences and exploration of remote outdoor areas. Small groups of about ten to fifteen students are accompanied by several adult leaders. The small group size allows each person to get to know and trust the other members, and ensures that the leaders can provide all of the students with technical instruction. Teamwork is a key part of adventures—group members have to help and support each other through all of the physical and emotional challenges involved.

Unlike a wilderness camp, adventure programs are mobile. You'll move around quite a bit, setting up temporary camps as you go. Adventures also include *a lot* of physical activity. In fact, most programs have an athletic focus, like sailing or backpacking. The pace may be quick and the activity level strenuous. You may find yourself hiking with a heavy pack, kayaking down a river for days at a time, or biking up and down hills and mountains. Some adventure programs have a solo component, where you need to rely on your own wits to survive for a few days in the wilderness.

F. Y. I.

It's best to be in good physical condition before signing up for an adventure. Even if you're toned and fit, you may need to strengthen your muscles or increase your endurance level before your departure.

Locating an adventure program is easy. You can look on the Internet to find listings of hundreds of adventure programs especially geared toward teens. An excellent online resource for any kind of summer program—camps and adventures included—is *www.petersons.com/summerop/ssector.html*. Here, you'll find Peterson's Summer Programs for Kids and Teens, a huge database of summer programs for your review. Just type in a name or general category such as "Adventure Programs," and you've got plenty of Web page links to browse. Another alternative is to talk to your guidance counselor about program options or check with local adventure-gear stores to see if they post listings of adventure programs that teens can join.

SPOTLIGHT ON

Niki Bartkow
Greenwich Academy
Greenwich, Connecticut

When I was eighteen, I did a NOLS (National Outdoor Leadership School) Alaska Mountaineering course, where the main goal was to reach the summit of the highest peak in the Chugach Mountain Range. At the time, I was already familiar with rope systems, but I had never traveled on a glacier or used crampons, devices that clip to your boots for better traction. My instructors on the trip were skilled and knowledgeable. I love the snow and cold weather, so the Alaska challenge suited me perfectly.

On my trip, I learned basic survival skills—how to survive on a glacier, how to keep warm, what foods to eat for maximum energy, and how to live in a place where you can't depend on electricity every day. I also discovered how to rely on and communicate with other people, because on a trip like this teamwork is crucial—especially when you're working with rope systems on a crevasse (a deep open chasm in a glacier). When you're thousands of feet above the ground and the temperature is below freezing, you really have to keep the lines of communication open and watch out for each other. That was an amazing lesson to learn.

The costs of adventure programs vary, but they usually range from a few hundred to several thousand dollars. Most don't include transportation to and from the starting site, so you'll need to figure out how you'll get there yourself. Make sure that you look over the promotional materials carefully before making a final decision. It can be very helpful to call a few past participants to find out whether they enjoyed their experience. (You can ask the sponsoring company to provide the names and phone numbers of these teens.) When you talk to a past participant, you may want to ask the following kinds of questions:

- What kind of training did the leaders have? How many leaders were there?

- How many group members were there?

- Did the ratio of leaders to group members seem fair?

- How did the group get along? Was there a good sense of teamwork? Did the leaders help foster a team-building atmosphere? How?

- Was there an orientation? Was this helpful?

- What do the group members need to provide in the way of accommodations? A tent? Sleeping bags?

- Was the level of physical activity too high, too low, or just right?

- Should group members prepare themselves physically in any way before the adventure?

- Are there any special skills that group members need to have?

- Is there any advice you'd give to would-be adventurers who want to go on this program?

If you find a program that sounds like the right match for you, you can request an application online or through the mail. Most applications are pretty basic (name, address, etc.), although some may require a recommendation letter or an essay—particularly if you're applying for financial aid or if the program is designed for teens who are especially motivated.

Before finalizing any arrangements, consider whether you truly want to set out on the adventure you've chosen. Determine whether you're comfortable with the idea of going for days without a shower, going to the bathroom in the woods, testing your wilderness skills on a daily basis, and pushing your body to new limits—all with a group of strangers. It's important to be honest with yourself and to have realistic expectations. If you're ready to face all the challenges that await, go for it! An adventure will strengthen your body, increase your confidence, teach you team-

F. Y. I.

Start an appropriate exercise program before you go. If you'll be mountain biking, practice at home on your own bike and get yourself used to long-distance rides. If you'll be hiking, strap on a backpack and trek through the outdoors to get used to the feel of the weight on your back.

work, and give you a new sense of what you're capable of in life. These are priceless lessons.

Some teens feel that they gained more from an adventure program than they did from any other high school experience, because they stretched their minds and bodies like never before. Think of how proud you'll feel at the end of the journey, knowing that you've accomplished something most teens—or adults, for that matter—wouldn't ever dare to attempt.

FIND OUT MORE

Peterson's Summer Opportunities for Kids and Teenagers 2000 (Princeton, NJ: Peterson's Guides, 1999). Jam-packed with over 2,500 summer opportunities, this guide gives information on camps, teen tours, academic programs, wilderness adventures, arts and sports workshops, community service programs, and more. You'll find details like dates, costs, financial aid, and accreditation.

Travel That Can Change Your Life: How to Create a Transformative Experience by Jeffrey A. Kottler (San Francisco: Jossey-Bass, 1997). Travel is not only fun but also can encourage personal growth. In this book, the author leads you on an exploration of the many ways you can benefit from travel.

Adventures Afloat, Teen SCUBA Diving & Sailing Camp, Ltd.
5439 Heather Ridge Path
Lecanto, FL 34461
(352) 527-3366

If you're interested in learning to sail or dive, Adventures Afloat might be worth checking out. On this program, you'll live aboard a 46-foot catamaran and sail in the Caribbean for three weeks. You'll sail and dive near the British Virgin Islands.

The Archaeological Institute of America
656 Beacon Street, 4th Floor
Boston, MA 02215
(617) 353-9361
www.archeological.org

If you're into archaeology but don't know where to go, contact this organization. It publishes the Archaeological Fieldwork Opportunities Bulletin, which is a great guide if you're interested in working on a dig.

Bike-Aid
333 Valencia Street, Suite 101
San Francisco, CA 94103
1-800-RIDE-808 (1-800-7433-808)
www.bikeaid.org

Looking for a unique way to spend the summer? If you enjoy biking, consider Bike-Aid, a program that sends teens on nine-week bike trips to learn about community involvement. During the trip, you'll engage in experiential learning as you meet with various grassroots organizations to understand different issues and struggles. Then you'll take your knowledge to Capitol Hill (each bike ride ends in Washington, D.C.) where lobbying appointments will be made for your group. Takeoff sites include Seattle, San Francisco, and Boston.

Close Up Foundation
44 Canal Center Plaza
Alexandria, VA 22314-1592
1-800-CLOSE-UP (1-800-256-7387)
www.closeup.org

The Close Up Foundation is the nation's largest nonprofit citizenship education organization. Built on the belief that textbooks and lectures alone are not enough to help students understand the democratic process, Close Up offers trips to U.S. federal, state, and local government centers. Some of the opportunities include the Close Up Washington Program, which gives high school students and teachers the chance to study the process of government in Washington, D.C., for a week and the Close Up Pacific Basin Program—a six-day program for students in grades ten to twelve in Honolulu, Hawaii, that focuses on the environmental, economic, and national security issues in the Asia-Pacific region.

EarthWatch
3 Clock Tower Place, Suite 100
Box 75
Maynard, MA 01754
1-800-776-0188
www.earthwatch.org

EarthWatch is a nonprofit organization that recruits people for field research expeditions in a wide variety of areas. You must be at least sixteen to join any of 135 expeditions in 54 countries and 24 states. The sessions are one to three weeks long and are directed by university scholars. You'll need to pay all your expenses to participate unless you're accepted into the highly competitive Student Challenge Awards Program, a two- to three-week expenses-paid summer program that allows teens to work side by side with scientists in the field or lab.

National Outdoor Leadership School (NOLS)
288 Main Street
Lander, WY 82520-3140
(307) 332-5300
www.nols.edu/NOLSHome.html

Outdoor lovers unite! NOLS operates nine branch schools around the world and its courses explore some of the wildest reaches of five continents. Prior outdoor experience is not a prerequisite for most courses, which last anywhere from two to fourteen weeks. You can try sea kayaking, mountaineering, white-water boating, sailing, rock climbing, horsepacking (traveling by horse), and more. Scholarships and financial aid are available.

Outward Bound
100 Mystery Point Road
Garrison, NY 10524
1-800-243-8520
www.outwardbound.org

If you're up for the challenge of surviving in the wilderness, consider Outward Bound, the largest and oldest adventure program in the world. The program provides group trips in Oregon, Minnesota, North Carolina, Maine, and Colorado. You'll work with your group to complete tasks, learn about your surroundings, and have fun. Most trips also offer the opportunity to go out solo into the wilderness and put all the survival skills you learned into practice.

Pangaea Quest: Teen Adventure School
8169 East Via De Viva
Scottsdale, AZ 85258
(602) 684-9370
www.pangaeaquest.com

Looking to explore the wilderness this summer? Consider Pangaea Quest. Pangaea offers trips for teens ages fourteen to eighteen to Arizona and Colorado. You'll explore remote areas, backpack through the mountains, and learn rock-climbing and white-water rafting skills.

Sail Caribbean
79 Church Street
Northport, NY 11768
1-800-321-0994
www.sailcaribbean.com

Love to sail? Think you would if you tried? If so, consider contacting Sail Caribbean. You'll learn the ropes (no pun intended) while you live, work, and sleep on a yacht. The camp is open to students between the ages of thirteen and eighteen and a variety of program lengths are available.

Weissman Teen Tours

517 Almena Avenue
Ardsley, NY 10502
1-800-942-8005
www.weissmantours.com

Enjoy a forty-day U.S./Canada trip or a five-week tour in Europe. Weismann Tours plans the itinerary, which you can check out at the Web site.

Westcoast Connection Travel Camp

154 East Boston Post Road
Mamaroneck, NY 10543
1-800-767-0227
www.westcoastconnection.com

Westcoast Connection offers fifteen summer tours for teens ages thirteen to sixteen and separate programs for students ages seventeen to eighteen. Programs visit the western United States, Canada, Europe, and Israel. Travel focuses on active and outdoor adventures; trips range from eighteen to forty-two days.

Wilderness Inquiry

808 14th Street SE
Minneapolis, MN 55414
(612) 379-3858
www.wildernessinquiry.org

Wilderness Inquiry sends people with disabilities and those without on wilderness trips, which include canoeing and kayaking in Canada. Trips can last from three days to two-and-a-half weeks. Need-based scholarships are available.

Traveling Overseas

If you're up for the idea of going to camp or heading off on an adventure, you may want to take an even bigger risk: traveling overseas. This option *isn't* for beginners. Before

> "Your world is as big as you make it."
>
> —**Georgia Douglas Johnson**

trying out this kind of alternative learning experience, you'll need some practice being far away from home for a period of time and adapting to a new environment. If this kind of thing doesn't faze you, then read on.

Here's a list of overseas experiences that may entice you to pack your bags and throw yourself a going-away party:

- **Camps abroad:** Being a camper abroad is an entirely different experience from being one in your home state or country. That's because you'll be in a foreign environment, where you'll interact with teens from a variety of countries. Plus, you'll have the added challenge of adapting to a new lifestyle and set of customs. Like camps in the U.S., overseas camps can be expensive, unless you find one that offers a scholarship or financial aid.

- **Adventures abroad:** Adventure programs that involve travel abroad give you a chance to learn about the culture of the country by participating in community life, eating the same food as the people who live there, heading out on travel adventures, and even participating in festivals and ceremonies. In other words, you won't be seeing tourist attractions from the comfort of an air-conditioned bus.

- **Voluntary service/work programs:** If volunteering is your thing, there are plenty of opportunities for you to flex your community-service muscles and see a new part of the world. You can join a work camp with other volunteers to assist people in overseas communities. As an assistant or trainee, you'll learn plenty from this kind of eye-opening experience, especially while working alongside the community members as they improve their living conditions. The programs usually include modest living arrangements—tents, dormitories, or churches. For more information and resources, see the section called "Volunteering Abroad" on pages 30–33.

- **Study tours:** Study tours are short-term travel opportunities (a few weeks to a few months) that include an educational theme. On a study tour, you'll learn a bit and travel a lot. Your guide may give educational lectures, but the emphasis is mainly on tourism. Participants usually stay in hotels or hostels.

- **Travel tours:** If you want to see a foreign country with a group of teens, you could try a travel tour. Some cover the well-traveled tourist areas; others specialize in more out-of-the-way locales. The focus is mainly on having fun and learning about a new place. Most travel tours are expensive, but they include everything—food, lodging, field trips, transportation, and so on.

- **Homestays:** There are two kinds of homestays—those that are part of a study abroad program (read more about these in Chapter 8, "Study Abroad") and those that aren't. A homestay that isn't affiliated with a study abroad program includes a short-term visit with a host family. The focus is on daily living, not on education or meeting with other students. These homestays can last anywhere from a week to a few months. If you choose this kind of program, you'll have the opportunity to concentrate solely on living with your hosts, free from the responsibilities of schoolwork.

- **Interning abroad:** Some internships are offered through special programs for teens. However, there is the possibility of arranging an internship in a foreign country on your own. You may be able to find an American company that has branches overseas; or you may want to pursue a foreign company in your particular field of interest. Either way, it helps to be fluent in a foreign language and to have a solid background in computers. You can look on the Internet to find the company or organization's Web site, or write to the company for information. As with any internship you apply for, you'll need to start with a résumé and a cover letter. (See Chapter 5, "Find an Internship," for everything you need to know about becoming an intern.) Keep in mind that overseas interns aren't paid for their work, unless they're over eighteen and have gotten a work permit. If you're on a tight budget, you may want to consider other options.

SPOTLIGHT ON

Joseph Killenmeyer
Appalachian State University
Boone, North Carolina

My internship took place the summer after my first year of college. From childhood I had always had a hard time in school. I was diagnosed as having ADD (attention deficit disorder), and attended several different schools before settling in for high school at an all-male boarding school in Chattanooga, Tennessee. Though I enjoyed being there, I never felt I was getting the right overall learning experience. I took a year off to work on a horse farm and travel in New Zealand between high school and college, but at the end of my freshman year in college I still didn't have a sense of what I wanted from life or how school could help me get there.

During this time a friend showed me an article about the Center for Interim Programs, run by Cornelius Bull (Neil). I contacted the center, and they sent me some questionnaires to fill out so they could get an idea of what to start looking for. They showed me lots of options, from working in Nepal with villagers to interning as a bicycle repairman in Ghana. What caught my interest was a position in a private arboretum in Turkey. My family has been involved in the nursery industry in Lexington, Kentucky, for more than 150 years, so I grew up with a love of plants and a desire to help my father in the family business. When Neil offered me an opportunity to work at the tree farm in Turkey, I jumped at the chance.

The arboretum consisted of ten acres of privately owned gardens and a small five-acre tree nursery. All of the employees worked both as gardeners and on the tree farm. The land was owned by a famous Turkish businessman named Heyrettin Karaca. The arboretum and nursery were a hobby for him. Karaca was also the founder of an environmental organization called TEMA. TEMA reforests land and concentrates on erosion problems that are caused by deforestation. For these efforts, Karaca had received a Medal of Honor from delegates at the World Environmental Conference in Rio de Janeiro, and had been named Man of the Year in Turkey.

I didn't have a consistent schedule of tasks. The work changed daily, and this kept it interesting. I did everything: pruning, planting, weeding. I lived in an apartment connected to the nursery offices. A cook there fixed my breakfast and prepared lunch for thirty workers.

When I arrived in Turkey there was one woman in the area who spoke English. I'd expected to study Turkish with her, but the first thing she told me was that her plans had changed and she'd be leaving in two weeks. I knew that if I wanted to talk to anyone, I had to learn as much Turkish as possible, and when she left for England, I didn't know quite what to do. I began to study voraciously. I pestered the people at work with my pidgin Turkish. They laughed a lot, but so did I, and eventually I started to grasp the language.

I've never met nicer people in the world. I was taken into town to eat out every night. They refused to let me pay for anything—at times I really wanted to, but they would *not* relent. The food in Turkey was heavenly. I indulged in some of the best meals I've ever eaten, and I felt really spoiled.

Besides working at the arboretum, I traveled throughout Turkey on my own for a month-and-a-half. I saw amazing things and met amazing people. I saw the ocean, and I saw the desert. I visited underground cities that went eight floors under the earth, and cities carved into the sides of cliffs up to 100 feet high. I also visited some of the best-known ruins of the ancient world, such as Ephesus. Now it seems almost unreal.

My internship in Turkey had a very important impact on my life. It gave me a chance to combine my two loves of traveling and horticulture. It allowed me to see that I could live comfortably in a completely foreign place and learn to speak a language that had been utterly strange to me. Unfortunately, I also learned about grief. Three days after I left Turkey, a horrible earthquake struck, and Yalova, the town I had lived in, was hit hard. I soon learned that two very close friends had been killed.

When I returned to the States, I spent one more year in college studying solar technologies. Now I'm back in Lexington running one of our family's garden centers. I'm extremely pleased with what I'm doing, and I feel that my experience in Turkey played an important role in giving me both the confidence and the skills I need to operate my business.

 ## FIND OUT MORE

AFS International Intercultural Programs
198 Madison Avenue, 8th Floor
New York, NY 10016
(212) 299-9000
www.afs.org

AFS is an international not-for-profit organization that promotes international exchange of high school students from over sixty countries. It offers year-long, semester, and summer programs, as well as programs for high school graduates.

Center for Interim Programs
P.O. Box 2347
Cambridge, MA 02238
(617) 547-0980
www.interimprograms.com

The Center for Interim Programs is a service that enables people to pursue structured alternatives to formal education or work by matching interests with over 3,000 internships, apprenticeships, volunteer positions, and cultural study programs worldwide. There is a fee to use this service.

CET Academic Programs
1000 16th Street, NW
Washington, D.C. 20036
1-800-225-4262
www.cetacademicprograms.com

CET Academic Programs, formerly China Education Tours, specializes in sending students overseas and helping them integrate into the society in which they're living. CET currently offers programs in China, Japan, Vietnam, Italy, France, and the Czech Republic.

The Experiment in International Living
World Learning Inc.
Box 676, Kipling Road
Brattleboro, VT 05302
1-800-345-2929
www.usexperiment.org

The Experiment in International Living is a program that provides summer homestays with host families in over twenty countries. You must be between the ages of fifteen and eighteen to participate, but in most cases, there is no minimum language requirement. Financial aid (based on family need) is available.

International Association of Lions Clubs
300 West 22nd Street
Oak Brook, IL 60523-8842
(630) 571-5466
208.35.130.10/Lions/Index.html

Individual Lions Clubs may take part in the Lions Youth Exchange Program and/or the Lions International Youth Camps. The exchange program allows selected teens to visit other countries as guests of host Lions Clubs. The association's international youth camps are organized to bring teens of different nationalities together for educational, recreational, and cultural activities. The camps last from one to six weeks.

International Teen Camp Lausanne
P.O. Box 400
1000 Lausanne 12
Switzerland
41-56-222-6778
www.itc-ijc.com

If you're between the ages of fourteen and nineteen and would like to camp abroad, consider this organization. You'll enjoy a camping experience in Switzerland on beautiful Lake Geneva as you take language classes, participate in cultural experiences, go on field trips, and more.

The Irish School of Landscape Painting
RiverRun Studio
Nuns Cross, Ashford
Co. Wicklow
Ireland
35-34-044-0197
aoife.indigo.ie/~ swebb

This "school" offers students the opportunity to paint outside while observing the beautiful landscape of Ireland. Students take one-week classes that have different starting times throughout the summer.

Operation Crossroads Africa
475 Riverside Drive, Suite 242
New York, NY 10115
(212) 870-2106
www.igc.org/oca

Operation Crossroads Africa offers educational and cultural exchanges in Africa, the Caribbean, and North America. Crossroads also offers a special program for those ages fourteen to eighteen: the Caribbean Workcamp, where students spend six weeks in the summer working on community projects in Central America and the Caribbean. No special skills are required (an orientation is held before the program starts). Some scholarships are available.

Outward Bound City Challenge
Chestnut Field, Regent Place
Rugby, CV21 2PJ
United Kingdom
44-51-707-0202

This organization is the urban cousin to the outdoor-adventure group, Outward Bound. In City Challenge, participants work with inner-city residents on a variety of projects. The programs take place in Liverpool and Coventry, England, and are two weeks in length.

The Student Hosteling Program
Ashfield Road, Box 419
Conway, MA 01341
1-800-343-6132
www.biketrips.com

This program offers bike trips for teens to a variety of countries, such as France, the Netherlands, Ireland, and Spain. Excursions are between two and ten weeks in length.

Where There Be Dragons

P.O. Box 4651
Boulder, CO 80306
1-800-982-9203
www.gorp.com/dragons

Dragons offers off-the-beaten-path expeditions in small groups to Laos, India, Thailand, Pakistan, China, Mongolia, Tibet, and Nepal. The trips are rugged and challenging, combining trekking, wilderness exploration, service projects, and more. The organization offers more than just a tour—you'll experience the culture through interaction and immersion in the society.

Youth Leaders International

4429 Faroe Place
Rockville, MD 20853
301-933-5211
www.leaders.org

A worldwide organization, Youth Leaders International provides teens with an opportunity to interact and gain global experience. Students can apply for membership when they're between the ages of thirteen and fifteen, and if accepted, begin a three-year program. The program focuses on leadership skills, community awareness development, and global vision. The program also includes a two-week student exchange to a foreign country to perform civic service while meeting members from around the world.

Legacy International

www.legacyintl.org

If you want to learn more about and receive training in cross-cultural understanding, global issues, leadership, community action, conflict resolution, and environmental awareness, check out Legacy International's Web site.

Youth for Understanding International Exchange

www.yfu.org

Youth for Understanding is a nonprofit international exchange program for high school students between the ages of fifteen and eighteen in thirty countries around the world. Take a look at the Web site to learn more.

SPOTLIGHT ON

Joe Akel
St. Ann's High School
Brooklyn, New York

At the end of my junior year of high school, I joined an adventure program with an organization known as Where There Be Dragons and traveled to the western region of Tibet near the border of Nepal. The program, called "Kailas Sojourn," took place in the most remote region of Tibet, which was desertlike and barren. We planned to hike up Mount Kailas for six weeks. The mountain is regarded as one of the holiest places in the universe to the Buddhist, Hindu, Sikh, and Jain religions. In fact, in the Buddhist religion, Mount Kailas is the symbolic center, or "navel," of the universe.

I chose this program because I knew I wanted to do something completely out of the ordinary; I wanted to push myself and have a spiritual experience. Where There Be Dragons sponsors many excursions to Tibet and Nepal, so students can see Asia on a local level. These adventures are nothing frilly—you interact with the locals and sleep in tents. Going off to this far-flung region of Tibet was a cultural experience like no other. We stayed with families in refugee camps and learned some of the Tibetan language, which made the experience even more meaningful.

Before the trip began, I received a list of supplies I'd need for a trek of this magnitude, including a hardcore backpack and quality boots. The program directors suggested that everyone start exercising to prepare for the difficulty of hiking at such high altitudes. They recommended jumping rope for an hour every day, which I did; I also took yoga classes.

On the program, my group (ten of us total) was made up of sixteen- to nineteen-year-olds. Because of the small group size, we were close-knit and it seemed like there were few barriers among us. We worked together and gave each other advice, especially if anyone felt homesick. We had three guides, plus two Sherpas (professional climbers who went to Sherpa training school). The Sherpas knew about medicine and weather patterns, and they were able to advise us when we needed to take a break or camp for the night.

Climbing a mountain is a very spiritual journey. I knew I'd have to overcome many obstacles and push myself. Even so, the hiking was more difficult than I'd expected. We'd hike for thirteen hours a day and rest for four, with little breaks here and there. We persevered through rainstorms, hail, and cold weather. If anyone got sick, everyone else in the group helped by taking some of the weight of that person's pack. The person then continued the hike unencumbered, or if very ill, continued the journey riding on a yak. These animals are temperamental like wild horses—you wouldn't want to ride one unless you had to.

At the higher altitudes, it was hard to breathe, and we'd all get short of breath. Getting up to 18,000 feet as we circled the mountain was extremely hard, but I pushed myself. Coming down, I felt euphoric as the oxygen level gradually increased. Overall, it was a difficult trip but very rewarding. Reaching those heights was an amazing feeling—not many things in life can compare to it.

Traveling to Mount Kailas provided me with a chance to search deep within myself. The difficult nature of the trip, coupled with its intense spiritual element, allowed me to form a better understanding of who I am. It is through Dragons that I was able to have such an experience, and for that I am forever thankful.

SPOTLIGHT ON

Evan deSieyes
Falmouth High School
Falmouth, Maine

As the spring semester of my senior year in high school rolled around, I found myself wondering more and more about whether college was the place I should be heading in September. I was confident that I could handle college life, but I craved something more adventurous.

In early May, I headed down to Boston, Massachusetts, to talk with an organization that arranges international work experiences. My interview provided me with many possible choices in foreign adventures, but none so exciting as working at Jardin Gaia, a wildlife rehabilitation center on the Pacific coast of Costa Rica. From the time I set foot on Costa Rican soil, I began an experience that changed my life, strengthened my personality, and opened my eyes to a world I'd never imagined.

Costa Rica is one of seven Central American countries. It's bordered by Nicaragua to the northwest, the Caribbean Ocean to the northeast, Panama to the south, and the Pacific Ocean to the west. The weather is tropical, with humidity levels averaging in the 80–100 percent range year round. Biologically, Costa Rica plays host to six levels of forest, thirteen active volcanoes, myriad waterfalls, and hundreds of species of mammals and birds. I can't imagine a more ecologically attractive area than the jungles of Costa Rica.

During high school, I had become increasingly interested in wildlife behavior, so Jardin Gaia—Costa Rica's first official government-funded wildlife rescue and rehabilitation center—was definitely the place for me. Since it was founded, Gaia has helped return over 600 wild animals to their native environment. There's a full-time veterinarian on hand, with vet students from around the globe constantly dropping by to study wildlife veterinary medicine. Jardin Gaia is literally Costa Rica's wildlife hospital.

I flew down to Costa Rica with few expectations. I hoped to attain as much veterinary knowledge as possible and to help the animals in whatever way I could. Both of my goals were met, and then some. I immediately fell in love with all Jardin Gaia had to offer. My daily routine consisted of cleaning cages, preparing food, taking care of general maintenance (sweeping, painting, repairing fences, and the like), constructing cages, providing guided tours of Gaia in Spanish and English, and doing some botany work. When I had spare time I would help the veterinarian perform necropsies (autopsies), stabilize injured animals, and assist the staff in the vet clinic. I became captivated by veterinary medicine, and I found myself wanting to learn more and more. After twelve years of formal education, I had finally discovered something that excited me as a possible future profession!

It was at Jardin Gaia that I experienced the single-most motivating moment of my life. As I held a dying endangered species of wildcat in my hands, I realized that I was ultimately of no use to that animal because I lacked the knowledge I needed to help keep it alive. As the wildcat's breathing grew labored and its eyes slowly shut, I could do nothing but watch it die. I've never wanted something more than I did then: I wanted the training and qualifications to become a wildlife veterinarian.

I went to Costa Rica looking for adventure and motivation. What I found was desire. That desire has led me to enroll in Colorado College as a pre-veterinary student.

At this point, you may have one big, important question on your mind:

"Sure, I want to see the world... but how in the world am I supposed to PAY for it!?"

Going abroad, on an adventure, or to a camp can be a big expense, taking into account the program costs, airline tickets, general travel expenses, meals, and so forth. The good news is that some programs are free or low cost; many offer some sort of financial aid to students who need it. Financial aid usually means either (1) loans that you have to pay back with interest or (2) a combination of loans and grants—grants are funds that you *don't* have to pay back. Some students are eligible for grants and scholarships that help fund their education or learning experiences.

As you begin researching opportunities, keep your eyes open for programs that offer financial aid. In most cases, in order to qualify for financial aid (including scholarships), you'll need to demonstrate:

1. your financial need

2. a strong academic background

3. a willingness to go somewhere that may not be your first choice

Another alternative is to look for student scholarships available through your faith organization, your local community center, or your mom or dad's employer. If these aren't possibilities for you, you may want to contact a group that's associated with the place you'd like to visit. For example, the American-Scandinavian Foundation, located in New York, promotes cultural and educational exchange between Scandinavians and North Americans; the Foundation awards more than $600,000 in grants and fellowships each year. If you're interested in traveling to a Scandinavian country, you could apply for a scholarship through the Foundation.

Public funding sources are another option—though a competitive one—for students who want to go overseas. You can head to your local library to look at the *Annual Register of Grant Support,* a directory of grants that anyone can apply for. Look for an organization that might be interested in offering a grant to a high school student who wants to visit a specific country. You'll most likely have to fill out a grant application, write an essay, and even have a personal interview. (For tips on acing an interview, see pages 142–149.) Some of the organizations listed in the directory will probably request a proposal that outlines what you plan to do with the grant money. And some organizations will require that you have special qualifications, like a college degree or proficiency in a particular language. Be sure to read the criteria carefully before putting energy into applying. Also, keep in mind that application deadlines occur once or twice per year, so you'll need to plan far in advance to have a good chance of securing the grant you want.

Even if you receive financial aid, a scholarship, or a grant, there still may be some expenses associated with your trip. There are plenty of ways to raise money, and if you've got the desire and determination to pursue an alternative learning experience, you've probably also got the drive to creatively fund it. Besides, if you use your initiative and keep thinking "outside the box," the process of raising funds isn't just about money—it's an alternative learning experience in and of itself!

- **Find a sponsor:** You'll have to get out there and pound the pavement, but the results can be worth the effort. Finding a sponsor involves contacting an organization that might be willing to help fund your trip—your place of worship, a local community center, or a nonprofit organization, for example. Suppose you were to ask your church to sponsor a trip to Kenya? What might you offer in exchange for funds? Once you return, could you put together a display that includes writings and photographs of your trip? Could you give a presentation to members of your church's youth group, sharing what you learned? Could you do a slide show? You'll have better luck finding a sponsor if the organization you contact has some kind of connection to the place you plan to visit or if you're able to make volunteering a part of your mission when you travel.

- **Fund-raise:** Student groups often fund their school-sponsored trips this way, so take a cue from them. How about organizing a bake sale, a garage sale, or a car wash to raise money? For example, if you decide to hold a garage sale, you could ask your parents and neighbors if they have any stuff they want to get rid of, and then sell these donated items for a profit. See if your friends and family are willing to lend a hand on the day of the sale. Make posters and signs that explain that the proceeds earned will go to a good cause—your trip.

- **Get a job:** (The old tried-and-true way to earn money.) If you're planning your trip far enough in advance, you may have time to get a job to earn money to pay for it. Lots of teens find work in fast-food restaurants or other local establishments. Newspaper routes and regular baby-sitting jobs are also a good source of income. Open a savings account to keep your money in a safe place, where you won't be as tempted to spend it.

- **Be vocal:** Go out of your way to let everyone know that you're looking for odd jobs and trying to save money for a trip. People will think of you when they want to hire someone to do chores or help with a project. Some family members may even be generous enough to make a donation to your "cause."

- **Start a business:** Perhaps some of your learning experiences and creative projects have led to finished products: artwork, crafts, or writings. If you're willing to part with these treasures, you just may be able to find people who will buy them. If you don't have a product to sell, consider whether you've got an area of expertise to share. Could you teach people to build birdhouses, do tricks on their in-line skates, sponge-paint their walls, or play a musical instrument? Another alternative is to base your business on a service. You could take care of people's plants and animals when they're on vacation, clean houses and apartments, run errands or start a delivery service (if you drive), put together unassembled furniture, or troubleshoot when people have computer problems or questions. There are plenty of options open to you, depending on your skills and interests—and many don't even require start-up money or entrepreneurial savvy. All you have to do is hang some fliers advertising your business and spread the word at school and in your community. And don't forget: once you've earned the money you need, SAVE IT!

FIND OUT MORE

Annual Register of Grant Support 2000 (Los Angeles: Academic Media, 1999). This thick guide is divided into subjects areas (such as languages, performing arts, and international affairs) and can be found in the reference section of your local public library. As the title suggests, the book is published annually, so make sure to find the latest edition.

Financial Aid for Study and Training Abroad 1999–2001 by Gail A. Schlachter and R. David Weber (San Carlos, CA: Reference Service Press, 1999). Each year hundreds of organizations in the U.S. and other countries set aside millions of dollars to fund the considerable expenses associated with studying or training abroad. You can get information on that funding by using this guide, which describes more than 1,000 scholarships, fellowships, loans, and grants that you can use to support structured and unstructured study abroad. Armed with the information in this directory, you're sure to find study abroad affordable and maybe even free!

Peterson's 2000 Summer Jobs for Students: Where the Jobs Are and How to Get Them (Princeton, NJ: Peterson's Guides, 1999). Want to land the perfect summer job? This guide will tell you what you need to know! State-by-state and Canadian listings give you details about employers, benefits, and any pre-employment training (if it's required). The book also includes valuable information on how to write a résumé and cover letter specifically for summer jobs along with tips on working for the national park service.

Whiz Teens in Business: Enjoy Yourself While Making Money! by Danielle Vallee (Kansas City, MO: Truman, 1999). This is a thorough book for young entrepreneurs who want to start their own small business. It covers topics such as choosing the right business, establishing credibility, obtaining financing, communicating with parents, juggling business and school workloads, and more.

The Young Entrepreneur's Edge: Using Your Ambition, Independence, and Youth to Launch a Successful Business by Jennifer Kushell (New York: Random House, 1999). A young entrepreneur who has been in business for herself since she was thirteen, Kushell discusses how to approach a business plan, tap into the right resources, deal with being new to the business world, and keep your life in balance. The book is full of advice and stories from the author and other young business owners.

The Young Entrepreneur's Guide to Starting and Running a Business by Steve Mariotti (New York: Times Books, 2000). If you'd like to be a young entrepreneur, check out this book. You'll learn how to do everything from writing your own business plan to making a return on your investments to marketing and advertising effectively. Lively stories of famous entrepreneurs and case studies of real teens who've started their own businesses make this book inspiring and practical.

Rotary International
One Rotary Center
1560 Sherman Avenue
Evanston, IL 60201
(212) 982-3900
www.rotary.org/programs/youth_ex/index.htm

One of the most popular ways for teens who need full financial aid to go abroad is through Rotary International. The organization, which focuses on humanitarian service and fostering goodwill and peace between nations, has chapters in most major cities in the world. Students ages fifteen to nineteen who have not yet started college can participate in an exchange between any two countries that have Rotary Clubs. Local Rotary branches sponsor long- and short-term exchanges, offering full-tuition scholarships plus room and board. For those who participate in a long-term exchange (one year), a small stipend is given to cover living expenses. Applications must be made through your local Rotary Club, and there's a rigorous application and selection process. To find the branch nearest you, look in your phone book under "Rotary Club" or visit the international Web site.

Youth Venture
1700 North Moore Street, Suite 2000
Arlington, VA 22209
(703) 527-8300
www.youthventure.org

Youth Venture is a nonprofit organization that assists teens in creating and operating businesses that meet their needs. These businesses must fall into three categories: community service groups, small business ventures, or after-school clubs. Youth Venture helps teens create a business plan, ensures a support network, and furnishes start-up funds in the form of grants and loans.

International Education Financial Aid
www.iefa.org

IEFA is a premier Internet information resource on financial aid information for students wishing to study in a foreign country. At this site, you'll find a comprehensive listing of grants, scholarships, loan programs, and more—as well as links to other study-abroad information.

Young Entrepreneurs' Organization (YEO)
www.yeo.org

People under twenty-five make up the fastest-growing segment of business starters. As a global, not-for-profit educational organization for young entrepreneurs, YEO strives to help its members build upon their successes through an array of educational and networking opportunities. YEO has members in ninety chapters around the world.

"When young people travel, the world becomes real. All the places that they've learned about in their classes at school and watched on television become more than dots on maps or paragraphs in texts. The foreign language that they may have been 'forced' by a requirement to learn is suddenly practical, and they are able to communicate with the people that they meet. The works of art that they'd seen only as slides on pull-down screens are suddenly in front of them in brilliant color and texture. And when they return, their learning doesn't stop, at least not for most. Once a world has been enlarged by travel, it's hard to shrink."

Nicole Rosenleaf Ritter, Managing Editor, *Transitions Abroad*

Chances are, you'll start noticing changes in yourself as soon as you make the decision to head out on an adventure or travel to a foreign country. You'll probably feel a little scared at first, wondering if you're making the right decision (or worrying that you aren't). Then, as you get more used to the idea that you've chosen a different path from your friends in high school, feelings of excitement and independence will set in. Soon you'll be busy planning your trip and preparing yourself physically and mentally for your departure. Days that used to seem routine will now be packed with activity—that's all part of the fun!

Chapter 8

Study Abroad

"All serious daring starts from within."

Eudora Welty

Have you ever wanted to ditch gym class and study tai chi in China? Or gain a deeper understanding of marine biology while observing sea life in Australia's Great Barrier Reef? Each year, high school students participate in hundreds of study abroad programs in Europe, Asia, South America, Central America, North America, Africa, Australia—just about any place on the map you can imagine. Through participation in travel programs, these students have discovered how exciting the world can be thousands of miles outside the walls of their high school classroom.

Some of the programs focus on a specific discipline—often, the study of a particular language. Others are more interdisciplinary in nature and combine the history, literature, and politics of a country into one cohesive program. Some programs fall under the category of an "exchange," in which you attend classes at a high school abroad and live with a host family. (So you "exchange" your school and family in America for a school and family in another country.) Language programs in particular operate on the principal that the best way to learn the language is to speak it morning, noon, and night; for this reason, most of these programs include a homestay with a host family whose members are, of course, fluent speakers. Other study abroad programs may include a stay in a student dormitory. The programs can last anywhere from a few months to a whole year.

Perhaps you've never known anyone your age who has studied abroad. Just possibly, you may wonder if these programs are risky, scary, or out of your reach. It's true that going abroad is a big deal. I found it pretty mind-boggling to make all of the travel arrangements and plan to be away from home for an extended period of time. My head was filled with hundreds of what ifs: What if I get lonely? What if I run out of money? What if my friends forget about me when I'm gone? What if I don't like the program, the director, or the other students? What if they don't like me? What if I miss all my friends? What if something major happens at school, and I'm not there to see it or be a part of it? What if I get sick and I'm thousands of miles from home? You may be filled with questions like these yourself.

Look at it this way: *What if you're having such a great time that you never want to leave?* Study abroad is a chance of a lifetime—especially as a teen, when you're young and you're learning so much. Sure, you'll miss your friends and family while you're gone and you'll probably even miss a few high school social events, like dances. But you'll have fun times overseas, too. And in the long run, you'll have more memorable experiences from travel. Instead of feeling overly anxious about the prospect of going abroad, you can focus on the unforgettable, fun-filled experiences that await you.

F. Y. I.

The idea of study abroad took root after World War II ended. European and American leaders encouraged student exchanges that would allow high school students from the U.S. to attend school in Europe and vice versa—to promote cross-cultural understanding and friendship.

"I was expecting to be homesick. After all, I had never been away from home for more than a few nights. But I had a wonderful time and wasn't homesick at all—and I experienced so much! I was seventeen. I watched France win the World Cup in soccer, dyed my hair red, and enjoyed French food, which cannot possibly be overrated."—Heather

16 Good Reasons to Study Abroad

1. You'll meet new people and see new places. Imagine studying in Brazil, one of the most diverse countries in the world, with its mixed population of Mexican, African, European, and other nationalities. While interacting with teachers, students, or other people of diverse origins and backgrounds, you'd most likely realize that the world is more varied than you ever would have thought. Exposure to more people and places broadens your understanding of the world we live in. Besides, seeing the Eiffel Tower, the Great Wall of China, or other amazing sites close-up is a hundred times more powerful than peering at them in books or viewing them on a Web site. Only through travel can you get a firsthand look at what the world has to offer.

2. You'll broaden your personal outlook and your view of the world. Suppose you've lived your whole life in a small town or rural area; then you decide to study abroad in Tokyo, one of the world's largest cities, where rush hour is so crowded that special conductors called "pushers" have to physically shove people onto the subways. The sheer number of people and the hustle and bustle of the city could give you a whole new perspective on life. That's what happened, in reverse, to Candace, a student who had grown up in the city and decided to get away from it all by studying abroad in a small town in Germany. She felt less stressed and more at ease in the serene surroundings of the German countryside. What you learn about the world—and yourself—through travel just might surprise you.

3. You'll be more cultured and worldly. Becoming fluent in a foreign language—or simply knowing insider vocabulary, like the British *queue* for line or *skivvies* for underwear—can make you seem like a jet-setter in the eyes of your friends back home. Plus, it's cool to know the ins and outs of a faraway city or country. While overseas, you'll become familiar with the sites along your usual bus or subway route, and you may know the best dishes to order from the menu at your favorite cafes. Knowledge like this will make you feel more connected to a place than memorizing information off a map or from a textbook. Once you return home, you'll probably stay interested in any political developments in your host city or country—you may even find yourself scanning the weather section of the newspaper to see what the weather's like in the place you visited.

4. You may be exposed to a new language. Just imagine how much more interesting language study will be when you get to talk with native speakers who can help you become fluent more quickly. You may even get to explore a language that isn't offered at your school, such as Portuguese, Russian, or Japanese.

5. You'll experience a different way of life. While living in a foreign country, you may find that each day brings surprises. You'll learn all sorts of new words, slang terms, and foreign phrases. You'll have the chance to wear different clothes, sample un-familiar foods and beverages, and watch or try new sports and recreational activities. You'll even see different cars, road signs, homes, buildings, trees, and plants. In other words, you'll be looking at the world with fresh eyes.

"While biking one day in France, I dined on a just-laid egg omelet and wild mushrooms with a farmer I met when his cows wandered across the road. Another time I found a rat in my ratatouille."—**Stefan**

6. You'll see your own culture in a whole new way. After spending some time in a foreign country, you'll have a new way of putting your own culture into context. You'll witness different traditions, beliefs, and behaviors; you'll find out what other people think of your culture and way of life—a truly eye-opening experience!

7. You'll become more mature. Students who study abroad are often told by friends and family that they seem more mature when they return. When you live on your own for a period of time and have to adjust to a new environment, you naturally become more self-sufficient. Plus, you may come back better equipped to deal with social situations, because you've spent time interacting with students you've never met before and who may not even speak the same language as you. When you share a home with a host family, as many students do while studying abroad, you learn how to cope with family life in an entirely new way as well. You may find that you become more accepting of people—a sign of maturity and increased tolerance.

8. You'll go far beyond your usual comfort zone. When you travel to an unfamiliar place and have to adapt to a new environment, you're forced to rely on yourself more than ever before. You won't always have your family or friends there to help you figure out what to do. You'll most likely face everyday challenges—communicating with your host family, tasting new foods, using foreign currency—that force you to grow and get more comfortable taking risks. Some students are surprised at how much they learn about their own strengths and weaknesses when adjusting to a foreign culture. You'll most likely come home with better people skills, a higher confidence level, and a newfound sense of independence.

9. You'll be taking advantage of a great opportunity. Let's face it—probably at no other time will you be so free of responsibilities that you can leave home to pursue a program of study that interests you. Right now, you're young and (pardon the cliché) you've got your whole life ahead of you. You don't have a full-time job to prevent you from taking time off, and you probably don't have a spouse or kids to consider. You're at the prime of your youth, so you most likely have few health problems and lots of energy. This is a great time in your life to travel and seek adventure!

10. You'll feel energized. A change of scenery can do wonders for your outlook. If you're feeling unmotivated at school or frustrated at home, spending some time away from your friends, family, and usual surroundings might be a positive solution. Many students who study abroad say that their spirits were renewed through travel.

11. You'll have a way to explore your interests and develop new ones. As a teen, you're becoming your own person, a process that involves defining your interests and thinking about your future. Study abroad can be a key part of your development by giving you the chance to pursue an interest while growing as an individual. You never know: following a specific interest overseas might ultimately give you a greater sense of purpose or even change your life's course.

12. You'll gain valuable skills. Fluency in a foreign language can be an asset in the future, as you decide what career to pursue. So can experience with other cultures, peoples, traditions, and ways of life. Because the world is rapidly becoming more connected through computers and the Internet, people in leadership positions need the kinds of skills that come from time spent abroad, including greater awareness, tolerance, and understanding of others.

13. You'll have something exciting to add to your college applications. If college is a path you eventually choose, you'll soon be filling out applications and writing the required "personal statement" or essay(s). Your applications will be more impressive if you can describe a study abroad experience. Admissions officers will see that you had both the initiative and courage to leave home and travel to a distant land as a teen. You'll seem more diverse and culturally aware.

14. You'll become more self-reliant. It's difficult to leave behind friends and family, no matter how excited you may be about your travels. Even though you may miss your loved ones a lot, you'll be busy getting to know your host family or making new friends. Being away from the people you're closest to gives you an opportunity to learn to handle the ups and downs of life on your own. Plus, if college is in your future, you'll be separated from your family even longer then; breaking away from them now for a shorter period of time can be good preparation for what's to come. Some teens use their time abroad to reinvent themselves. They feel more free to change their look or outlook; this kind of experimentation can be a positive, healthy form of self-expression.

15. You'll learn things you simply can't learn in school. No matter how engaging your teachers are, you probably have your moments of thumb-twiddling and clock-watching in class. Study abroad can add some much-needed excitement to your high school experience. While studying abroad, you may not even be in a classroom with walls! Instead, you'll probably go on field trips where you're free to explore ruins, view famous relics, talk to the people you meet, practice your language skills, learn new customs, and get a taste of everyday life in foreign places. These independent, hands-on activities teach you more about life and learning than facts on a chalkboard *ever* could.

16. You'll change in ways you can't anticipate. Maybe you'll discover that you're braver or more independent than you ever thought you could be. Maybe you'll grow closer to your family as you keep in touch through long letters or emails describing how much you miss each other. Maybe you'll meet someone overseas who becomes a friend for life. Study abroad means a change of environment, a change of pace, and a change in the path you've been on so far. Without a doubt, you'll be a different person when you come back, forever changed (in a good way) as a result of all your experiences.

SPOTLIGHT ON

Sidsel Overgaard
Penn Yan Academy
Penn Yan, New York

Having the ability to say *rod grode med flode* has been my lifelong claim to fame. To an American, this guttural phrase meaning "red sauce with cream" sounds like the desperate cry of someone about to choke on her cornflakes. But in Denmark, these words carry a huge significance—anyone capable of pronouncing them correctly is obviously a Dane, no DNA test required. I am, in fact, legally half Danish and have always been able to spout off these words as proof of my heritage. But at the age of seventeen, after spending almost my entire life living in a small town in western New York, I decided that knowing one phrase wasn't enough. I wanted to be able to carry on a conversation with my Danish grandparents, and I sought a better understanding of my father's home country.

So, I packed my bags and headed off to spend the fall semester of my senior year studying at a folk high school in Denmark. It's difficult to describe the Scandinavian folk high school system because there's no American equivalent. Folk high school students take classes in the arts, humanities, and sciences, but they rarely have homework, they don't take tests, and they don't receive grades. Rather than forcing students to memorize details (which often seem meaningless to teenagers grappling with much larger questions in their own lives), teachers demonstrate how different courses relate to one another and how students can find broader relevance in what they're learning. For example, one of the courses offered at my folk high school, "The Good Life," combined philosophy, oral history, and writing to help students explore their own definitions of a well-lived life. My stay at Egaa Ungdoms Folke Hoejskole, outside the city of Aarhus, turned out to be one of the best experiences of my life.

While at Egaa, I lived in one of six houses with twelve students each—all Danish. The seventy-two of us ate, sang, and hosted parties together. Not only did I learn Danish in record time (missing all the jokes everyone was telling served as excellent motivation), but I also got my first solid lesson in people skills. One of the principle tenets of the folk high school system centers on the idea that "finding yourself" has as much to do with exploring social relationships as it does with introspection.

Living with twelve housemates for five months, I definitely got to experience all kinds of social interaction. Trying to divide household cleaning and cooking duties among a dozen people led to definite moments of frustration. We all soon learned the art of tactful discussion and conflict resolution. Also, for the first time in my life I had a long-term roommate, which proved to be excellent preparation for college life. All in all, while tensions may have run high at times, I have never felt so close to such a diverse group of people. I quickly learned that I had much in common with the nose-, eyebrow-, and tongue-ringed girl, the thrasher boy next door, and, most surprisingly, my teachers (all of whom we called by their first names).

Before going to Denmark, the thought of entering a room full of people that I didn't know would have caused a mild panic attack. Now I enter new situations much more easily with the knowledge that, because we're all human, there's always something to talk about. And if at some point in our relationships we face a disagreement, there's always a way to resolve it. These realizations have helped me countless times, and I know that they'll continue to be invaluable lessons for the rest of my life.

SPOTLIGHT ON

Shanna Kirschner
Loy Norrix High School
and the Kalamazoo Area
Math and Science Center
Kalamazoo, Michigan

When I was fifteen, I spent my sophomore year in the America Israel High School Exchange program on Kibbutz Beit Hashita. (A kibbutz is a community where property is owned collectively.) Beit Hashita is a large kibbutz, located in the Valley of Jezreel, midway between the towns of Afula and Beit She'an. The area is breathtakingly beautiful, with rolling hills covered by fields and Mount Gilboa in the background. Periodically, the kibbutzim are filled with a riot of color as the bougainvillea or some other prominent plant comes into bloom.

There were twenty-eight American and Canadian students in my class. We lived in small buildings in the center of the kibbutz, close to where the older Israeli high-schoolers live when they move out of their homes. (Kids at Beit She'an move out of their family home when they reach twelfth grade to go live in a dormitory on the kibbutz.) We studied at the regional school at Kibbutz Ein Harod, about ten minutes down the road. Our classes were separate from those of the Israeli kids, and were held in English. The curriculum was designed to be much the same as in an American school, with standard courses such as British literature, American or European history, chemistry or biology, and math. There were also classes on the Bible and Israeli history and geography, as well as intensive Hebrew lessons each day.

Everyone on the kibbutz does some kind of work to support the community. Thursday was our work day. (We didn't attend school that day, but classes were held on Sunday, so we were still in school five days a week.) People worked in a variety of areas, including the petting zoo, the cow sheds, the dining hall, and the laundry. In addition, Beit Hashita has a large factory for canning olives, pickles, and cocktail onions, and many students worked there. I worked in what was called the old-age home, and it was an incredible experience. Some of the people in the home were Holocaust survivors who had helped build the state of Israel and the kibbutz, and they all had interesting stories to tell. The job was emotionally draining because I came to love the residents, and it was hard to watch them dying. At the end of the year, they threw a goodbye party for me and the other student who worked there. The obvious love that they felt for us touched me deeply, and I still treasure a picture they gave me.

We took many trips over the course of the year, which gave us a great opportunity to see more of the country and apply some of what we were learning at school. My favorite trip was one we took with all of the older kids from the kibbutz. We spent five days camping and hiking in the Judean desert. Being on foot in the heat was hard work—we got very hot and tired. By the last day of the trip, we were completely filthy and exhausted, but the feeling of accomplishment was amazing.

All of us in the exchange program were "adopted" by families who lived on the kibbutz; although we didn't physically live with them, we usually ate dinner at their houses and would spend some time together with them each evening. As an only child, I really loved having two younger brothers and a little sister. My family was one of the best things that happened to me in Israel. The love, warmth, and generosity they showed got me through many tough times.

When I left the States, I thought I knew what I was getting into: I was going on this program to get away from home, have fun, and spend some time in Israel. I had visited the country briefly once before and loved it. But this time was different. The first few months were very hard. I had trouble adjusting to the unfamiliar dining hall food and the dorm-style living. Academically, things moved much more slowly than I would have liked, so I was often bored in my classes, even though the teachers let me work independently some of the time. I was homesick, too—a lot of us were, and I don't know that there's any way to prevent that. My adopted family helped me through this, and it also helped to be part of a group of Americans who were feeling pretty much the same way.

Many close friendships developed among the kids in our exchange group. It was difficult, though, to form friendships with the Israeli kids. We were the tenth class from the U.S. and Canada to participate in the program, and I think that the kids on the kibbutz were getting tired of making friends and then watching them leave each year. While some of the Americans and Israelis formed individual friendships, two of my biggest regrets are that we didn't become close as groups and that I didn't make any Israeli friends my age.

People who read and watch reports of terrorism in Israel may wonder if it was dangerous for me to be there, and I want to stress that it was *not.* Many people have asked me whether I was afraid to go live in Israel and asked my parents how they could let me do it. The truth is, the overall crime rate in Israel is extremely low, and the program took all possible precautions to ensure our safety. However, we did come into contact with terrorism. A girl from my kibbutz was killed in a bus bombing and there was a kidnapping as well as two other bus bombings during the year. Israelis are deeply affected by these incidents, and people all over the country are in mourning following every attack. As Americans living in Israel, we also experienced these emotions.

I do think that the program heightened my Jewish awareness. Though there were exceptions, pretty much everyone in the program was Jewish. Judaism is a part of the everyday culture in Israel, so it's hard not to develop a sense of Jewish pride and identification when you're there. One tough thing to readjust to when I came home was all the materialism in the United States. I think this was made harder by the fact that I no longer had my American friends from the program nearby.

I would definitely recommend a program like this to other kids. Although, academically, the time I spent on Kibbutz Beit Hashita wasn't as enlightening as I'd expected, I feel strongly that the other experiences I had there more than made up for that, changing my life completely and making me a far better person. I grew up a lot. As I learned to survive on my own and overcome homesickness, I found strength in myself I didn't know I had. Working in the old-age home and coming into contact with the effects of terrorism matured me and made me much more serious.

My year in Israel completely changed my outlook on life and the world. I met many incredible people and had experiences, both good and bad, that I'll remember for the rest of my life. I journaled from time to time—mostly when I was frustrated, even despairing, from some of my experiences. Today, those notes serve to remind me that there is a world very unlike the one in which I live, yet at the same time, with people much like me.

Choosing a Program That's Right for You

So you've decided to go somewhere. What now? The possibilities are endless. Before you start packing, take a moment to think about what kind of program might interest you most. Part of the independence you'll gain from studying abroad begins before you even set foot on foreign ground—when you take charge of your experience from the start. You can rely on yourself to scout

out the programs that interest you, gather the application materials, and turn them in on time. Ideally, planning should begin a full year before the day you jet off to another country.

There are two main types of study abroad programs: *traditional* and *language study.* Traditional programs involve study in a group setting, whether in a classroom, in a meeting room, or out in the field (at historical sites, for example). Most of these programs have themes—biology, ecology, culture, peace studies—plus some language instruction, if applicable. (For instance, my program in London focused on British literature and theater. We saw many Shakespearean plays, read the works of British writers, and toured famous authors' childhood or ancestral homes.) The programs may last anywhere from a few weeks to an entire year; many occur in the summer, a popular time for high school students to go abroad. Students may homestay with a local family or reside in a dormitory, apartment, hostel, or hotel, depending on what's offered. Some study abroad programs have an independent study component, like a project or final paper.

Language study programs focus primarily on teaching a foreign language. Some of these programs are sponsored by organizations or universities; most are sponsored by language institutes that are open to students of all ages and backgrounds. The classes cater to all levels of proficiency—from beginner to advanced—and may last for three or four hours each day. A homestay is usually part of the experience because one of the best ways to learn a language is to be immersed in it twenty-four hours a day.

What exactly is a homestay? It's an opportunity to stay with a host family in the country you're visiting. Host families come in many varieties, but what they all have in common is a willingness to extend their hospitality to a foreign student. Most host families choose to welcome a student because they're interested in cross-cultural understanding and enrichment. As a guest of your hosts, you're exposed to the culture, traditions, and family rituals of the country. The idea of participating in the daily activities of a host family may not appeal to you, especially if you feel that there's too great an element of the unknown. After all, you'll be living in close quarters with people you've never even met, and you won't know ahead of time what their expectations and habits are. On the other hand, maybe you'd enjoy the chance to form a bond with a foreign family, instead of living with other students in a dorm or hostel. Both alternatives have advantages, so think carefully about what type of environment you might be most comfortable in.

DIRECT ENROLLMENT AND STUDENT EXCHANGES

Direct enrollment programs offer students the chance to enroll directly into a high school in a foreign country. This type of cultural immersion is intense and requires fluency in the language. Another option is the student exchange, which provides the opportunity to travel to a foreign country for a year, go to school there, and live with a host family. The following year, you return and a foreign student comes to live with your family and attend your high school. (Direct enrollment *doesn't* involve an exchange.) With both options, you find yourself in a completely new academic setting, where everyone else speaks the language with fluency. If you're considering these alternatives, be sure to talk to past participants to get the scoop on what it's like to adapt to a different place and spend such a long time away from home.

The choices for study abroad may seem overwhelming at first. Before looking at program brochures and guides, ask yourself what you hope to gain from this learning opportunity. What are your main goals? Do you want to:

• become more proficient in a language?

- become fluent in a language?

- tour a specific part of the world?

- gain new skills?

- meet people?

- help people?

- live with a host family?

- get some work experience?

- get an insider's view of a foreign country?

Is your goal altogether different from these?

Once you've made a list of your goals, ask yourself where you want to go. What place will best help you meet your objectives? These questions are key:

- Would you feel better sticking with an English-speaking country, like England, Ireland, or New Zealand? Or do you want to focus on learning another language through immersion?

- Do you want to go to a remote place that you may never again have the chance to visit?

- Are you interested in a program that lets you visit only one country or one that allows you to see many?

- Do you want to visit a developing country? Or would it be too difficult for you to live someplace that may or may not have reliable electricity and indoor plumbing?

- Are you adaptable? How easy is it for you to adjust to new surroundings and leave behind the comforts of home?

If you're the adventurous type, you might prefer a remote area of Africa. If you're a person who likes things to be mostly the way they are at home, then Western Europe might be a better choice for you. Maybe you want to explore the land where your ancestors originally hailed from. Maybe your family once had a foreign exchange student, and you want to visit his or her homeland. Perhaps you'd prefer to stay in North America, in which case a summer in Montreal or a year in Mexico might be a good bet for you.

Next, think about the kind of person you are and what kind of academic experience you want:

- Can you handle coursework (lectures, readings, assignments) in a foreign language? Or would you prefer classes that are taught in English?

- Are you able to work under minimal teacher supervision? Or do you prefer regular lectures, papers, and assignments?

- Does structure appeal to you? Can you deal with a less-structured day? Will you find creative ways to use your time, or do you think you'll feel bored without a specific plan?

- Are you looking for lots of academic challenge, or are you more interested in seeing sites, meeting people, and having a relaxed pace of learning?

- Do you want to be gone for a summer, a semester, or a full year?

Consider when may be the best time to go. Freshman year may not work, since you're just getting accustomed to high school and may need that time to make friends. Second semester of sophomore year might be the right time, as by then you've gotten used to the high school routine. Junior year seems to be the most popular time to go abroad. (Many juniors feel that they're at the right age to go, plus they don't have to worry about the college-application process quite yet.) At the beginning of senior year, you may be too busy applying to college; at the end of senior year, you may not want to miss prom or graduation. It's up to you to decide when travel may fit your schedule of academic and social activities.

Don't overlook your budget when deciding what kind of study abroad program may be right for you. When calculating the budget for your trip, make sure you take into consideration all of the program fees, the transportation costs, and the personal spending money you'll need. Some programs offer scholarships or financial aid, which may be of help. You can also find ways to raise money on your own. See pages 210–215 for more information about funding your trip.

Keep in mind, too, that your parents, teachers, and relatives may be skeptical when you bring up the idea of going abroad. Be prepared to answer their questions about your motives for studying abroad, instead of getting defensive. If you handle this part of the process with independence and maturity, you'll show the adults in your life that you're determined and serious about this experience.

Begin your search for the right study abroad program by seeing what kind of information your school may have. Talk to your guidance counselor, foreign language teacher, or principal. You may come away from these conversations with brochures and applications, or just a few program names—a good starting point either way. Another alternative is to seek out directories of study abroad programs, which may be available at your local library or bookstore. Typically, these guides are organized by the name of the country, so it's important to have an idea of where you'd like to go. The Internet is another good source for listings of study abroad programs.

Once you've checked out the directories or found some possibilities, narrow down your list to four or five programs to pursue. You can contact the programs by phone, fax, email, or snail mail to express your interest and request further materials.

It's important to sit down and talk with your parents before beginning this information-gathering process, if you haven't already told them about your desire to study abroad. Your mom or dad will no doubt be curious when you start receiving informational materials—brochures, viewbooks, catalogs, applications—in the mail. Many teens find that, at first, their parents are reluctant about letting them join a study abroad program, and your parents may be, too. Your mom or dad might say you're "not responsible enough," you're "too young," or "you don't know what you're getting into." They may worry about the costs or feel anxious about your being away from home for an extended period of time. They may believe that you'll miss out on too many important social activities or that you won't meet your high school graduation requirements if you go abroad.

To reassure your parents, make sure you've got answers to any potential issues they may bring up. This means doing your homework ahead of time by reviewing the program guidelines and talking to your school about whether you'll get credit for your study abroad experience. Make sure that you're in good academic standing and will still be able to graduate on time with your class. If you're well informed when you approach your parents, you'll more easily turn those raised eyebrows into handshakes of congratulation.

It may also be helpful to involve your parents in the research process, so they don't feel left out. As you gather materials, show your parents the following:

1. proof that the study abroad program will be supervised
2. the names and credentials of the program directors, teachers, and administrators
3. the number of students accepted
4. a description of the orientation
5. information about housing, food, and other accommodations
6. information about the courses, field trips, and special events that are included
7. the screening process for host families, if applicable
8. the program costs and how you intend to pay for them
9. the quality of health care in the country you plan to visit, plus how the program handles the medical-care needs of students

Once you receive the catalogs or brochures in the mail, look at them closely. Which program has the features you want? Which one looks the most professional? Which fits your budget? Which one is in line with your goals? As you further narrow your options, share the information with your parents and ask them which program they have the

F. Y. I.

Having your parents talk to past program participants is one of the best ways to sway their opinions in your favor. When your parents hear what a life-changing experience someone else your age had, they may be more enthusiastic about your plans.

best feeling about. Sit down together and make a list of the pros and cons of each one.

Decide which program(s) you want to pursue, and then request an application online or by mail. (Check the deadline first, so you leave yourself plenty of time to get your materials together.) Most study abroad applications ask for your contact information—name, address, phone number, and so on; many also include an essay portion in which you describe why you want to go on the program. Your essay should be unique, professional (don't hand-write it), and neat. Use the same care in applying to study abroad programs as you would to colleges or jobs.

Now that you've done the hard part, all you have to do is sit by the mailbox and wait . . .

SPOTLIGHT ON
Rosha Forman
Riverdale County School
Hastings-on-Hudson, New York

The summer after my junior year, I participated in a SIT (School for International Training) World Learning program in Kenya. The program was six weeks long, and had different sections to it. The first week was an introduction to Swahili and an orientation. During the orientation we got to know other participants and discussed our goals for the program. Then we spent two weeks on the coast doing community service, working in villages every day. While we did the community service, we stayed in youth hostels or hotels. For one project we worked with the villagers, digging a hole in the ground to build a water catchment tank. I liked the fact that the program emphasized so much contact with the villagers—that was why I'd chosen this program.

The next two-and-a-half weeks was the homestay component. The program's philosophy is that you can't experience a culture without living with a family. Members of our group stayed in a variety of different villages. Before going to Africa, I had two conceptions about the climate: *hot* and *dry*. I was wrong and wrong again. The cities and villages that our group visited had varying climates and different styles of homes. Some, like Nairobi, were urban. Others were coastal. A few did have a dry landscape and climate. However, of all the places I visited in Kenya, my favorite was my homestay village on the border of Uganda where it was wet, leafy, and cold at night.

The houses there were square huts with tin or thatched roofs. Almost every home had a cow outside, tied to a tree. My house was an exception to all the others, because it was blue. Bright, light, clear blue, like the color of the sky on a perfect summer's day. The roof was a sheet of tin, so when it rained at night, the sound of the rain was so loud that it kept me awake.

My host mother was a teacher and my host father was unemployed, which gave the family an average socioeconomic status in Kenya. They had a concrete hut with separate rooms, dirt floors, and no running water. When I walked into my house for the first time, I saw a very sparsely decorated, dark living room with a small couch, a little table surrounded by five wooden chairs, and a coffee table. We had been told that only the richest of the families would have electricity, and I was both relieved and disappointed to see a bare light bulb hanging from the ceiling. "You have electricity?" I asked my host mother. "No," she said. "Then why the light bulb?" I asked. "For decoration," she replied.

From the living room an outside hallway led to the open kitchen, which had a wooden fireplace for cooking and a door that opened to a bedroom. This was my room. It belonged to the oldest boy in the family, who was living in Nairobi while attending college. The room had one window and a bed. On the walls were magazine cutouts of pop stars from the 1980s. There was a small bedside table with a bowl of bananas and a small chair. The bathroom was an outdoor outhouse, and the bathtub was a small cement closet with two buckets of water, one cold and one that my host mom would heat. I liked this simple living. I wanted to experience the typical Kenyan lifestyle, and that's what I did.

I noticed that there was no real place for storage: no closets, very few shelves, and no extra rooms. The family simply did not have extra stuff. That was very different from the homes of my family and friends in the States. I realized that Americans buy a lot of needless things. Before my trip, I had lived only in the U.S., where people drive cars everywhere, constantly work to be efficient and productive, and need to have the things they want NOW. Nothing in my experience had suggested to me that things should be any other way. Until Kenya. In my homestay village, being efficient and productive, driving fast cars everywhere, and using lots of high-tech equipment weren't possible—yet the people were living good lives. Experiencing this helped me put American values into perspective, and realize that there are other valid ways to live.

FIND OUT MORE

Academic Year Abroad 2000–2001: The Most Complete Guide to Planning Academic Year Study Abroad by Sara J. Steen (New York: Institute of International Education, 2000). The guide describes almost 2,500 programs representing over 70 countries worldwide. Many, but not all, of the opportunities listed are available to high school students. Learning options range from lecture courses and intensive language immersion to internships and voluntary service.

The Exchange Student Survival Kit by Bettina Hansel (Yarmouth, ME: Intercultural Press, 1993). If you're thinking seriously about becoming an exchange student, this book was written with you in mind. It will help you understand the unique experience of international exchange programs and avoid many of the common misunderstandings and problems that can occur.

Peterson's Learning Adventures Around the World, edited by Peter Greenberg (Princeton, NJ: Peterson's Guides, 1998). Are you looking for a unique traveling experience? Check out this book. Whether you want to work, study, experience a new culture, or just relax, you'll find plenty of ideas.

The Student's Guide to the Best Study Abroad Programs by Greg Tannen and Charley Winkler (New York: Pocket Books, 1996). As study abroad veterans, the authors bring helpful information about available programs. Their "Top 25" highlights the programs they deem most worthy of attendance. The descriptions are presented in great detail and include interviews with program participants. You'll find information on financial aid, atmosphere, housing, workload, and more.

Study Abroad, 2000–2001 (UNESCO, Paris:1999). This biennial guide is the United Nations Educational, Scientific, and Cultural Organization's international guide to study opportunities and scholarships offered in 129 countries. It includes over 2,000 entries on courses and scholarships including addresses (with Web sites), admission requirements, application deadlines, financial aid, fees and living expenses in each country and, in some cases, work opportunities for students.

ASSE International Student Exchange Programs
228 North Coast Highway
Laguna Beach, CA 92651
www.asse.com

ASSE offers exchanges in a variety of countries to promote international understanding and cultural exchange to students ages fifteen to eighteen. There are three possibilities for U.S. students going abroad: the Academic Year Abroad, Summer Abroad, and Language Adventure. Scholarships are available.

EF International Language Schools
1 Education Street
Cambridge, MA 02141
1-800-992-1892
www.ef.com

EF offers year-long and shorter programs in twelve different countries. While abroad, participants live with a host family, attend high school, and can go to an optional language and culture camp held before the program actually starts. Financial aid is available and based on both need and academic performance. EF also offers school-based scholarships, for participants of schools that take in exchange students.

The Experiment in International Living
World Learning Inc.
Box 676, Kipling Road
Brattleboro, VT 05302
1-800-345-2929
www.usexperiment.org

The Experiment in International Living is a program that provides summer homestays with host families in over twenty countries. You must be between ages fifteen and eighteen to participate, but in most cases there is no minimum language requirement. Financial aid (based on family need) is available.

Intercambio Internacional de Estudiantes
16 Broadway, Suite 107
Fargo, ND 58102
1-800-437-4170

Intercambio sponsors exchanges between the U.S. and countries in Central America for students ages eleven to sixteen who speak some Spanish. The homestay is the focus of the program, and students whose families host Intercambio students from abroad receive a deduction in the program fee.

International Youth Hostel Federation (IYHF)
(202) 783-6161
www.iyhf.org

IYHF is a nonprofit agency that runs a worldwide network of hostels. Check out the Web site to find out more about hostels by country or to order a Hostelling International Guide.

Nacel Open Door
3410 Federal Drive, Suite 101
Saint Paul, MN 55122
1-800-NACELLE (1-800-622-3553)
www.nacelopendoor.org

Nacel Open Door offers various programs in the U.S. and abroad for teens ages sixteen to eighteen. Nacel also administers the Congress-Bundestag Vocational Exchange to Germany, which offers full one-year scholarships to graduating high school seniors with a vocational background. Participants receive two months of language preparation following their arrival in Germany, and then are able to pursue their vocational interests abroad. The scholarships cover the homestay and a professional training opportunity in Germany, but do not cover round-trip travel from the participant's home to Washington, D.C., or spending money. You must be nominated by your high school to apply for the program.

Get Ready, Get Set, Go

Once you've been accepted to a program, you can let out a yelp of joy, call your friends and neighbors, and let everyone know that you're going to study abroad. After the initial excitement has passed, sit down and make a list of all the things you'll need to take care of as soon as possible. Your list might look something like this:

1. Get a passport. If you don't already have one, you must get a passport if you want to travel out of the country. You'll need to apply in person to the passport agent at the U.S. Department of State. You can find agencies in Chicago, Honolulu, New York City, Miami, New Orleans, Boston, Houston, Los Angeles, Seattle, Washington, D.C., Philadelphia, San Francisco, or Stamford, Connecticut. You can also apply for a passport with a clerk of any federal court or state court of records, as well as through selected post offices. You need proof of U.S. citizenship (birth certificate, naturalization certificate, or previous U.S. passport), two recent photographs, and a current I.D. (such as a driver's license). Apply early, because processing an application can take four to six weeks.

2. Get a visa. A visa is written permission granted by the government of your country to visit your host country. Visa requirements vary from country to country and are fully described in *Visa Requirements of Foreign Governments* (Publication M-264), available at any passport agency or by writing to the Office of

Passport Services, Room 386, 1425 K Street NW, Washington, D.C. 20524. If you're planning to study in a country for an extended period of time, you may need to get a special student visa. Information relating to all visas may be obtained from the nearest embassy or consulate of the host country. You'll probably need to supply passport-type photos with your visa application. These may be kept on file or incorporated into the visa itself. Keep in mind that you may not need to obtain a visa on your own—some programs take care of this for their participants.

3. Visit your doctor. It's important to make sure your vaccinations are up to date, as well as to find out what vaccines you'll need for your particular trip. Some countries require visitors to have vaccination certificates to prove they've had certain shots. Check with your local health department for your host country's regulations; otherwise you could risk getting seriously ill while abroad or not being let into the country at all. Make sure any prescription drugs you bring are labeled by the pharmacy and in the original bottles. It's also a good idea to bring along extra medication, because your prescription drugs may not be available in your host country. If you wear glasses, make sure you buy an extra pair or have extra contact lenses. Leave a copy of your prescription with your parents and bring one for yourself, in case you need to get corrective lenses abroad or phone home to get them.

4. Get an International Student Identity Card (ISIC). This fabulous piece of plastic gets you discounts on everything from airline tickets to museum admissions. The ISIC is issued by the Council on International Educational Exchange. Basically, it's a card that students ages twelve and up who are enrolled in a study program can use both in the U.S. and abroad. To obtain an ISIC, visit any Council Travel office. You'll need to submit an application with the following: one passport-size photo (with your name in pencil on the back), a check or money order to cover the fee, and some sort of proof of student status (contact Council Travel for more details on this). For the location of an office near you, call 1-888-COUNCIL (1-888-268-6245) or go to: *www.counciltravel.com*.

5. Buy the right clothing and supplies. Appropriate clothing for your host climate is crucial, especially if you're traveling to a very warm or cold area. Read up on your host country's clothing restrictions and recommendations. You may also want to talk to the program directors about what to wear and how much to bring. A good rule of thumb: PACK LIGHT. Keep in mind that you'll be carrying everything yourself, so don't overload your bags. One important purchase to make is a money belt, which is a pouch that ties around your waist or hangs from your neck and closes with a zipper at the top (it should be large enough to hold your passport, credit cards, and cash). A money belt is much better than a fanny pack or purse, which can be cut off without your even knowing it, especially in crowded places like buses or train terminals. One final essential: a foreign-language dictionary!

"When I arrived in Beijing, with a small rolling suitcase and a backpack, I was ashamed to see that although I thought I had 'packed light' there was nowhere to put all my belongings. Suddenly my practical clothing seemed too flashy; my Chinese sister only had one set of clothes besides her blue school uniform. She insisted on giving up her bed for the three months I was there, and slept on a couch in her parents' bedroom. My sister's bed, so generously offered, was a platform with some horsehair pads and a bag of rice in a pillowcase."—**Susannah**

6. Bring presents for your host family. In exchange for your host family's hospitality, bring along small gifts, such as a book about your home state or another souvenir. When I studied abroad in Japan, I brought the students who hosted me T-shirts from Minnesota, a couple of state postcards, and a picture book with photos of the Twin Cities. They loved the gifts because they had never been to the U.S. before; even though they didn't know English, they could look at the pictures and get an idea of where I was from. Your host family will also be interested in seeing photos of your family, home, school, and friends, so be sure to pack a small photo album. It's a good idea to contact your host family before you leave home. Write a letter or an email introducing yourself and letting them know how excited you are about your visit.

7. Figure out your financial arrangements. Talk to your mom or dad about whether it's best to use traveler's checks or an ATM card while abroad. You'll most likely also want to bring along a credit card for emergencies. Before you go, make a photocopy of everything in your wallet and leave the copy with your parents (this will be useful if your wallet or money belt is lost or stolen). Be sure to change some U.S. dollars into the currency of your country before you leave home, so you have some quick cash for food or other necessities when you arrive.

8. Make your travel plans. In some cases, the program fee will include your transportation costs (plane ticket) to the host country, but if not, you'll need to make your own arrangements. For overseas travel, make your reservations at least one to two months in advance to get a better price. You can contact a student travel agency or look for discounted plane tickets online.

9. Prepare yourself mentally. You're about to embark on a journey of gargantuan proportions, so be sure you're ready for it. If you don't know the language of your host country well, get some books and tapes that can help you learn more. You can also read books and magazines (*Transitions Abroad* and *Student Travels* are good ones) about life overseas. And you can do research about your host country's culture, history, politics, literature, and music. It's also helpful to brush up on the history, politics, and pop-culture scene of your own country because the people you meet will probably ask you lots of questions.

10. Get ready to say good-bye. Your friends, family, and girlfriend or boyfriend will definitely miss you when you're gone, and vice versa. To stay in touch, sign up with a long-distance calling plan before you leave home and get a calling card or special access number. Collect the home addresses and email addresses of everyone you want to keep in contact with. You may want to take photos of your loved ones right before you go, so you have current pictures to look at and show to the new people you meet.

You've got a lot to look forward to in your travels, and before you know it, your departure date will be here. Bon voyage!

SPOTLIGHT ON

Jesse Twain
Mount Desert Island High School
Mount Desert, Maine

My experience abroad took place on the island of Falalop in the Ulithi Atoll of Yap state, in the Federated States of Micronesia. My host family, and indeed the entire local populace, constantly went out of their way to make me happy. Still, there were many little things that made my adjustment very hard. I showered every morning with rainwater that ran off my roof through a gutter and emptied into a trash can. I spent quite a bit of time on nearby islands that had no electricity at all—and even on Falalop having electricity didn't mean we had all of the everyday American-style utilities. What helped me through this experience? With anything of this nature, a person needs most of all to be adaptable. The ability to just go with the flow got me through the year. It was difficult, but once I got used to the food, adjusted to the hot, humid climate, got comfortable with the living conditions, and learned some of the local language, I found it was well worth the effort. In fact, I'm going back to Micronesia for a second year!

FIND OUT MORE

Americans Traveling Abroad: What You Should Know Before You Go by Gladson I. Nwanna (Baltimore: World Travel Institute Press, 1996). If you have questions about cultural do's and don'ts, vaccinations, or any other topic, you'll likely find an answer here. A comprehensive guide to safe and knowledgeable travel, this book discusses everything from being stranded to standard tipping.

Health Information for International Travel, 1999–2000 Edition (Atlanta: International Medical Publishing, 1999). This reference book is published annually and advises international travelers about the risks they might encounter when traveling abroad. It specifies the required vaccinations of different countries and includes information on measures travelers can take to protect their health.

The Packing Book: Secrets of the Carry-On Traveler by Judith Gilford (Berkeley: Ten Speed Press, 1998). If you can't imagine taking anything less than your two largest suitcases on a trip, then check out this book. The author offers information on getting the most out of packing, from choosing the right kind of luggage to selecting what clothes to bring. You'll find plenty of checklists, detailed instructions (including illustrations), and a whole lot more.

The Pocket Doctor: A Passport to Healthy Travel, Third Edition by Stephen Bezruchka, M.D. (Seattle: Mountaineers, 1999). *The Pocket Doctor* provides you with all the information you need to prepare for a trip, stay healthy while traveling, and care for health problems that may arise during the journey. Topics include finding medical help abroad, common and not-so-common illnesses, general health advice, and life-threatening emergencies.

Centers for Disease Control and Prevention Hotline
1-877-FYI-TRIP (1-877-394-8747)
www.cdc.gov/travel

This toll-free automated travelers' hotline is accessible from a touchtone phone or on the Web twenty-four hours a day, seven days a week. It provides information on requirements and recommendations for the international traveler and is updated as needed.

Government Printing Office
travel.state.gov/asafetripabroad.html

The U.S. government releases several publications related to traveling outside of the country. Visit the Web site to review *A Safe Trip Abroad*, or order specific documents such as *Tips for Travelers to the Middle East and North Africa* or *Tips for Travelers to the People's Republic of China*. A listing of publications can be viewed at the Web site.

International Student Travel Confederation (ISTC)
www.istc.org

ISTC is a nonprofit confederation of student travel organizations around the world whose focus is to develop, promote, and facilitate travel among young people and students. ISTC members provide student flights, other forms of transportation, student and youth cards, travel insurance, work exchange programs, and lots more.

Penpals.net
www.penpals.net

Pen pals from other countries are a great way to get an introduction to life abroad. You can ask all sorts of questions, and your pen pal will probably be more than happy to respond. Penpals.net is a free service that links you up with another person who's interested in communicating. You can choose pals by country or age.

Making the Most of Your Experience

"I am naturally shy, and I worried a lot about how to be more out-going so I could make friends with the other participants on my program. Instead of holding back and waiting for others to make the first move, I got together all my courage and went up to them. It paid off because I made lots of friends and had a great time."—**Abby**

It's an exciting and scary feeling to arrive in a new country where you don't know anyone. You may feel a mix of emotions: fear, loneliness, exhilaration, anxiety, exhaustion. You may think,

"What in the world am I doing?" one moment and "I can't believe how cool this is!" the next. It may take a few days to calm down and begin the process of adjusting to your new environment.

One of the first things you'll probably do is meet your host family or the other students in the program. Depending on how familiar you are with the language, conversation may be awkward at first. Many students who've been through this experience before recommend keeping an open mind and staying positive. Make an effort to talk, introduce yourself to others, and explore your new home, school, and community. The more involved you are in school or community activities, the more confident you'll feel about the whole experience.

If you're in a country that's completely different from your own, you may experience culture shock, or sensory overload, at first. Culture shock includes feeling irritable, moody, and disoriented. If you get culture shock, don't hesitate to talk to one of the program leaders. He or she may be able to help you work through your feelings and can help bridge the gap between the two cultures. Keep in mind that feeling overwhelmed is normal and that interacting with your host family or the other students is a good way to adjust. Writing in a journal can also be of help.

"As soon as I got to Japan, I felt completely disoriented. I was blown away by how many formalities exist in the Japanese culture: people bow to each other all the time, even to people they're talking to on the phone. And the Japanese language has all sorts of honorifics (words used to convey respect). The food was different too: lots of raw fish, tea, and rice. I felt I was in over my head big-time for the first month or so. Sometimes I'd feel so out of place that I'd just sit in my room for hours, alone, trying to sort things out. Eventually it got better, though."—**Jon**

It's also important to have a sense of humor about what happens on a day-to-day basis. You may have to communicate with your host family mainly in gestures. Or you may be at a foreign restaurant with all your new classmates and mistakenly ask someone to please pass the "toilet paper" instead of the salt. If you goof up, laugh it off. At other times, you may feel a bit helpless in your new surroundings. What if you realize that you have no idea how to count your money, read the train schedules, or find your way to the nearest drug store? Instead of panicking, try to take it all in stride. Ask for help when you need it and keep your outlook positive. Gradually, you'll adapt to life abroad.

While adjusting to your new city or country, you may feel especially vulnerable. You might wonder if you're in danger or imagine all sorts of terrible things happening to you. If you're concerned about your safety, take some precautions. Dress like the locals and avoid wearing clothing that identifies you as a tourist (shirts with American symbols or logos on them, for example). Unless you're taking photographs, keep your camera tucked away. On the streets, follow the same commonsense rules you would in the United States: Walk with confidence and keep your eyes open for anything suspicious. Stay with a group when possible. If you plan to go somewhere alone, tell people ahead of time so they know where you'll be and when to expect you back.

How NOT to look like a local!

Most likely, you'll have a great experience abroad, and your initial sense of anxiety will be replaced by self-assurance and self-reliance. Each day, you'll feel a little more confident about your routine, your ability to converse with others, and your willingness to get out there and explore. But not all students have a positive experience while overseas. It's possible that you may run into obstacles you aren't prepared for and aren't sure how to handle. No matter how bad things may seem, you *do* have options other than taking the next flight home. Talking to your program leaders is the first step. You have the right to speak up if the program isn't meeting your basic needs or living up to your expectations. Most likely, the program leaders will do what they can to work with you and handle any problems that occur.

SPOTLIGHT ON

Molly Levin
Mountain Heritage High School
Burnsville, North Carolina

Coming from a strong, communicative family in rural North Carolina, I thought that I could get along and live with anyone. When I was placed with a family through my study abroad program, I was anxious about living in their home for six months, but confident that it would be a great experience.

Upon arrival in Bolivia, I was treated in a most *un*friendly way, especially by my host mother, who found fault with everything I did. At first, I thought this was because of cultural differences, but things got progressively worse. I wasn't allowed to have friends over to the house unless Mama was home to prepare a proper tea for them. She yelled at me when the hiking boots I wore every day left imprints (not dirt) in the plush pink carpet. I offered to help out in the house as often as I could, and otherwise I kept my mouth shut. Slowly, though, my sense of who I was and of what rational behavior was eroded. I slept a lot, stayed in my room as much as possible when I was home, and went out as often as I could.

The exchange program I was with refused to set me up with another host family. Luckily though, they had set me up with a contact—someone my age who was supposed to make sure everything was all right. At first, I didn't know whether I could trust Ana, but I eventually spilled all that was inside my head and heart to her. Ana was sympathetic and began to look for a family for me, but things were not coming along fast enough. In a fit of anxiety, I packed all my bags, set them by the front door, and asked my host father how I might call a taxi. I was planning to go to another Bolivian friend's house until a new family was found. My host father told me not to be so rash and to wait for things to work out in their own time. I agreed to do that, but kept everything packed until Ana gave me the news that her aunt had agreed to host me. However, the agency said I couldn't move until the housing and family situation had been checked out.

Almost to prove I still possessed free will, I decided that I would not spend one more night in that household. I took all my packed bags and moved to Ana's house until her aunt was approved as my new host mother. Ana's mother was so welcoming and supportive of me. "No one should have a bad experience in my country," she said. A few days later, I was officially told I could move into Ana's aunt's house. I was welcomed with open arms and hearts. In this household I began to regain what I had lost of myself and my sense of reality while in the first household. One uncle in the family invested much time in discussion with me and taught me a lot about the country, its people, and its language. I came to love and feel a connection with this second family of mine in Bolivia. This is what I had been searching for.

Do what you can to make your trip meaningful and memorable. Ask questions of your hosts, put your best effort into your classes, get to know the other students, visit all the sites you want to see, and most of all, focus on enjoying the time you have there. You may want to record your impressions in a travel journal that you can look back on later. If you bring along a camera (highly recommended), take pictures not only of the sites but also of the people you meet and your daily surroundings, so you'll never forget them. When you leave, be sure to collect home addresses and email addresses, so you can always stay in touch your newfound friends.

"The perfect journey is circular—
the joy of departure and the joy of return."
Dino Basili

Even though you'll feel glad to be back, you'll probably have many fond memories of your trip and you'll want to share them with others. You can continue making the most of your time abroad by finding ways to keep the experience alive. You could write an article for your school paper or talk to your classmates about your travels. If you're applying to college, you could describe your trip in the essay portion of the applications. If you're looking for an internship or part-time job, update your résumé to reflect your study abroad experience; discuss your travels when you're interviewing as well. What if you loved being abroad and you're itching to travel again? If it's within your means, maybe you could return to your host country or even plan an all-new trip. Once you've been bitten by the "alternative learning bug" (like I was), you may always be on the lookout for new and life-changing experiences. I hope you find them!

A Final Word

Alternative learning is about starting something. What you start may be small-scale or large-scale—the size of it isn't crucial. The most important thing is that you make an effort to take charge of your life. Many of the alternative learning experiences that you've read about in this book involve reaching outward—connecting with others at school; through your faith community or a community center; at local colleges or universities; in corporations or businesses; in your neighborhood, town, or city; or in other parts of the world. Making connections helps you learn and grow, but there are other ways to increase your learning and enrich your life. Following are some examples of learning experiences that you can initiate on your own—to boost your mind, body, and spirit *any* day or *every* day.

- **Keep a journal.** A journal is a great place to store your innermost thoughts and to work through personal problems. And if you secretly harbor a wish to be a famous writer someday, you can use your journal for practicing your writing techniques, storing memories, and creating kernels of wisdom.

- **Work out.** Countless studies have shown that teens who exercise on a regular basis are healthier, more fit, and more energetic—*and* have sharper minds. Take long walks, go for a run a few times a week, in-line skate, and find other ways to keep your body active. Working out not only teaches your body new moves but also improves your brain's ability to think clearly.

- **Feed your spirit.** Maybe you're part of a faith community or maybe not. Either way, there may be times when you question the meaning of life or feel a need to commune with someone or something larger than yourself. Your search for answers can involve saying a prayer, talking to a religious advisor, meditating, or spending time alone in nature— whatever feeds your spirit.

- **Become a family historian (of your own family).** Have you ever asked about a family tree or seen old photographs of your ancestors? Finding your roots can be a fascinating experience: you not only learn about your family but you may gain insights into yourself. Your local library should have books on how to trace your family's genealogy. You ma also want to talk to your parents, aunts and uncles, a grandparent, or distant relatives.

- **Become a letter writer (a lost art).** In the age of email, fax machines, and instant communication, fewer people are writing letters the old-fashioned way: in longhand. Staying in touch with people through the mail can be fun and creative, especially if you write long, expressive letters or send your own handmade cards.

- **Create a 'zine.** Do you have interesting ideas, strong opinions, a penchant for graphics, or a favorite topic of interest? Then create your own mini magazine, or 'zine. Do-it-yourself publishing could be your entrance to a new circle of friends and marketable computer skills. You could turn your 'zine into a mini business and charge a small fee per issue, or make it entirely free.

- **Develop your own Web site.** Whatever interests you for a 'zine is also ripe material for a Web site (many sites being nothing more than high-tech 'zines). Any search engine should be able to get you started. Try "Angelfire" (*www.angelfire.com*), which has a do-it-yourself approach to building personalized sites, including funky cursors, online image tools, and so on. Or take a look at "LissaExplains" (*www.lissaexplains.com*)— built and maintained by thirteen-year-old Lissa. This helpful site clarifies the process of building a Web site and gives you the technical tools to start one from scratch.

- **Start a collection.** Collections say something about what interests and intrigues you. Whether you collect stamps, coins, comic books, rocks, old books, shells, or something more unusual, it's the thrill of the hunt that makes the pursuit worthwhile. Some people remain collectors all their lives; over time, they amass a wealth of interesting treasures that keep them connected to their past and give them something memorable to pass on to future generations.

- **Learn a craft or an art.** What interests you most: woodworking, watercolor painting, sculpting, ceramics, collage, "found art," calligraphy, mixed media, jewelrymaking, leatherwork, decorative painting, stained glass? Why not teach it to yourself? You can find how-to books and Web sites on just about every art or craft under the sun.

- **Use your mind.** Read, build scale models, do crossword puzzles, test your knowledge of trivia, play chess or other board games, play a challenging video game . . . all of these activities boost your brain power and encourage you to learn something new.

Your days will never be dull when you make the most of the time you have and continue to be a curious, creative individual, now and always. In fact, this is known as being a lifelong learner. This approach to living can sharpen your mind, keep your body active, hone your creative-thinking skills, and help you to be a more interesting, inquisitive, and intriguing person—throughout your life.

Index

A

Aaronson, Josh, 47–48
Abosh, Paul, 105–106, 189–190
Academic Year Abroad 2000–2001, 238
Academy of Art College, 45
Acceleration programs, 56
Advanced Placement (AP)
    classes/exams, 54–55, 56
Adventure Careers, 108
Adventure programs
  athletic focus of, 191
  benefits of, 193–194
  examples of, 190
  finding more information about, 194–197
  making the decision, 192–193
  obtaining program listings, 191
  organization of, 191
  overseas, 198
  personal story about, 192
  reasons to consider, 178–179
Adventures Afloat, Teen SCUBA Diving &
    Sailing Camp, Ltd., 194
AFS International Intercultural Programs, 202
Akel, Joe, 206–207
Alternative learning
  benefits of, 2–5
  connecting with others through, 252
  deciding what you want to learn, 59
  definition of, 1–2
  self initiated
    challenging your mind, 254
    creating a magazine, 253
    developing a Web site, 253–254
    feeding your spirit, 252–253
    keeping a journal, 252
    learning a craft/art, 254
    researching family history, 253
    starting a collection, 254
    working out, 252
    writing letters, 253
  as a way of taking charge of your life, 252
Alternatives to the Peace Corps, 31
America Israel High School Exchange
    Program, 225–228
American Camping Association, 186
American Farm School, 32
American Friends Service Committee Youth
    Programs, 32
American Red Cross, 17–18
American-Scandinavian Foundation, 210
Americans Traveling Abroad, 245
America's Top Internships, 127
Amigos de las Americas, 33
Angelfire (Web site), 253
Annual Register of Grant Support 2000,
    210–211, 213
AP (Advanced Placement) classes/exams,
    54–55, 56

Apprenticeships, youth
  benefits of, 160–162, 176
  benefits to employers, 160
  controversy over, 163
  definition of, 158–159
  examples of, 159–160
  finding more information about, 173–174
  informal programs
    arranging coursework for, 168
    being persistent, 172
    developing a proposal, 170–172
    finding contacts for, 168–170
    formalizing the agreement, 172–173
    outlining your goals, 168
    personal story about, 174–176
  making the decision, 162
  through your school
    applying for, 166
    co-op programs, 164
    example of, 163
    personal story about, 166–168
    talking with your principal/counselor,
      164, 165
    tech prep programs, 164
  vs. career mentoring, internships, and job
    shadowing, 92–93
  vs. four-year degree programs, 161, 162
  vs. regular apprenticeships, 159
  See also Internships; Job shadowing;
    Mentoring
Apprenticeship Training Employer Labor
    Services offices, 173–174
Archaeological Institute of America, The, 194
ASSE International Student Exchange
    Programs, 238

B

*Back Door Guide to Short Term Job Adventures,
    The*, 128
Barron's Guide to Distance Learning, 54
Bartkow, Niki, 192
Bierma, Aisha, 110–111
Big Brothers Big Sisters of America, 72, 87
Bike-Aid, 195
Boston University's Sargent Camp, 187
Boy Scouts of America, 89
Brock, Henry, 174–176

C

California Mentor Foundation, 79
Camp Fire, Inc., 89
Camps, summer. *See* Summer camps
Career Choices, 108
Career Exploration on the Internet, 128
Career mentoring. *See under* Mentoring
Center for Creative Youth (CCY), 187
Center for Interim Programs, 200–202

Centers for Disease Control and Prevention Hotline, 245
CET Academic Programs, 203
Chapin, Hannah, 21–22
CLEP (The College Level Examination Program), 55, 56
Close Up Foundation, 195
Clubs, school service, 16–17
College Board Advanced Placement Program, 56
College classes, taking. *See* Distance learning; Dual enrollment; Early admission; Summer coursework
College Credit Without Classes, 46
College Degrees by Mail & Internet, 54
College Level Examination Program (CLEP), The, 55, 56
Communities in Schools, 72
Community-based learning, 57–58
Community Service for Teens, 24
Community service requirements, 17–19
Concordia Language Villages, 187
Connecticut Mentoring Partnership, 79
Co-op programs, 164
Corporation for National Service, 25
Correspondence courses, 53
Council on International Educational Exchange, 33
Cover letters. *See under* Résumés
Cover Letters They Don't Forget, 141
CTY Challenge Awards Program, The, 187–188

D

Delaware Mentoring Council, 79
deSieyes, Evan, 208–209
Devine, Katie, 51–52
Distance learning
    availability of, 53
    definition of, 53
    finding more information about, 54
    reasons to consider, 35–36, 53
    vs. correspondence courses, 53–54
    See also Dual enrollment; Early admission; Summer coursework
Do Something!, 25
Dual enrollment
    benefits of, 37, 38–39
    definition of, 37
    earning dual credits, 39
    making the decision, 37–38, 41–42
    managing your time, 42–44
    paying for college courses, 39
    personal story about, 40–41
    reasons to consider, 35–36
    See also Distance learning; Early admission; Summer coursework

E

Early admission
    example of, 48–49
    making the decision, 49–51
    personal story about, 51–52
    qualifying for, 49

reasons to consider, 35–36, 48
    See also Distance learning; Dual enrollment; Summer coursework
EarthWatch, 195
EF International Language Schools, 239
Enrichment programs, 55–56
eteen (Web site), 89
Everything Résumé Book, The, 139
Exchange Student Survival Kit, The, 238
Experiment in International Living, The, 203, 239

F

Ferguson's Guide to Apprenticeship Programs, 173
Financial Aid for Study and Training Abroad 1999–2001, 213
Foreign travel. *See* Traveling overseas
Forman, Rosha, 235–237
Free (and Almost Free) Adventures for Teenagers, 46
Free and Inexpensive Career Materials, 108
Future Is Ours, The, 24

G

Generation React, 24
Girl Geeks (Web site), 68
Girl Scouts of the USA, 89
Government Printing Office (Web site), 246
Governor's Mentoring Initiative, 79
Governor's Mentor Initiative, 80
Greisman, Erika, 23
Groundhog Job Shadow Day, 109

H

Habitat for Humanity, 10–11
Health Information for International Travel, 1999–2000, 245
Hendler, David, 18–19
Hewlett-Packard International Telementoring (Web site), 68
Hillenmeyer, Joseph, 200–202
Homesickness, 185
Homestays, 199, 229–230

I

Indentures, 166
Independent study, 56
Interact Club, 16
Intercambio Internacional de Estudiantes, 239
International Association of Lions Clubs, 16, 203
International Directory of Voluntary Work, The, 31
International Education Financial Aid (Web site), 214
International Partnership for Service-Learning, 33
International Student Identity Cards (ISIC), 241
International Student Travel Confederation (ISTC) (Web site), 246
International Teen Camp Lausanne, 203
International Youth Hostel Federation (IYHF), 239
Internship, Practicum, and Field Placement Handbook, The, 128

Internship Bible, The, 127
InternshipPrograms.com (Web site), 128
Internships
　applying for
　　building your résumé, 129–132, 135–136
　　chronological format résumés, 132, 133
　　finding more information about cover
　　　letters, 141
　　finding more information about résumés,139
　　functional format résumés, 132, 134
　　posting your résumé online, 138
　　tips for effective résumés, 137–138
　　writing your cover letter, 139–141
　benefits of
　　acquiring letters of reference, 121
　　demonstrating your reliability, 120
　　getting job experience, 120
　　improving your résumé, 120
　　learning new information, 119
　　learning to use new tools, 120
　　making better choices, 120
　　making professional contacts, 114, 119
　benefits to employers, 118
　brainstorming ideas for, 122–123
　clarifying your goals, 121–122
　definition of, 118
　examples of, 113, 115–116
　finding contacts for, 126–127
　finding more information about, 127–128
　getting paid for, 124
　interviewing for
　　finding more information about, 149
　　personal story about, 147–148
　　preparing for the interview, 142–145
　　tips for successful interviews, 145–147
　making the most of the experience
　　accepting additional responsibilities, 152
　　clarifying expectations, 150
　　finding more information about, 157
　　learning your job, 151
　　making the final decision, 149–150
　　personal story about, 154–156
　　resolving problems, 152–153
　　surviving the first day, 150–151
　　taking advantage of opportunities, 153
　　working independently, 152
　overseas, 199
　personal stories about, 116–117, 125–126
　reasons to consider, 114
　through your school, 123–124
　vs. apprenticeships, career mentoring,
　　and job shadowing, 92–93
　See also Apprenticeships, youth; Job
　　shadowing; Mentoring
Internship Success, 157
Interviews
　arriving on time, 145
　asking questions, 142–143, 146
　checking the place out, 145
　dressing properly, 145
　finding more information about, 149
　keeping a positive attitude, 142
　maintaining eye contact, 146
　making a good first impression, 145
　personal story about, 147–148
　practicing for, 144
　preparing mentally for, 144–145
　relaxing before, 144
　responding to questions, 144
　selling yourself, 146
　standard questions used in, 143
　taking notes, 146
　writing thank-you notes, 147
Irish School of Landscape Painting, The, 204
It's Our World, Too!, 24

J

Jobs for the Future, 109
Job shadowing
　approaching contacts about, 99–100
　benefits of, 92, 93, 95, 112
　brainstorming ideas for, 95–96
　definition of, 92
　examples of, 93–94
　exploring all of the options, 96–97, 108
　finding contacts for, 98–99
　finding more information about, 108–110
　making the most of the experience
　　being friendly, 103
　　being on time, 103
　　bringing money for lunch, 103
　　communicating, 103–104
　　dealing with downtime, 103
　　dressing properly, 102–103
　　greeting your host professionally, 102
　　maintaining eye contact, 102
　　projecting yourself into the job, 104
　　saying thank you, 104
　personal stories about, 105–106, 110–111
　preparing for the big day
　　clarifying your goals, 101
　　doing research, 102
　　making a list of questions, 100–101
　reasons to consider, 91
　requesting follow-up sessions, 106
　sharing your experience, 107
　through your school, 97–98
　vs. apprenticeships, career mentoring,
　　and internships, 92–93
　See also Apprenticeships, youth; Internships;
　　Mentoring
Job Shadowing Handbook, The (Web site), 109
Job Shadowing Month, 109
Junior Achievement, 109

K

Key Club International, 16, 26
Kirschner, Shanna, 225–228
Kiwanis International, 16

L

Legacy International (Web site), 205
Leo Club, 16
Letters of reference, 121
Levin, Molly, 249–250
Lions Club, 16, 203
LissaExplains (Web site), 253–254

M

Maine Mentoring Partnership, The, 79
Make a Difference Day, 27
Mass Mentoring Partnership, The, 80
Mentoring
    becoming a mentor
        benefits of, 86
        finding more information about, 88–89
        making the decision, 86–87
        options for, 87–88
    benefits of having, 62–63
    career mentoring
        benefits of, 76
        benefits to mentors, 78
        definition of, 62
        ending the relationship, 84
        examples of, 74–75
        finding more information about, 79–80
        importance of communication, 83–84
        making arrangements for, 76–78
        personal story about, 81–83
        reasons to consider, 73–74
        results of, 78
        tips for success, 83
        vs. apprenticeships, internships, and job
            shadowing, 92–93
        (See also Apprenticeships, youth;
            Internships; Job shadowing)
    definition of mentor, 60, 68
    finding more information about, 64
    having more than one mentor, 64
    informal mentoring
        approaching your potential mentor, 66–67
        clarifying expectations, 67
        definition of, 61
        finding what works best, 67–68
        online mentoring, 68
        tips for selecting your mentor, 65–66
    making the experience rewarding, 85–86
    mentoring at-risk youth
        benefits of, 69
        definition of, 61–62
        finding more information about, 72–73
        results from, 68
        things to do with your mentor, 70
        personal story about, 71–72
Mentoring, 88
Mentoring Partnership of Minnesota, 80
Mentorship, 88
Merrell, Dante, 71–72
Middlebury College, 47–48

N

Nacel Open Door, 239–240
National Commission for Cooperative Education
    (Web site), 164
National Directory of Arts Internships, 128
National Directory of Internships, 128
National Mentoring Partnership, 79
National Outdoor Leadership School (NOLS),
    192, 196
National Service Act, 28

National Service-Learning Clearinghouse, 26
National Youth Leadership Council, 26
National Youth Science Camp (NYSC), 188
National Youth Service Day, 27
Neel, Rebecca, 40–41
North Carolina Promise, Office of the
    Governor, 80

O

100 Black Men of America, 71–72, 73
150 Ways Teens Can Make a Difference, 25
Online mentoring, 68
Operation Crossroads Africa, 204
Oregon Mentoring Initiative, 80
Outward Bound, 196
Outward Bound City Challenge, 204
Overgaard, Sidsel, 223–224
Overseas travel. See Traveling overseas

P

Packing Book, The, 245
Pangaea Quest: Teen Adventure School, 196
Passports, 240
Peace Corps and More, The, 31
Penpals.net (Web site), 246
People for the Ethical Treatment of Animals,
    10–11
Person Who Changed My Life, The, 64
Peterson's Learning Adventures Around the
    World, 238
Peterson's Summer Opportunities for Kids and
    Teenagers 2000, 194
Peterson's Summer Programs for Kids and Teens
    (Web site), 191
Peterson's 2000 Summer Jobs for Students, 213
Peterson's 2001 Internships, 128
Pocket Doctor, The, 245
Points of Light Foundation, 26
Princeton Review's Student Advantage Guide to
    Summer, The, 186

R

Résumés
    building your résumé
        chronological format résumés, 132, 133
        deciding on a format, 132
        functional format résumés, 132, 134
        identifying responsibilities held, 130–131
        identifying skills learned, 130–131
        listing basic information, 130
        organizing your information, 132–134
        using active verbs, 136
    cover letters
        example of, 140
        finding more information about, 141
        tips for writing, 139, 141
    definition of, 129
    finding more information about, 139
    listing references, 135–136
    posting résumés online, 138
    producing a draft, 135
    tips for effective résumés
        editing carefully, 137

finding and correcting errors, 137
keeping them current, 138
keeping them short, 137
printing your résumé, 138
taking your time, 137
Rising Star Internships (Web site), 128
Rotary International, 16, 214

S

Sail Caribbean, 196
Saint Peter's College, 45
Save the Children, 72
School-to-Work Act of 1994, 163
Schwartz, Scott, 147–148
Scott, Beth, 116–117
Service clubs, school, 16–17
Service-learning
  benefits of, 29
  celebrating your achievements, 29–30
  definition of, 28
  origins of, 28
  vs. community service requirements, 28
Sierra Club, 17–18
Simon's Rock College of Bard, 48–49
SkillsUSA-VICA, 80
So You Want to Join the Peace Corps, 32
Student Hosteling Program, The, 204
Student's Guide to the Best Study Abroad Programs, The, 238
Study Abroad, 2000–2001, 238
Study abroad programs
  answering the "what if" questions, 217
  benefits of
    becoming a different person, 222
    becoming more cultured, 218–219
    broadening your view of the world, 218
    developing greater self-reliance, 221–222
    experiencing a different way of life, 219
    exploring interests, 221
    feeling energized, 221
    gaining maturity, 220
    gaining valuable skills, 221
    getting out of your comfort zone, 220
    having an adventure, 220
    improving college applications, 221
    learning a different language, 219
    learning new things, 222
    meeting new people, 218
    putting your culture into context, 219
    seeing new places, 218
  choosing a program
    applying for a program, 235
    choosing your academic experience, 232
    clarifying your goals, 230–231
    deciding where to go, 231–232
    direct enrollment programs, 230
    estimating your budget, 233
    gathering information, 233–234
    homestays, 229–230
    language study programs, 229
    overcoming skepticism, 233–234
    picking a time to go, 232
    student exchanges, 230

traditional programs, 229
examples of, 216
finding more information about, 238–240
making the most of the experience
  dealing with jet lag, 247
  handling culture shock, 247
  keeping a sense of humor, 248
  preserving memories, 251
  registering with an embassy, 248
  resolving problems, 249–250
  staying positive, 247
  taking safety precautions, 248
personal stories about, 223–224, 225–228, 235–237, 244–245, 249–250
preparing to go
  bringing presents, 242–243
  buying clothing/supplies, 242
  finding more information about, 245–246
  getting an International Student Identity Card (ISIC), 241
  making financial arrangements, 243
  making travel arrangements, 243
  obtaining a passport and visa, 240–241
  preparing mentally and emotionally, 243–244
  visiting your doctor, 241
Summer camps
  applying for, 185
  being a counselor-in-training, 185–186
  choosing a camp, 183–184
  dealing with homesickness, 185
  finding camp listings, 183
  finding more information about, 186–188
  overseas, 198
  personal story about, 189–190
  reasons to consider, 178–179
  types of
    art, 182
    day, 180
    sleep-away, 180–181
    special interest, 182–183
    sports, 182
    traditional, 181
    wilderness, 181
    writing/journalism, 181–182
Summer coursework
  benefits of, 45–46
  finding more information about, 46
  personal story about, 47–48
  reasons to consider, 35–36, 45
  See also Distance learning; Dual enrollment; Early admission

T

Take Our Daughters to Work® Day, 110
Tech prep programs, 164
Teen Tours of America, 188
Thomas, Tammy, 166–168
Time management
  avoiding procrastination, 43–44
  becoming self-reliant, 43
  importance of, 42–43
  learning from others, 43

making to-do lists, 43
rewarding yourself, 44
understanding your work style, 44
using a planner, 43
Traveling overseas
benefits of, 215
finding more information about, 202–205
paying for
finding more information about, 213–215
finding sponsors, 211
getting a job, 212
obtaining financial aid, 210–211
organizing fund-raisers, 211–212
public funding sources, 210–211
starting a business, 212–213
personal stories about, 200–202, 206–207, 208–209
preparing for, 197
reasons to consider, 178–179
types of experiences
adventure programs, 198, 206–207
camps, 198
homestays, 199
internships, 199, 200–202
study tours, 198
travel tours, 199
voluntary service/work programs, 198, 208–209
Travel That Can Change Your Life, 194
Twain, Jesse, 244–245

U

United Way, 10–11
Unofficial Guide to Acing the Interview, The, 149
Utah Mentor Network, 80

V

Van Gundy, Kate, 125–126
Virginia One to One: The Mentoring Partnership, 80
Virtual Volunteering Project, The (Web site), 27
Visas, 240–241
Volunteer America, 25
Volunteering
age restrictions on, 12
benefits of
discovering new talents, 14
exploring possible careers, 16
having new experiences to share, 15
helping others, 34
learning new skills, 15
making new friends, 13
putting life in perspective, 14
seeing life differently, 15
seeing other ways of life, 13
understanding different viewpoints, 13–14
watching others respond to adversity, 14
brainstorming ideas for, 11–12
dealing with problems
feeling overwhelmed, 23
helping parents understand, 22–23
making mistakes, 24

overcoming first-day fears, 22
finding more information about, 24–27, 31–33
getting started, 10–11, 13
in other countries
benefits of, 30
examples of, 30, 198
finding more information about, 31–33
personal stories about, 18–19, 21–22, 23
at school
to meet community service requirements, 17–19
service-learning, 28–30
through service clubs, 16–17
showing volunteer experience on college applications, 15, 30
tips for success
being a good team member, 20
communicating, 20
discussing expectations, 19
keeping a log, 20
making contacts, 20
taking things slowly, 19
taking your duties seriously, 20
vs. paid work, 15
Volunteering, 25
Volunteers for Peace, 33
Volunteer's Survival Manual, The, 25
Volunteer Vacations, 32
VonGruben, Kristen, 154–156

W

Washington State Mentoring Partnership, 80
Weissman Teen Tours, 197
Westcoast Connection Travel Camp, 197
Where There Be Dragons, 205, 206–207
Whiz Teens in Business, 213
Wilderness Inquiry, 197
Winning Cover Letters, 141
Wolff, Lindsay Bell, 81–83
Woods Hole SEA Programs, 188
Work Force Investment Act, 163

Y

Yale Daily News Guide to Internships 2000, The, 128
Yale Daily News Guide to Summer Programs 2000, The, 46
YMCA of the USA, 17–18, 73
YMCA Teen Leadership Programs, 27
Young Entrepreneur's Edge, The, 213
Young Entrepreneur's Guide to Starting and Running a Business, The, 214
Young Entrepreneurs' Organization (YEO) (Web site), 215
Your First Interview, 149
Your First Résumé, 139
Youth for Understanding International Exchange (Web site), 205
Youth Leaders International, 205
Youth Service America, 27
Youth Venture, 214
YWCA of the USA, 17–18, 73

About the Author

Photograph © 2000 Catherine Golden

Rebecca Greene graduated from Carleton College in 1999 with a B.A. degree in English literature. While in high school and college, she gained the experience that inspired this book—internships at a newspaper, magazine, and TV station; job shadowing days with professionals in a variety of fields; volunteer work at a science museum and a senior citizens' care center; and study abroad in London, Germany, and Japan.

Rebecca is also a freelance writer who has written extensively for various newspapers, and she is currently at work on another book. She will attend law school starting in the fall of 2000. In her free time, Rebecca enjoys reading, art, and travel.

Other Great Books from Free Spirit

What Teens Need to Succeed

Proven, Practical Ways to Shape Your Own Future
by Peter L. Benson, Ph.D., Judy Galbraith, M.A., and Pamela Espeland
This book empowers teens to build their own assets, discover they have the power to change their lives for the better, and make a difference in the lives of people around them. It includes over 1,200 asset-building ideas plus hundreds of inspiring true stories, facts, checklists, quizzes, resources, and much more. For ages 11 & up. *$14.95; 368 pp.; softcover; illus.; 7¼" x 9¼"*

The Kid's Guide to Service Projects

Over 500 Ideas for Young People Who Want to Make a Difference
by Barbara A. Lewis
This guide has something for everyone who wants to make a difference, from simple projects to large-scale commitments. Kids can choose from a variety of topics including animals, the environment, friendship, hunger, politics and government, and much more. For ages 10 & up. *$12.95; 184 pp.; softcover; 6" x 9"*

Making Every Day Count

Daily Readings for Young People on Solving Problems, Setting Goals, & Feeling Good About Yourself
by Pamela Espeland and Elizabeth Verdick
Each entry in this book of daily readings includes a thought-provoking quotation, a brief essay, and a positive "I"-statement that relates the entry to the reader's own life. For ages 11 & up. *$9.95; 392 pp.; softcover; 4¼" x 6¼"*

Making the Most of Today

Daily Readings for Young People on Self-Awareness, Creativity, & Self-Esteem
by Pamela Espeland and Rosemary Wallner
Quotes from famous figures guide you through a year of positive thinking, problem solving, and practical lifeskills—the keys to making the most of every day. For ages 11 & up. *$9.95; 392 pp.; softcover; 4¼" x 6¼"*

*To place an order or to request a free catalog of SELF–HELP
FOR KIDS® and SELF–HELP FOR TEENS® materials,
please write, call, email, or visit our Web site:*

Free Spirit Publishing Inc.
**217 Fifth Avenue North • Suite 200 • Minneapolis, MN 55401-1299
toll-free 800.735.7323 • local 612.338.2068 • fax 612.337.5050
help4kids@freespirit.com • www.freespirit.com**